Jump Start

Your Business Brain

Jump Start
Your Business Brain

**The Scientific Way
To Make
More Money**

Doug Hall

CLERISY PRESS

CINCINNATI, OHIO

THE PURPOSE OF THIS BOOK

This book is written to help small business owners and those with a small business owner attitude win more, lose less and make more money.

I have been wonderfully successful in my thirty years of small business ownership. And with that success comes a responsibility to give back.

This book is my effort to share the wisdom I've acquired with the broadest possible audience. My goal is to teach others the scientific laws they need to know to "thrive" instead of merely "survive" in the world of business.

For those reading this book outside of the United States of America, this book is also intended as a guide for how to "win" in the American marketplace.

Life is meant to be lived and enjoyed. In my mind there is no finer feeling than the sense of personal accomplishment that comes from founding a profitable new business.

THANK YOU

A complete listing of the many people who helped make this book possible is provided on pages 299-301.

Jump Start Your Brain with David Wecker (Warner Books, 1995).
    A fun and entertaining excursion into the world of innovation. It's a motivational anthem for those looking to shake up their thinking.

Maverick Mindset: Finding the Courage to Journey from Fear to Freedom (hardcover; Simon & Schuster, 1997) and *Making the Courage Connection: Finding the Courage to Journey From Fear to Freedom* (paperback version; Fireside, 1998). Both with David Wecker. Inspiring stories and lessons for generating the courage to take action with your life.

TABLE OF CONTENTS

INTRODUCTION Good News! 3

PART I **The Three Laws of Marketing Physics**............... 19
Quick Quiz: Getting Your Mind Engaged

CHAPTER 1 The Science Behind Marketing Physics............ 25

CHAPTER 2 How to Triple Effectiveness of Salespeople,
Advertising and Marketing Efforts 40
First Law of Marketing Physics: Overt Benefit

CHAPTER 3 How to Find Your Overt Benefit 66

CHAPTER 4 The Secret to Doubling Effectiveness at
"Closing the Sale".................................. 88
Second Law of Marketing Physics:
Real Reason to Believe

CHAPTER 5 Proven Strategies for Real Reason to Believe 100

CHAPTER 6 How to Design Your New Product, Service
or Business for Power Profits...................... 125
Third Law of Marketing Physics: Dramatic Difference

CHAPTER 7 How to Craft a Dramatic Difference 149

CHAPTER 8 Frequently Asked Questions About
Marketing Physics................................ 158

PART II   **The Three Laws of Capitalist Creativity** 167

CHAPTER 9   The Science Behind Capitalist Creativity 168

CHAPTER 10   How to Fuel Your Brain for Maximum Productivity. . 177
First Law of Capitalist Creativity: Explore Stimuli

CHAPTER 11   Multiply Your Brain by Borrowing Others. 224
Second Law of Capitalist Creativity: Leverage Diversity

CHAPTER 12   Go for It! Turning Thoughts Into Reality. 254
Third Law of Capitalist Creativity: Face Fears

CHAPTER 13   Frequently Asked Questions About
Capitalist Creativity 284

Eurkea! Ranch Services. 295

Bibliography 296

Thank You 298

Index 301

Three Options for How to Read This Book

Chapter eight outlines how each person learns and creates differently. In that spirit, you have three options for how to read this book. Pick the one that best fits your style and jump in.

Option 1 Begin at the beginning. The beginning of this book gives the scientific basis for all of the learnings and teachings. If you're the type of person who wants (or needs) that level of understanding, then start at the introduction and proceed through the book in sequence.

Option 2 Go straight to the tactics. If you are in urgent need of ideas, have no patience for background understanding, and trust that this is all based on hard scientific data, then jump directly to chapter two. This is where the practical tools for increasing your odds of success begin.

Option 3 Read the book in reverse order. This book teaches what a high-probability idea looks like (Marketing Physics), then it teaches you how to create one (Capitalist Creativity). Research has shown that this is the most effective learning sequence for most people. If, however, you are more interested in creating than evaluating ideas, feel free to start at chapter ten and then come back to the beginning.

Doug Hall has put me in a . . . HORRIBLE POSITION. (I'll not soon forgive him.) He asked me to "write a Foreword" to this book. That means . . . one thousand words or so. BUT . . . I can't do it. No . . . it's not that I don't like the book. To the contrary . . . I LOVE IT. And . . . there's my problem.

HOW AM I SUPPOSED TO BE RATIONAL? All I want to say is . . . I LOVE IT. IT'S SUPERCALIFRAGILISTICEXPIALIDOCIOUS.

(There . . . I said it.) Every damn practical question Doug poses, and there are dozens, is . . . simply . . . ESSENTIAL .. to creating a Cool/Profitable/Wildly Different business.

Here's how he hooked me, in a word (two, actually): DRAMATIC DIFFERENCE.

Dramatic Difference. PAYS OFF. Big Time. That's true . . . and his new quantitative models prove that . . . as never before.

But it goes beyond that. I, of course, am thrilled that his Quant Studies PROVE what I've long believed: SERIOUSLY COOL . . . WINS . . . BIG. (P.S. And takes Guts! Big Time!)

It's . . . THE PASSION . . . for the IDEA . . . of . . . D-R-A-M-A-T-I-C DIFFERENCE. (And . . . those COMPELLING/STUNNING/HARD NUMBERS ... to back it up.)

I LOVE IT. (OK?)

AND. As in . . . AND. Every Chapter is brimming with . . . PRACTICAL QUESTIONS and EXERCISES: None of us can escape from his . . . INEXORABLE LOGIC.

This ain't a book for Wimps. It is a book for those who will Never Rest until they have Set the World on Its Ear. With a local auto-body shop. Or a 23-table French restaurant. Or Mega-corp. (Or a one-person window-washing service.)

You see, there's another thing Doug and I agree on. BIG TIME. (Again.) We don't think "branding" is limited to Coke or Pfizer. We believe "branding" is . . . AVAILABLE TO ALL . . . WITH VISION AND NERVE AND VERVE. We believe that "dramatic difference" and Brand Position is as plausible at $1,000,000 as at $1 billion. NO BULL.

DD is a FOM. (DRAMATIC DIFFERENCE . . . is a . . . Frame Of Mind.)

PERIOD.

Doug provides GAJILLIONS of Practical Examples. (No Barren Desert of Theory here!) And . . . YOU MUST READ THEM ALL. (Trust me. Please.)

I LOVE THIS BOOK. (And I rarely—never before, truth be told—go that far.) It SOARS . . . and provides PRACTICAL STUFF . . . worth its weight and price 1000x over. PLEASE. P-L-E-A-S-E. Read—and ingest—this book. PLEASE.

You may end up making a ton of money. Far more important . . . your life will take on Meaning as never before. (Meaning that flows from the Relentless Pursuit of Dramatic Difference.) How Liberating!

Thank you, Doug, for allowing me a few lines in this masterwork.

Palo Alto
May 14, 2001

INTRODUCTION

Good News!

I bring you good news! Business success is not random. There are patterns to the universe of business. There are reproducible scientific lessons and laws that, when applied with diligence, can help you win more, lose less and make more money with your new products, services, sales and advertising efforts.

Sadly, most businesspeople don't understand these laws. As a result, businesses large and small fail daily. Declining sales surprise business owners, companies are shut down and employees are put out of work. And worse yet, people's dreams for businesses of their own die.

By applying the findings repeated in this book, you will significantly increase your odds of business success. I want to be very clear on this point. I'm not guaranteeing success. Just as there are no foolproof systems for winning a lottery, so, too, there is no such thing as a miracle secret for guaranteed business success. What is being promised are a set of scientific lessons and laws that can dramatically increase *your odds of success*.

Estimates of new product or service success rates vary widely depending on the industry studied and the definition of success. A review of academic studies and U.S. census data found that on average about 75% of new businesses, products or services fail and are discontinued within two to five years. This means that you basically have only a 25% probability of success with your new advertising, product, service or business concept.

A venture capitalist told me that 17% of the companies his firm invests in succeed. This would actually be an improvement over the 10% rate reported by Greg A. Stevens and James Burley in "3000 Raw Ideas—1 Commercial Success," their May-June 1997 *Research Technology Management* review of the results of ten major venture capital firms.

A 10 to 25% chance of success is terrible odds. Most business owners would have a greater probability of success if they went to a Las Vegas casino and gambled their investments. The following chart details the various probabilities of winning at gambling games.

Game	Probability of Winning
Slot machines	32%
Horse racing	41%
Blackjack (as usually played)	45%
Roulette	47%
Blackjack (perfect strategy and card counting)	50%

What is most amazing is Las Vegas studies indicate 68% of the people who gamble play slot machines—the lowest probability game-most often!

The goal for this book is humble. At a minimum it is to help you win more than you lose, to help you double your probability of success from the current 25% to some 50 to 75%. In effect, the goal is to move your business thinking from low odds slot machines to the higher probability blackjack with perfect strategy and card counting. The odds presented below are for concepts that enter the marketplace. The odds are even longer if we back up a bit and start from moment of creation of raw ideas.

Business Idea Source	Probability of Winning
Current new business success rate	25%
Applying the scientific laws on these pages	50 to 75%

Stevens and Burley also reported that for common industrial products it takes about 3,000 raw ideas or 125 formal projects to generate 1 success. Translate these numbers into odds similar to those listed above and it's clear that the odds of any individual idea being a success are a fraction of one percent.

Idea Stage	Odds of Winning
Raw idea	0.03%
Formal projects explored	0.80%

Generating successful ideas for growing a business is similar to Charles Darwin's famous theory of survival of the fittest. With odds like these, success seems to be a numbers game. If you want to grow, your only choice is to create more ideas—6,000, 9,000, 12,000 ideas. Then if you are lucky, you will have enough energy, time and money to stumble upon a success or two.

This book is dedicated to helping defeat this "survival of the fittest" approach. The goal is to have "thriving" replace "surviving" through the use of data-validated scientific laws.

Stop the Madness

The failure rates described above are true insanity. To repeat, the facts indicate that there is a higher probability of profits from playing a Las Vegas slot machine than investing in the average new product, service or business. This is ridiculous!

This book is my attempt to help stop the madness and tangibly improve your odds of success. To this end, the lessons and words on these pages may seem severe, blunt and uncompromising. They are meant to be. If a true difference is to be made, it is time for a revolution in our thinking.

Emotional preaching to "work harder" won't do it. Entrepreneurs in general work extremely hard—eighty, ninety, even one hundred hours a week. Rather, we must learn to "think smarter." And thinking smarter means we must ground our thinking in the scientific laws and marketplace probabilities associated with true success.

Finally, casting a spell or even reading this book will not miraculously make success occur. This book is merely the alphabet's twenty-six letters selected and arranged in a particular order. To realize a true return on your time invested in reading it, you must take action with what you've read. It cannot be done for you. **You are the only one capable of changing your business.**

Bottom Line: It's a Book About Ideas That Can Drive Success

Jump Start Your Business Brain is focused on helping you discover, develop and identify ideas—ideas for new products, services and businesses as well as ideas for advertising and marketing communication in support of your existing business. Go back to the origin of virtually any company and you'll find someone with an idea for delivering products or services that were more effective and or efficient that those currently available.

Ideas are the only true fuel for winning customers and grow-

ing profits. In fact, the idea is, at its essence, the core reason for being for any business enterprise. Without an idea, nothing else matters. You can have the most cost-efficient manufacturing process, most outstanding customer service system and distribution system on earth. Without an idea that excites customers, you will soon no longer be an operating business.

The synergy between the strength of an idea and bottom line results is immense. When an idea is strong, everything else falls into place. One client friend put it this way: "I've found that when I'm working on projects where the idea is right it's like hitting beach balls with a baseball bat. You can't miss. Everything we do from packaging to advertising to sales and operations just works."

What this means to you is that when you focus your energy on the right idea, you dramatically enhance your skill at execution. If your idea is focused, clear and persuasive, each business task is executed in a focused, clear and persuasive manner. If your idea is foggy, obtuse and hard to understand, then everything you execute will be foggy, obtuse and hard to understand.

Business success is dependent on three elements: (1) your idea, (2) your passion and (3) your plan. Of these, I believe the most important is your idea. **It is from the idea that your passion flows. When the idea is aligned with your heart and soul, your passion is a natural.** When the idea is clear, distinct and smart, crafting a business plan for successful execution is easy.

Conversely, when the idea is wrong, working harder at execution can never make it right. High levels of passion can sustain the life of a poor idea, but when energy eventually dies, so, too, does the idea. With a bad idea, the part of the business plan that will eventually become the most important is the portion detailing an exit strategy.

Most new venture business plans are impressive in their depth of documentation and level of "banker" wisdom. Most are highly unimpressive in their level of "shopkeeper" wisdom.

Banker wisdom is the knowledge of money and markets. Bankers buy and sell companies, like modern-day slave traders, while keeping a clear distance from the front lines where companies come face-to-face with customers.

Shopkeeper wisdom is the knowledge of customers. It's focused first and foremost on what is offered for sale to customers. **True shopkeepers are driven with a passion to fulfill their customers'**

needs, dreams and aspirations. Over the long haul, because of this faith in serving customers, shopkeepers are rewarded tenfold in sales and profits versus bankers.

The bottom line isn't very complicated. Customer-focused ideas drive sales and fundamental valuation of your company. Ideas are the secret weapon that allows small businesses to compete with and beat larger companies. A recent Arthur D. Little survey, reported in *The Innovation Premium* by Ronald Jonash and Tom Sommerlatte (Perseus Publishing, 1999), found that 95% of stock analysts felt that, with large companies, the innovative companies are worth higher shareholder premiums.

Encouragingly, managers know this, since some 84% of company leaders in the study felt innovation is a much more critical business success factor than it was five years ago. Discouragingly, less than 25% of respondents were happy with their current performance on innovation.

Small Business Owners Are the Focal Point of This Book

As mentioned earlier, this book is written to help the millions of small business owners generate greater sales with less effort. It's also written to help those who have dreams of founding their own small businesses find the courage and conviction to take the leap and succeed.

When small businesses are mentioned, I think it's worth defining what is meant. Despite the media hype behind fast growth companies, most business is small business-very small business. This fact is supported by U.S. census data (http://www.census.gov).

- 17 million proprietorships, partnerships and subchapter S corporations exist in the USA-total gross sales equal $3.3 trillion annually.
- 97% of all businesses have less than $1 million in sales per year.
- 69% of owners report annual personal income of under $50,000 per year.
- 60% of business owners with employees work over forty hours a week.
- 25% of business owners with employees work over sixty hours a week.

At first glance, those in large corporations may look at these numbers and say, "Why bother?" The answer is simple: freedom. Small business owners are driven by a desire to be their own bosses and, more importantly, have the freedom to explore their ideas. If all companies gave employees the freedom to spend a significant portion of their time and energy exploring ideas they have a passion for there would be far fewer small business start-ups.

The passion to explore ideas is the cornerstone of small business start-ups. This innovation spirit is well documented. Babson College reports that small entrepreneurial firms have created 95% of all the radical innovations since World War II and some 50% of all innovations.

Interestingly, small business owners often start their enterprises when employed. Data from the U.S. Department of Labor indicates that three-quarters of those who start new businesses are also employed in wage-and-salary jobs at start-up. And, some 60% of new firms begin at home.

Few small businesses fail because of bankruptcy. In fact, only one in seven small businesses that fails leaves unpaid debts. Rather, they fail because the owners come to the conclusion that it's just not worth the effort relative to the return they are receiving.

My experience shows that as a small business owner you are probably a true brain at your chosen field, be it cooking, woodworking, computer programming, landscaping or investments. However, the business and marketing part of your brain may lack education and discipline. My friend Dan is a classic example. Dan always had a passion for photography. He worked for seventeen years at a newspaper working up the ranks to be one of the top news photographers in the state. When he turned forty he decided it was time to be his own boss. He quit the paper and opened up a photography studio, taking portraits and selling fine art photographs. Sadly, Dan knew photography but he didn't know business. Sales were slow and hours were long. He hung in for two years then gave it up and went back to working for a newspaper. His dream of freedom died in the process.

It didn't need to be that way. With the principles in this book, Dan could have been a success. He is clearly skilled at photography. He just doesn't understand the business of customers.

Another reason this book is addressed directly to small business owners is because all of us, in our own ways, are running small businesses, whether those enterprises are restaurants, day-care centers or small departments within worldwide corporations. We all have customers to satisfy.

The classic definition of "customer" is "a person who is interested in buying your product or service." In *Jump Start Your Business Brain*, that definition is broadened. A customer can also be a person in the next department whose cooperation you're seeking. Or it could be the boss you're trying to convince to give you a raise.

Until you start to think like the leader of your own small business, you're destined to arrive at age sixty-five and look back on a career filled with woulda's, coulda's and shoulda's. It's your life, your career, your history that you are making each and every day. Life is too short and precious to be wasted on executing tasks and efforts that don't work. Now is the time to increase your impact on the world by thinking smarter and more creatively about how to grow your business.

The scientific laws outlined in this book are for those who market products, as well as those who market services. The strategic principles for growing consumer products are similar to those for growing services and industrial products; however, the latter are an order of magnitude more difficult to be successful with. In large part, this is because of the intangible nature of services and industrial market segments.

The laws articulated in *Jump Start Your Business Brain* are important for all who are involved in your company's growth. For large companies, this means technology, production and operations departments. For small businesses, this means your key advisors, spouse, accountant and key supporting suppliers. At one of our training programs, one engineer put it this way: "For the first time, I understand what the marketing people really do. I now understand how we in technology can more directly drive customer sales."

Scientific Laws, Not Personal Opinions

What makes this book unique is its backing in original, scientific data. Disciplined statistical analysis supports all teaching. This research has been made possible because of the generous support of many of the world's leading corporations. Their visits to the Eureka! Ranch have been utilized as laboratory experiments for discovering and quantifying truth when it comes to inspiring and identifying big ideas.

- Over 6,000 client groups have provided quantitative and qualitative feedback while in the process of creating ideas to grow their businesses.
- Over 1,200,000 customer reactions to new business concepts have been measured and analyzed to identify the core truths that define winning customer ideas.
- Over 60,000 data points have been collected and analyzed as part of an expert innovator survey to provide even further depth and understanding of the true dynamics of how breakthrough ideas are really invented.

With the help of the Eureka! Ranch R and D Team—Jeffery Stamp, Ph.D., Chris Stormann, Ph.D., and Mike Kosinski—the research has been distilled into practical lessons and laws for helping you increase your odds of business success. The original data, analysis and research behind the findings could fill a half-dozen doctoral dissertations. On the pages of this book, the discoveries have been packaged in such a way as to maximize accessibility to the broadest possible audience. For those with an interest in the original data and analysis that supports the principles, feel free to contact me directly at the address listed in the back of the book.

Today's marketplace has a way of creating instant gurus, experts and messiahs. They often preach but rarely practice. In the case of the laws detailed on these pages, the learnings are a result of scientific measurement during frontline inventing projects.

Scientific Laws Provide a Calm From the Marketplace Storm

Albert Einstein believed nature was a mystery waiting to be solved and the world could be explained. "God does not play dice with the universe," he said. "The eternal mystery of the world is its comprehensibility." The work of most pure scientists is based on a faith that there are actionable patterns in the world around us waiting to be discovered. These patterns are in effect big-picture views that can provide us with grounding in all that we do.

The quantified patterns, or laws as they are called on these pages, provide yardsticks we can use to determine the bases for dozens of minor and major decisions. The laws give us an ability to act as a team. Much of the debate between employees is because of a lack of common vision for what success looks like. Without a common vision, we revert to what is success in our area of responsibility, be it finance, production, sales or technology development. We use the standards that we are measured by in our functional job area to measure ideas in the absolute. This can result in endless circular debates and a corresponding lack of speed and productivity.

Contrast this chaos with a business run by proven, scientific laws. All employees and suppliers know what really matters. Energy is focused on what really drives customer excitement in the product or service that is offered.

Scientific laws provide a foundation for making decisions and taking action in the face of chaos. Without principles, we're destined to a world of second-guessing our actions and investments in growing our business.

And the greater the uncertainty, the greater the potential for becoming like Don, a telecommunications executive who came to work with us in the early days of the Eureka! Ranch. Don was the newly hired "big cheese" of a division focused on exploiting a new networking technology. As the project progressed, it became clear that Don was also a perpetual motion machine of indecision. Every time he reviewed the set of ideas that had been developed, he changed them endlessly.

Don just couldn't make a decision. Finally, about eleven o'clock in the evening, as we were going around the bend for another lap of changes, a junior engineer on Don's team said what all had been thinking but dared not say: "Don, how will you know a great idea when you see it?" The room got quiet. It was like the little boy declaring the emperor was naked. Don stopped, stuttered and then for the first time in nearly fifteen hours of discussion that day was honest: "I don't know." He admitted, "When I was with my former company [a large financial services company], I knew what worked and what didn't. To be honest, this industry confuses me."

Eureka! Now the root problem was on the table. Over the next two hours, the conversation turned to defining what the team thought great ideas looked like. The room was filled with a new energy. At one o'clock we called it a night. The next morning we met again. This time we had a collection of principles to guide our decisions. In three hours we did what we hadn't been able to do in fifteen hours the day before.

The guiding truths we used that day ten years ago were crude. But the lesson learned was clear: Without a clear set of strategic laws for guiding our business thinking, we are destined to a life of chaos.

Deming Provides the Inspiration

The fundamental inspiration for the research behind this book came from the work and writings of Dr. W. Edwards Deming. Deming was a statistician who was recruited by the supreme command for the Allied powers to help rebuild Japan following World War II. At the time, that country had a negative net worth. What businesses existed were focused on the seemingly "easy" business of selling low-cost, cheap goods. Low price also meant low profit margin. Thus, it was not a great way to generate the levels of trade needed to fund the importation of the food and goods necessary for the Japanese people.

Deming encouraged them to move from a low-cost orientation to a high-quality customer-focused orientation. He viewed messy production processes as eminently definable. Through systems analysis and statistical control charting, he showed them how the "art" of manufacturing could be quantified and managed through scientific methods and measurements. Deming's theories, training and consulting efforts had great effect. In recognition of his contribution to Japan, the Union of Japanese Science and Engineering instituted the annual Deming Prizes for contributions to quality and dependability.

My father worked with Dr. Deming at Nashua Corporation, the first U.S. company to embrace his philosophies. At the time, I was studying for a degree in chemical engineering from the University of Maine. The discussions with my father about Deming's teachings profoundly impacted my view of business management.

Dr. Deming taught that the only way to improve manufacturing quality was to improve the process through better systems, worker training and systemic improvement. When the process is improved, Dr. Deming maintained, a chain reaction of reduced waste, less rework and greater customer satisfaction inevitably results. Fix the system, Deming said, and you fix the factory. With our Eureka! Ranch efforts a similar philosophy has been followed. Instead of focusing on the manufacture of products, the focus has been on the manufacture of successful business-building concepts. Deming's statistical measurement methods have been used to identify laws for success in the "messy" world of creating and evaluating ideas to excite customers.

If you are not realizing outstanding business results with your small business, your department or your division, it is likely that you are not the problem. Most likely, it's  also not your employees, your competition or the marketplace. Rather, the source of your failure lies in the principles you consciously or subconsciously use to create and pick your ideas. The principles and thinking habits you've developed are what hold you back from great success.

Jump Start Your Business Brain Part I:
The Three Laws of Marketing Physics

Part one of this book details Marketing Physics, a collection of three scientific laws that can help you identify, improve and enhance your ideas to maximize their chances of marketplace success. With these laws, you will learn how to take what you offer currently and dramatically enhance the power of your customer communication. Often, all a company needs to grow sales is to sharpen its marketing message through overtly telling the remarkable story of what is behind the company's product or service enterprise.

This book assumes that you already have a business or a business idea you are seeking to market to customers. The first two laws of Marketing Physics (chapters two to five) detail how to enhance and improve the communication of your current idea. The third law (chapters six and seven) challenges you to step back and review what you have optimized. It is at this point that you will be coached ·

on how to honestly evaluate whether your idea is good enough to be successful in the marketplace.

Bravo if the answer is yes. Do not be discouraged if the answer is no. The second half of the book is dedicated to helping you think through how to re-create your idea to make it truly great.

Jump Start Your Business Brain Part II: The Three Laws of Capitalist Creativity

The three laws of Capitalist Creativity help you increase your effectiveness at creating a new business offering or reinventing an existing business concept. Don't let the word *creativity* scare you. This section is not about "howling at the moon" creative weirdness; Rather, its content is brass tacks centered on crafting customer-focused ideas that make a tangible difference on both top-line sales and bottom-line profits.

This focus on business innovation is an important distinction. The classic definition of creativity is "artistic creativity." This is the realm of the painter, the sculptor, the songwriter, the novelist set in a world dedicated to inspiring the soul and enlivening the spirit. This sort of creativity is not the focus of this book.

The focus here is on a brand of creativity called Capitalist Creativity, which is about inspiring ideas that tangibly grow sales and profits.

The first two laws of Capitalist Creativity (chapters ten and eleven) detail the strategic elements that fuel the creation of ideas. The third law (chapter twelve) reviews the key constraint that if not addressed can dramatically reduce your potential for success.

Organization of the Obvious?

In *Jump Start Your Business Brain*, fresh data and advanced research provide validation of fundamental principles to help you win more, lose less and make more money with your business growth ideas. In the process, much old wisdom has been found to be still valid. And, new principles have emerged for the modern marketplace. Given the overlap between old and new learning, some of the teaching described in this book may seem like organization of the obvious. The teachings may feel familiar. The learnings may seem like common sense.

As reported earlier, however, the obvious doesn't appear to be readily apparent to those starting new businesses. The U.S. Department of Commerce department reports that 75% of small businesses fail within five years.

The obvious doesn't appear to be readily apparent to those at large companies, either. A variety of studies estimate that 75% of new products and services are discontinued within an even faster two years. The patience of large corporations appears to be shorter than the patience of entrepreneurs.

The obvious doesn't appear to be readily apparent even to top advertising professionals. Obscure advertising that keeps the customer confused continues to be broadcast. The greatest showcase for meaningless advertising may be the most expensive one. At nearly $2 million for a thirty-second commercial, the NFL Super Bowl is one of the most expensive, most watched events of the year. During the 2000 Super Bowl, top advertising agencies, working for newly born Internet companies, flooded the airwaves with some of the most artistic, least effective ads in history. In April of 2000, *USA Today* reported the majority of these Internet companies realized no significant sustainable difference in the number of Web site hits despite their two-million-dollar commercials!

The challenge with the scientific laws outlined on these pages is not that they are obvious; rather, it's that in today's hyperactive marketplace, we don't stay focused on what really matters. The rapidly changing world of tactical changes, from the Internet to new manufacturing and marketing technologies, tends to consume our energies. We get to the point where we start believing the answers to our business challenges lie in technology. They don't. Success comes from harnessing technology to fulfill customer needs. In the end, the customer is all that matters.

Policy on Client Secrets

As noted previously, the laws outlined on these pages would never have been discovered without the assistance of clients. Each week clients come to the Eureka! Ranch, just outside Cincinnati, to invent ideas for growing their businesses.

Kindly, they also allow us to measure every action and reaction. They allow us to measure their states of mind before and during the actual inventing process. They also provide invaluable quantitative data on how each idea does with customers.

Each client project has intense secrecy surrounding it. Discovering ideas for a new computer, new toilet paper or a new credit card may not seem like a matter of national security; however, hundreds of millions of dollars and thousands of jobs are often at stake. To preserve client confidentiality, I have disguised identities and only used actual client names and identified industries when they have given permission. Your cue that an identity is disguised will be when a client is referred to by only a first name that begins with the letter D (for Disguised), such as Dave, Dan, David, Don, Daisy, Darleene, Donald, Darla, Deena.

For example, the scope of the challenge facing an old-line industrial corporation became clear when Dave, a senior vice-president protested a statement I made about the company's poor product quality: "Doug, we may not be great, but we're better than mediocre." It's a sad statement. A shocking statement. But there is nothing gained by identifying the executive, company or industry.

One other executional note: You will observe my liberal quoting from the writings of Ben Franklin. Franklin has always been my hero and business inspiration. He was an entrepreneur, writer, inventor, scientist and statesman. It's my humble hope that this book, with its blending of inspiration with scientific research, would have made him proud.

Now Is the Time to Increase Your Odds of Success

Business results are influenced by luck, effort and skill.

Luck can't be planned. You can increase your chances of luck only by getting into the marketplace quickly and efficiently and through being alert to opportunities.

Effort is a given. If you're expecting instant business success, give up now. Building anything worthwhile takes passion and commitment.

The third of the three influences on business success, skill, is what this book aims to enhance. You learned the skills of reading, writing and arithmetic in school. *Jump Start Your Business Brain* will teach you advanced principles and processes that empower you to make your business dream happen a little sooner, a little more easily and, almost certainly, far more profitably. **In the end, you'll learn how to work smarter to grow your business instead of working harder or relying on lady luck.**

In summary, this book is about providing you with the skills you need to take action and to take control over your probability of future success. It's time for everyone to take responsibility for her own destiny, time to stop whining about the challenges of today's hypercompetitive world, time to start focusing energy on learning the skills required to enhance odds of winning.

As much as there is science and research in this book, the overall message here is one of hope for the future—hope and faith that through applying the wisdom on these pages, you can make a dramatic difference in your business.

To paraphrase the author Copthorne Macdonald, whose writings and discussions have had a powerful influence on my thinking: "My impression is that all good writing uplevels our experience in some way. Either it produces uplifting feelings, or it helps us to know something or see something more clearly." That, my friends, is the recipe behind this semiliterary effort: a pinch of uplifting inspiration with a healthy serving of quantitative data that can help you see the world of business a little more clearly.

Doug Hall
Threshfield Farm, Springbrook
Prince Edward Island, Canada
March 2001

PART I

The Three
Laws of

Quick Quiz: Getting Your Mind Engaged

The next few pages contain a quick quiz designed to get your mind engaged in thinking about what makes for a concept with a high probability of success.

The quiz consists of three rounds. Each round presents three ideas. Your task is to read the three ideas in each round then rank them based on their probability of being successful in the marketplace.

The concepts you are about to read have a real-world pedigree. They are based on actual products that have been introduced into the U.S. marketplace. The actual brand names and packages have been modified to disguise their real identities.

In order to simulate the effect of making decisions under the pressure of the marketplace, give yourself just five minutes to complete all three rounds. Score any decision you don't make as a zero.

For each round, mark the ideas' ranks at the bottom of the last idea in the round with 1 indicating the idea with the highest probability of success and 3 the lowest probability.

ROUND 1

Redout Rust Stopper
Stops Rust Each Time You Flush

Redout Rust Stopper is a bowl cleaner that prevents rust with every flush. Its unique, innovative, time-release formula stops the formation of rust and hard-water stains in your toilet bowl and tank, eliminating waterline ring. Nothing else on the market works like Redout Rust Stopper. It contains no acids, chlorine bleach, caustics, phosphates or dyes and is safe for plumbing and septic systems.

Grandma Fricker's Organic Meals for Kids
Kids Meals Made From Organic Ingredients

Grandma Fricker's Organic Meals for Kids were developed to introduce children to the advantages of organic foods in a way they'll appreciate their whole lives. The recipes capture the flavor and fun of kids' favorite foods, using premium-quality, certified organic ingredients. Try all the flavors—including Pasta-Os in Tomato Sauce, Pasta-Os in Tomato Cheese Sauce and Beans and Veggie Franks.

StainSane
An Instant Stain and Spot Remover that Won't Harm You or Your Fabrics

StainSane Instant Spot and Stain Remover is safe for you and safe for your fabrics. Use StainSane to get rid of a wide range of stains-grass, blood, coffee, perspiration, grease, ink, pet stains, chocolate and more. Its nontoxic formula works on clothing, rugs, upholstery, vinyl and as a laundry pretreatment. Plus, it's biodegradable and nonflammable.

Rank the potential for each idea—number 1 having the greatest potential for customer success:

____ Redout Rust Stopper   ____Grandma Fricker's   ____ StainSane

TURN THE PAGE FOR ROUND 2 NOW.

ROUND 2

StepSafe Ice and Snow Remover
Melts Ice and Snow on Walkways in Super-Low Temperatures

Use StepSafe Ice and Snow Remover on steps, porches and walkways to melt ice, snow, sleet and freezing rain. Specially formulated for harsh winter conditions, it works immediately to melt ice in temperatures as low as -50 Fahrenheit to guard against winter slips—and it's safe on concrete, shrubs and lawns. StepSafe comes in a convenient shaker package that's easy to store in your car, kitchen, hall closet or office.

Jack Snack's Milwaukee Beach Snack Mix
A Tropical Party From Milwaukee?

It happened one January winter. The snow was piling and kids were whining. Jack was going a bit stir-crazy. Time for something different. Time to escape the same old same old.

O.K., O.K. It's true there is no Milwaukee beach with palm trees, umbrella drinks and beach cabanas. But we didn't let that get in the way of our imaginations.

Jack Snack's new snack mix is a tropical island blend with the tastes of the islands.

Microwave Sentry
Monitors Your Microwave to Insure Your Family's Safety

The Microwave Sentry is a reusable indicator that detects radiation leaks from your microwave. These leaks sometimes can be caused by basic wear and tear or food particles that become caught in door seals or hinges.

The Microwave Sentry has a laboratory-tested sensor that uses liquid crystal technology to change color to show if your microwave is leaking radiation. Full instructions are on the card, along with a toll-free number to call with questions.

Rank the potential for each idea—number 1 having the greatest potential for customer success:

____ StepSafe   ____ Jack Snack's   ____ Microwave Sentry

ROUND 3

Opti-roma
An Air Freshener That Lets You Choose From Three Fragrances

Opti-roma is the only air freshener that lets you choose between three attractive scents in one. Its innovative container is designed so that while the scent you select fights odors, the other two scents remain freshly sealed.

Opti-roma lasts longer, up to sixty days. The three distinct fragrances in the package are Sweet Strawberry, Tropical Exotic, Lemon Fresh Crush. Or you can choose a unit with fragrances of Spiced Lemon, Meadow Mist and Southern Potpourri.

HearthGlow
A Quick-Lighting Fireplace Log of All-Natural Peat

HearthGlow is a quick-lighting, long-burning fireplace log that's environmentally friendly because it's made of natural organic peat.

Made of peat compressed with wax, HearthGlow fireplace logs are soot-free, nontoxic and nonsparking. A compact 5-lb. log will burn brightly for more than three hours.

Ventin' Scents
Turns Your Room Vents Into an Air Freshening System

Ventin's Scents air freshener is an easy, inexpensive way to use your venting system to circulate a pleasant fragrance throughout your home or office. And it kills germs that can come from a ventilation system and make your environment unhealthy.

Place the patented Ventin' Scents fragrance cartridge just inside an air intake, and the free-flowing air from your central heat, air conditioner or heat pump gently releases aroma each time your system turns on. Ventin' Scents will keep the fragrance flowing all day long and for up to six weeks. Available in French Vanilla, Caribbean Breeze, Meadow Sweet Floral and Gardenia Potpourri fragrances.

Rank the potential for each idea—number 1 having the greatest potential for customer success:

_____ Opti-roma   _____ HearthGlow   _____ Ventin' Scents

Quick Feedback on the Quiz

Before reviewing the results, ask yourself how you feel about your answers. Would you feel comfortable investing your entire net worth in your decisions? Can you clearly explain to others the rationale behind your selections? Are your choices guided by principles or instinct?

Scoring You get three points for correctly picking the best idea and one point for identifying the worst idea.

> *Round 1*
> Score 3 points if you named Redout Rust Stopper as #1 _____
> Score 1 point if you named Grandma Frickers as #3 _____
>
> *Round 2*
> Score 3 points if you named Microwave Sentry as #1
> Score 1 point if you named Jack Snack's as #3 _____
>
> *Round 3*
> Score 3 points if you named Ventin' Scents as #1. _____
> Score 1 point if you named HearthGlow as #3 _____

Scoring Results Total your scores from all rounds. _____

• If you got a perfect score of 12: Forget idea generating. I suggest you consider leveraging your skill on the stock market.

• If you got a score of 9 to 11: Congratulations, you are above average. This book can provide some help; however, clearly you have some strong skills already in the area of identifying successful ideas.

• If you got a score of 0 to 8: Congratulations, you are average relative to the groups who have done this exercise. This book can help you dramatically. It will provide principles and processes for identifying top ideas. This will help you realize a greater profitable return on the ideas you pursue.

The explanation behind why each idea is the best and worst is given in detail in the next chapter.

CHAPTER 1

The Science Behind
Marketing Physics

This chapter provides the specific supporting credibility for the Marketing Physics laws that follow. This background is especially important if you have a rational or skeptical orientation. Readers who are more trusting or who have an allergic reaction to mathematics should feel free to skip ahead to chapter two where the conclusions and practical tactics are presented. Chapter one also provides a top-line overview of the Merwyn Simulated Test Marketing and Coaching system. This is important for readers to understand, as outputs from this system will be utilized in subsequent chapters.

The Medium Is Not the Message

Canadian philosopher Marshall McLuhan declared "The medium is the message." He felt that *where* you communicated your message was more important than *what* you were saying. McLuhan's teachings are often quoted by Internet and "new economy" messiahs who preach that by changing the communications medium a bounty of success will be yours. Wrong.

Our research has found **it's the message that motivates customers**, not the medium. It is *what* you say, not *where* you say it that matters most. In nearly thirty years of utilizing direct mail to promote my own businesses, I've found time and again the message is king.

Most businesspeople never learn this. They create one advertisement and run it in three different locations. Usually it generates no response, and they conclude advertising in those vehicles doesn't work.

The Eureka! Ranch approach is the inverse of that described above. We create three different direct-mail pieces and mail them to one list, split into three portions. Then we measure responses to find the winning message.

The difference in response rates from the best to worst is usually at least a difference of 50%. A doubling or tripling of responses is not unusual. The most effective direct marketers know this. To maximize success, they are continuously testing new messages to enhance effectiveness.

Sadly, often times small business owners get caught up on where, not what. Recently, I attended a meeting of small business owners. The discussion turned to which marketing vehicles worked the best. In the course of fifteen minutes, they collectively gave testimony to the ineffectiveness of brochures, direct mail, newspaper, radio and television ads. The collective conclusion was that marketing didn't work.

I then asked, "What was your marketing message? I'd like to see some examples, as it could be that the problem is what is being communicated not where it's being communicated."

I then gave a short talk on the laws of Marketing Physics, similar to what you're about to read. A look of revelation came over the group. As one woman said, "We're not trained in this stuff. I make pottery, not marketing stuff." My response was instinctive: "I make marketing stuff because I can't make pottery. Working together we could probably sell a lot more pottery." We all laughed and set forth transforming their message.

Marketing Physics Is Focused on the Content of Your Message

Marketing Physics focuses on enhancing the content of your message at the moment of truth: the magic moment when customers make the decision to place their hard-earned cash or their companies' cash on the counter and purchase your product or service.

Customer is defined on these pages as the ultimate consumer of your product or service. In business-to-business situations, the buyer and consumer are usually the same. With consumer products and services the end consumer is sometimes on the other side of a middleman or distributor. In the case of this book, the terms customers and consumers are interchangeable. Customers also refers to potential business partners, suppliers or even fellow employees within your company whom you need to "sell" on your idea.

The Power of Statistics as a Discovery Tool

Statistics is a powerful tool for helping us clear away the "noise" that exists in everyday business and, as such, see the truths that lie beneath. With statistics, we are able to see more clearly what is most likely to be cause and effect as opposed to a random chance relationship.

For example, assume you are thinking of entering a hot new small business service category. You read in a magazine about a lady named Sally who has been very successful with the concept in another city. As you're talking to a friend about your concept, he relates that Fred, in another city, has failed miserably with the same concept. What do you do now? What do you know now?

If you're an optimist, you'll assume that the idea is a customer winner and that successful Sally is just a more dedicated business person than unsuccessful Fred.

If you're a pessimist, you might assume that Fred did his best, the core customer idea is a failure and Sally just got lucky.

In an ideal world, a scientist would gather key data on Fred, Sally and a hundred others like them. The data would include market demographics, marketing support, service quality and any other key variables. Then statistical analysis would be utilized to determine which variables had and which did not have a statistically significant relationship with success. Then, based on the evaluation, the scientist would come to an objective conclusion about the customer potential of the core customer idea as well as an understanding of the few key factors that determine potential for success.

Whoa! I can hear you now. Doug, are you out of your mind? I don't have time for all that. Don't worry. In *Jump Start Your Business Brain*, we've done the statistics and analysis for you. Millions of data points have been analyzed to determine the laws of Marketing Physics and Capitalist Creativity at statistically significant levels. **All you have to do is read, think and take action with the results.**

History of My Interests

The search for reproducible marketing principles has been an interest of mine for over twenty years. Moving from the world of chemical engineering to Procter & Gamble brand management, I was surprised to learn of the lack of disciplined principles in the world of "big-time marketing."

My interests grew during the early 1990s when I owned a market research company called AcuPOLL Research. Reviewing results from thousands of tests for new products, services and advertising, we would often look for patterns to define and describe why customers reacted as they did.

In 1995, a very generous purchase offer was made for the AcuPOLL Research company and I sold it. The money from the sale made it possible for me to fund a long-term R and D effort to discover and define the laws of Marketing Physics.

In time, the effort grew into a full-scale company with multiple researchers involved in the quest and millions of customer data points being modeled using some of the most advanced statistical modeling techniques available.

The Research Process

The starting place in our analysis was a set of four thousand concept descriptions of new products and services. We had hard data on customers' reactions to the ideas in research, in the marketplace or in both.

We quickly learned it was easy to measure the tangible, concrete dimensions associated with each idea. These included brand category, pricing versus competition, sizing and function. However, this analysis didn't yield any significant correlation with actual customer behavior.

The Eureka! moment came when we moved beyond hard data and started to explore perceptual and strategic archetypes. We defined archetypes as the dimensions "running through customers' heads" when they were making decisions to purchase. Archetypes included benefits, features, credibility elements, focus, synergy, value perception, clarity of communications, believability, overtness of communication, emotional versus rational orientation.

The validity of the archetypes was determined by modeling them versus actual marketplace results using advanced statistical methods.

The statistical modeling was simple to execute with today's computers. The challenge was in discovering the proper archetype inputs. Identifying the proper archetypes involved thousands of test- and learn-experiments and millions of data points. We now fully understand what Thomas Edison meant when he said, "If I find 10,000 ways something won't work, I haven't failed. I am not discouraged, because every wrong attempt discarded is another step forward."

Defining Probability of Success

A key research decision was how to define business success. Success can be based on profits, sales, margin, net extra sales and so on. In the end, the decision was made to define success as a new product or service that maintains distribution or is actively marketed for at least five years. The assumption is that a product or service does not remain in distribution for five years unless customers like the offering and the company is seeing reasonable levels of sales, profits and return on investment. Using our definition of success, a 20% probability of success means that one out of five times the product or service will survive in the marketplace for at least five years. This purposely tough success standard was chosen to maximize focus on the true merits of ideas and to minimize the impact of short-term introductory hype.

From a small business perspective, another way to think about the probability of our success measure is as a relative measure of the return on effort expended. For example, if a concept has a 20% probability of success, it means that the business owner must work hard, long hours and spend lots of money and time on marketing in order to generate sales. Alternatively, if the business owners can double their probability of success to 40%, they can work half as hard for the same sales return.

A Few Words About Probability

On these pages, you will see probability numbers. In our binary yes/no world, it's common to see these numbers and to round off. For example, the weather forecaster predicts a 70% chance of rain and we round that to yes it will rain. When it doesn't rain, we assume the forecaster was wrong. This is not correct. The weather forecaster did not say it was going to rain. He said that if the current conditions existed one-thousand times, it is most likely that it would rain seven hundred times. In order for the probability to follow statistical distribution it must also not rain about three-hundred times. A 90% probability means that one time out of ten, the event won't happen. So 70% is not 100%. And 80% is not 100%. Even 99% is not 100%.

When making business and personal decisions, this concept is often missed. We round off to 100% on the top end and 0% on the bottom end. This is not reality. In life, high-probability winners lose and low-probability losers get lucky and win.

There is no such thing as a guaranteed lottery ticket. There is no person, no system, no entity on earth that can guarantee success. The best we can do is gain an understanding of our odds of success between various options. Then with this understanding, we can place our bets based on the highest odds of success.

As you review the probability estimates provided here, remember that, as detailed in the Introduction, on average only 10-25% of new business initiatives succeed and in some industries the average is as low as 10%.

Identification of the Three Laws of Marketing Physics

Repeated test- and learn-cycles eventually identified clear patterns among the archetypes. No matter what set of ideas, what industry, what customer segment it seemed that the same three overriding factors emerged. The three factors weren't based on a singular archetype; they were multidimensional, incorporating a cluster of eight to thirteen distinct yet related archetypes each with various weightings.

These three factors were named the three laws of Marketing Physics in honor of Sir Isaac Newton and to pay respect to my engineering education. As Newton's laws define and describe the physical universe of motion, the three laws of Marketing Physics define and describe the universe of customer purchase behavior. The principles help reduce the naturally foggy nature of the marketplace and help us see with greater clarity the core strategic elements that define big ideas that win in the marketplace.

We sorted the concepts to identify the impact of each of the three laws on overall success potential.

1. Overt Benefit

What's in it for the customer? The concept of focusing on benefits instead of features has long been known to be critical to success. The new news is how overt you need to be in today's cluttered market place. In order for customers to "get it" today, you must be direct.

	Probability of Success
High Overt Benefit	38%
Medium Overt Benefit	26%
Low Overt Benefit	13%

In round one of the Quick Quiz preceding this chapter, Overt Benefit is the defining point of difference. Of the concepts presented, the Redout Rust Stopper has the most Overt Benefit. The statement "Stops Rust Each Time You Flush" provides no doubt or mystery about what is "in it for me," the customer, when I purchase Redout. StainSane offers the next strongest Overt Benefit, followed by Grandma Fricker's Organic Meals for Kids. Grandma Fricker's promises "the advantages of organic foods," but it never defines what those advantages are. It is left to the customers to draw their own conclusions of why organic is important. In the busy marketplace, this "extra work" results in less sales.

In live training programs, participants often pick StainSane or Grandma Fricker's because they perceive the market to be bigger and they know things that are not written. This is wrong. As you'll learn, despite what you may think, data analysis indicates that the idea offered customers is dramatically more predictive of success than the size of the market. And customers cannot and will not read your mind. If a benefit isn't overtly articulated, it isn't there.

2. Real Reason to Believe

To convert the excitement generated by Overt Benefit into sales, customers require that you provide persuasive credibility that you will do as you promise. Credibility has long been known to be important. The new news is how important it is. Customer confidence is at an all-time low. Data analysis indicates that Reason to

Believe is as important as Overt Benefit. Success in today's marketplace requires clear, distinct credibility communication.

	Probability of Success
High Reason To Believe	42%
Medium Reason To Believe	29%
Low Reason To Believe	18%

In round two of the Quick Quiz, Real Reason to Believe is the critical dimension. Of the round two concepts, Microwave Sentry offers a clear description of how it works, as well as a scientific pedigree explaining the technology. StepSafe at least offers a special formula; however, it and Jack Snack's are both significantly less credible.

3. Dramatic Difference
Sales and profits explode when an Overt Benefit and Real Reason to Believe pair is offered with a Dramatic Difference. Without uniqueness, you have a commodity that sells for commodity-like profit margins. The new news is that for the uniqueness to be effective, it must be dramatic-ten times bigger than you think it needs to be—and the drama must be focused directly on the Overt Benefit and Real Reason to Believe.

	Probability of Success
High Dramatic Difference	53%
Medium Dramatic Difference	40%
Low Dramatic Difference	15%

In round three, Ventin' Scents is the winner as it offers the greatest Dramatic Difference of the three. The benefit it offers cannot easily be achieved in any other manner. Opti-roma and HearthGlow offer decreasing levels of uniqueness. HearthGlow provides many features; however, the end benefit of it versus competing logs is insignificant.

Students of marketing will note a great similarity between the three laws of Marketing Physics and the teachings of marketing and advertising icon David Ogilvy. In effect what we have found is that when it comes to persuading customers to purchase products or services, it is not enough to be popular or well liked. To generate sales, customers demand to know what's in it for them, why they should believe you and what makes you different from their current favored options.

In his classic book *Ogilvy on Advertising*, Ogilvy wrote, "When I write an advertisement, I don't want you to tell me that you find it 'creative.' I want you to find it so interesting that you buy the product." The mission of this book is the same: to help managers create products, services and advertising that persuade customers to spend money.

The Birth of Merwyn

The Laws of Marketing Physics were discovered using old-fash-
ioned research and development. The strength of these laws, in describing marketplace results, inspired us to create a very modern computer "brain" that would allow us to forecast probability of success for new business ideas.

After years of research and experimentation by a team of Ph.D.'s, a computer-based idea-assessment system was created and given the name Merwyn. Merwyn is my father's first name and the name I used through high school and college when I performed as a magician and juggler. And frankly, no matter how much the math and statistics behind the system are explained, it will still be "magic" to many people.

Merwyn is a Simulated Test Marketing and Expert Coaching System designed to help reduce the maddening 75 to 90% failure rate for new business initiatives. The patent-pending Merwyn decision "engine" uses many of the same advanced mathematical technologies that drive the "computer brains" that autopilot airplanes, navigate ships and manage NASA systems.

Merwyn's primary input is a written description of your idea for a new product or service, advertising or a sales pitch. The written description is translated into a series of strategic and executional archetypes that the Merwyn model uses to develop an independent risk/reward assessment.

Merwyn's predictive power was validated by tracking the success of nine-hundred new products over a five-year period. Analysis found a near one-to-one relationship between Merwyn's probability of success and actual marketplace survival.

	Merwyn Predicted Probability	Merwyn Predicted Rate (Difference)
Average for lowest 225 ideas	22%	23% (-1)
Average for next 225 ideas	30%	29% (+1)
Average for next 225 ideas	37%	36% (+1)
Average for highest 225 ideas	45%	47% (-2)

Merwyn was also given a vigorous review by clients during real projects. Clients that include Johnson & Johnson, Procter & Gamble, Frito-Lay, The Ford Motor Company, American Express and a collection of small businesses used the system while reviewing ideas for growing their businesses.

For further information on Merwyn Simulated Test Marketing, see page 302 or visit http://www.Merwyn.com.

Why Merwyn Beats Most Humans

Humans who study the learning on these pages and apply that learning with absolute discipline have no need for Merwyn. However, humans are "human" after all, and absolute discipline can be a challenge when faced with the day-to-day challenges of running a business.

Analysis has found that Merwyn has the following key advantages versus most businesspeople. Listen and learn from them, and you can increase your business wisdom and reduce Merwyn's advantage.

Modeling Market Behavior Instead of Customer Intentions:

Merwyn models *marketplace behavior*, as opposed to customers' *intent or popularity* as measured in classic market research. By modeling actual marketplace behavior, Merwyn takes on a level of wisdom that is often missing when we make judgments based on our perceptions of future behavior or of past experiences.

Throughout time, the telling of stories, fables and legends has been a means for passing wisdom through the generations. The business world has its own set of tortoise and hare fables. Business stories are called case studies. The challenge with these stories is similar to those of grand King Arthur legends: In the telling and retelling, they become polished to such a level of perfection and simplicity that if we're not careful they lose their authenticity. And, if we're not careful, we end up running our lives and our businesses based on a set of false laws.

Business distortions rarely start maliciously. They usually begin as little white lies that serve the purpose of protecting our emotions, our egos and our reputations when failures occur. With repeated telling, the lies take hold and become a part of our conscious and unconscious decision patterns. This growth of bad data is like a slow-growing cancer. The reason a change in leadership of any business is so powerful is that the new leader doesn't have the same cancer or wear the same blinders that many of the other employees do.

The challenge is to learn to temper our past learning with a clear understanding of the reality of today's customer behavior and needs. We must learn to temper our past knowledge with a sensitivity to the realities of the marketplace.

Success Algorithms:
Humans have a tendency to become distracted by short-term, or random, events. For example, if we see someone win at a slot machine we are tempted to gamble on slot machines even though we know that the odds are against our winning.

In some cases, business people lack true understanding of the reality of customer purchasing dynamics. Without a bigger picture view, the decision makers lack a basis for relevant decision making. In effect, "They don't know what they don't know."

A key purpose of this book is to define clearly the big-picture probabilities of various business approaches. You don't have to follow the highest probability strategies. You can take a chance on a long shot. All that is asked is that you recognize the reality of your chances.

Merwyn is not distracted by random experiences or opinions. Merwyn is driven by dozens of data-based algorithms. Each as been validated as having a statistically significant relationship with success based on analysis of four thousand concepts and some 1.2 million customer data points.

Maintaining Emotional Discipline:

Merwyn has no emotional or personal involvement in the success or failure of a project. Merwyn's evaluations are based solely on the idea as presented and the wisdom inherent in its algorithms. Merwyn focuses on scientific probabilities and nothing more or less. Contrast this approach with the human tendency to develop emotionally clouded judgment. A common example is when talking to a colleague who is so infatuated with an idea that no matter what you say, she is unable to see concerns that to you as an outsider are obvious.

Humans are notorious for allowing their emotions to run their decisions. At their root, the emotions involve fear or greed—fear that you have to make this idea work no matter what, greed of what it will be like if you win.

The other source of emotion-driven error is old-fashioned machismo or arrogance. As managers move up through the ranks or achieve small business success, they can catch this disease. Having achieved levels of success, they forget what got them to where they are. They enter the world of psychological delusions of grandeur. Instead of basing decisions on disciplined fundamentals, they believe that they have extrasensory perceptions of the marketplace.

Merwyn Example

During a recent Small Business Coaching program, I met a smart entrepreneur named Ed McKenna. Ed had recently purchased a company called Island Pewter that was near bankruptcy. When I met Ed, he was trying to decide where to take the company. Island Pewter had offered a huge line of pewter jewelry, frames and collectibles.

To start our efforts we tested the company's catalog using Merwyn to identify key strengths and weaknesses. The test generated the following ratings.

Overall Probability of Success: 14%

Laws of Marketing Physics
(Percentiles calculated versus Merwyn's benchmark database of 4,000 concepts)

1. Overt Benefit	**5th percentile**
Specifically, obviously, directly— What's in it for the customer?	
2. Real Reason to Believe	**5th percentile**
Why should the customer believe you will deliver on the promise made above?	
3. Dramatic Difference	**10th percentile**
How revolutionary and new-to-the-world is your benefit/reason to believe pair?	

It was no wonder the company was in such trouble. With a 14% probability of success the company lacked a fundamental concept or customer idea. There was no benefit, reason to believe or point of difference. Another challenge Ed faced was that he had but a few weeks before he had to have a new proposition ready to take to the winter trade shows for the craft industry.

A couple of hours of idea creation identified a simple and elegant idea: Ed would focus his energy on classic earring designs that he already had molds for. Instead of offering a wide line of products, all his efforts would go toward earrings.

To provide a clear Overt Benefit and Dramatic Difference for his earrings, an idea was crafted to offer his classic earring designs in sets of three. The earrings would be positioned as "your favorite pair and spare." Now when a customer lost one earring, she would already own a third earring to take its place.

The new concept was resubmitted to Merwyn to check its potential for success.

Eureka! It worked. Clearly the Overt Benefit and Dramatic Difference were clear and focused. Ed developed proto-type display pieces that leveraged the concept. He took the new proposition to two trade shows and sold over $50,000 worth of earrings! This is a dramatic improvement considering that the company, the year before Ed bought it, did under $10,000 in sales.

Overall Probability of Success: 84%

Laws of Marketing Physics
(Percentiles calculated versus Merwyn's benchmark database of 4,000 concepts)

1. Overt Benefit   **70th percentile**
Specifically, obviously, directly—
What's in it for the customer?

2. Real Reason to Believe   **40th percentile**
Why should the customer believe you will
deliver on the promise made above?

3. Dramatic Difference   **80th percentile**
How revolutionary and new-to-the-world
is your benefit/reason to believe pair?

Trust the Laws

The three laws of Marketing Physics were themselves discovered three years ago. Since that time, they've been challenged and examined by Eureka! Ranch staff and clients to uncover flaws or laws of greater importance. Nothing has shook their standing.

In study after study, and project after project, their truth has been validated. It's also become clear how difficult it is to stay focused on them. The moment anyone becomes emotionally involved in the creation of an idea, discipline leaves as the heart overrules the brain. The more you study and work with the learnings, the greater their complexity and the greater the challenge to master them.

The science of Marketing Physics is a truly new science. There is much more to be discovered and learned. However, with what we do know, dramatic differences can be made in virtually everyone's probability of business success.

CHAPTER 2

How to Triple Effectiveness of Salespeople, Advertising and Marketing Efforts

The first portion of the chapter defines Overt Benefit and provides evidence as to its importance. You will learn how to focus on this first dimension that customers consider when making purchase decisions.

First Law of Marketing Physics: Overt Benefit

Customers maintain established behaviors until they come in contact with an *overtly appealing* alternative benefit force.

Customers get excited and take notice of your product or service offering when they perceive that it offers them a benefit.

Benefits help make your customer's life easier, more enjoyable, more exciting, more rewarding—that is better in some fashion. Benefits are the solutions to the customer's day-to-day problems.

Customers are creatures of habit. The only way to get them to change from what they are currently purchasing is by offering an Overt Benefit that catches their interest. Ed Eggling, Director of Sales for Hot Off The Press explained it to me with this simple analogy: "People only listen to one radio station WII-FM (What's In It For Me)."

Analysis of thousands of new product and service concepts indicates that when an Overt Benefit is communicated, the probability of business success and the return on investment for the effort you expend will nearly triple.

This is good news! **By simply enhancing and improving your benefit communication, you can realize a dramatic improvement in your business results.**

	Probability of Success
High Overt Benefit	38%
Medium Overt Benefit	26%
Low Overt Benefit	13%

These findings also indicate straight talk wins. You don't need fancy, flowery or clever wordplay to win customers. Simply telling customers in a direct and easy-to-understand manner what you can do for them can nearly triple your chances of success.

In our journey together in this book, we will first seek to define the benefit you offer customers then to communicate it overtly. The cost to develop and implement this improvement is virtually nothing more than the cost of the book you already hold in your hands.

In working with small businesses, I've seen as much as a 45% increase in sales as a result of simply optimizing core communications as detailed in this chapter and the next. It's important to note, however, that I've also seen cases where no amount of communications enhancement can help a business. In these cases, the companies' core products or services are simply not competitive and the only way to generate significantly improved results is to more radically change the products or services as detailed in the balance of the book.

Benefits are what customers pay for. They are the only profitable way to bring new customers to your business. The other option—deep discounts—is not a profitable choice. Customers acquired via low pricing usually are discount shoppers, who just as quickly will leave for the next price deal that's offered. I have a friend who for two years switched long-distance phone companies every sixty days. He saved lots of money through special introductory deals. Was he worth the cost of the introductory price specials to the phone companies? Absolutely not!

The one pricing strategy that can be highly effective is to offer free samples. It's especially effective when you are offering something dramatically different from anything else on the market. In these cases, a free sample is often the fastest way to share the good news of your revolutionary product or service with potential customers.

Practical Tactic: Demonstrating Overt Benefit to Yourself

The goal of this tactic is for you to learn to understand the importance of Overt Benefit as a means for attracting customers' interest.

Grab a stack of magazines. Better yet, grab today's newspaper. Get a highlighter or marker. Quickly scan the advertisements or articles that catch your eye. Which headlines spark an interest, for whatever reason, for you to read further and learn more about what's in the article?

Keep your focus on the headlines and the opening paragraphs. Each time you see an article or advertisement that catches your eye, highlight the headline. Take no more than a minute or two to scan the entire newspaper or magazine.

Now go back to the publication and review the headlines that caught your eye. There will be many reasons why you made your selections; however, it's likely the majority of the marked items offered a benefit—a benefit that is relevant to you and your life.

If someone else had reviewed the paper or magazine, he would have probably marked a number of the same headlines you did, but his personal needs and interests that are different from yours would show up in additional marked ads or articles.

My wife, Debbie, volunteered to complete this process for me using a section from our local newspaper. Here are the headlines she highlighted. The parenthetical comments reflect my interpretations of the benefits.

- Midler in Search of a Better 'Bette'
  (Bette Midler is someone I respect; I wonder if what she's doing could help me.)
- Bootleg Contact Lenses Endanger Teens' Vision
  (Potentially important information for our teen who wears glasses now.)
- Latest Crop of Weight-Loss Books Filled With 'Sure-Fire' Plans on How to Be a Good Loser
  (I can always hope a miracle system has been discovered.)
- Techniques Speed Surgical Healing
  (Thank goodness we don't need it now. . . but it would be valuable to know about.)

To varying degrees, all of these articles offered a promise of news and information that could be of potential value to Debbie. They were relevant to her needs yet offered hope of new news.

Alternatively, many articles and headlines did not catch her eye. A review of these headlines indicates doublespeak and confusion. Here are a sampling of headlines and articles she didn't mark. Again the italicized comments are mine.

- Face. . . the Possibilities (Of what?)
- Factory Direct Windows, Siding, Patio Rooms (So what?)
- Get to It (?????)
- The Secret is Out (Mindless teasing that I just don't have time for.)
- Media Bridges Moving to New Site (I'm very happy for them but why should I care?)

Check your list. Compare the headlines you selected versus the ones you didn't. What was your motivation? What types of ideas were you more interested in? Less interested in? In most cases, you will find the ones you didn't select offered little hope of benefit to you.

More Ways to Learn the Importance of Communicating Benefits

For my scribbling on these pages to have a true impact on your business success, it is important that you internalize a full understanding of what a benefit is. Try the following three easy ways to practice recognizing benefits.

1. Review your credit card statement. As you pay your monthly credit card bill, review your charges. Think back and try to remember the benefit you received from each purchase. Was it something you were aware of before purchasing, or was it something discovered afterwards? By focusing on what benefits you received when making these purchases, you can learn a lot about how to communicate benefits when selling.

2. Shop for benefits. As you visit stores, look for how various merchandise is marketed. Look for Overt Benefits in sales pitches and on clothing hangtags, restaurant signage, menus, the jacket copy of books. Grocery stores are a particularly good place to learn about Overt Benefits, as the competing brands are lined up beside each other. Stop,

look and read the labels of competing brands to get a feel for how each company tries to communicate its benefits.

3. <u>Rate advertising.</u> Look for Overt Benefits in advertising on television, radio and billboards and in magazines. Explain the concept of Overt Benefit to your children or spouse, and rate advertisements on a scale of 1 to 10 regarding benefit communication.

An All-Too-Common Story of Not Communicating Benefits

As I was writing this chapter, I had an experience that demonstrated the need for communicating a benefit. Following a long morning of writing, I decided to go out for lunch. As I drove down the road, thoughts of benefit communication filled my head. At a stoplight, I looked to the left and noticed a restaurant I had seen many times yet never stopped to visit. As I looked at the signage, I suddenly realized why. The sign out front declared Dave's Place. On the building hung a banner announcing, "Now Open, Open, Open for Lunch." That was it. No benefit was communicated—overt, implied or otherwise.

I pulled into the parking lot and was surprised to see it almost full. Hmmm, I thought, this place must be better than it looks. Just inside the front door hung a reprint from a local newspaper. Here I thought would surely be the answer to what makes Dave's Place great. In the first paragraph, the reporter asked Dave what makes his place special. Dave explained, "Attention to detail and good value." Ugh, I thought, not much help here. Attention to detail and value aren't very specific, distinct or exciting. In fact, they sound incredibly generic.

As I entered the main dining room, I was struck immediately by the patrons: Fully 90% were senior citizens. Clearly Dave's value message had gotten around among this community of patrons.

A very polite and attentive waitress seated me and gave me a menu. "What's the specialty of Dave's Place?" I asked. "We have a Rueben sandwich for $5.95" she replied. I tried again. "What is Dave's place famous for?" She looked at me puzzled and said, "Nothing really. We don't have anything we're famous for. All the food's good."

A look at the menu showed clearly that Dave didn't overpay for his marketing help. The menu featured generic food offerings described as generic items: Ham and Swiss Sandwich, Caesar Salad, Chicken Salad, Cheeseburger.

Let's review what's happened so far. The sign out front communicated a generic restaurant inside. The staff and menu confirmed that they offer nothing special. A quick look at the prices confirmed that Dave offered great value as his prices were 20 to 40% below the cost of two national "fun food" restaurants just around the corner. I don't believe, though, that his cost of buying hamburger, chicken and lettuce were significantly below the competition's. Thus, Dave probably works for little to no profits.

Given that a cheeseburger is my all-time favorite food, I ordered one. I then scribbled some quick notes that became the words you just read. I fully expected a generic burger to go along with the generic perceptions I had observed. Boy, was I wrong!

The cheeseburger was spectacular, and I know a few things about cheeseburgers. Dave really does pay attention to details. The meat tasted fresh ground, not from a preformed frozen patty. The bun was a bulky roll that had been grilled. The cheese was a blend of three cheeses that had been shredded and blended together. And the taste was of a burger that had been flame grilled not fried.

Clearly Dave's Place was a place for locals who had discovered it. A check of the date of the article on the wall indicated the restaurant was three years old. However, because of Dave's lack of simple benefit communications, I had driven past his place for three years and never bothered to stop in.

It doesn't have to be this way. My guess is Dave has to work hard, long hours to make a living. He's clearly a great cook with a real passion for preparing great food. If he communicates that clearly to the world, he can dramatically enhance his return on effort expended.

If Dave is happy making low profits, then there's no problem. If, however, he wants to make more money per unit of effort he puts into the business, then he needs to communicate about what makes him great.

Think now about your business. If I came to your Web site or place of business, what would I see? What would your staff tell me makes you unique and great? Hanging a banner out front or instructing your staff on what to say costs virtually nothing. Do it. Do it now and you will be amazed what a difference it makes in getting customers to stop and take notice of you when you clearly articulate what's in it for them.

Practical Tactic: Self-Audit of Current Benefit Communications

Step 1 Gather the materials that communicate your core business offering. If you are an existing business, find materials that describe what your company is all about. Examples might include
- Yellow pages advertisement
- Company advertisement from a trade or consumer publication
- Company brochure
- Home page from your Web site
- Direct-mail prospecting letter
- Telemarketing script

If you're a retailer and have none of the above, simply take a photo of the front of your establishment showing your signage as representative of your core customer concept.

If you're not in business yet, use a previously written description from either an e-mail, business plan or even a napkin you might have scribbled your dream upon. If you have nothing written, then write it *now*. This is nonnegotiable. If you can't put it in words, you have no chance of long-term success. (It should be noted I am not prone to declaring absolutes. However, in the case of giving voice to your business in words, it's absolutely critical.)

Step 2 In a quiet place, read the best representation of your core business idea out loud with a full voice. Our research has found it's critical to read it out loud, as we want the ears to hear the message, just as we want the eyes to see it and the mind to think about it.

Step 3 Put away the materials. On a clean sheet, identify and explain in a single sentence what the materials described as "what's in it for the customer." Be honest. Don't add thoughts you didn't read. The purpose of this step is to simply translate what currently exists into a single sentence.

Step 4 With great honesty, look at the single sentence you have just written from the perspective of a customer who is being introduced to your business for the first time. Answer the following questions with a simple yes or no.

- Is the benefit communicated in a clear and obvious fashion?
- Is the message specific about what's in it for you?
- As a new customer, does the idea excite your interest?
- Is the concept clearly unique versus what the competition is offering?

If you don't have four resounding yesses, then the good news is the pages ahead will guide you to tremendous improvements in your marketing message. By making those changes, you can generate significantly improved business results.

Keep these materials together, as you will be using them again in the next few chapters.

Benefits, Not Features

A classic error is to mistake features for benefits.

Benefits are what's in it for the customer. A benefit is what your customer receives, enjoys or experiences in exchange for his time, trouble, trust or money.

Features are the facts, figures, technology and details that make up the structure of your product or service.

It's not uncommon for features to enable benefits. When they do, it's important that the benefit dimension of the feature be clearly articulated. Without communication as a benefit, it is left to the customer to derive and determine why the feature is of importance. And the more work required of customers, the less sales return you will realize.

Here's an example from a brochure from a client of mine that details the features and benefits resulting from a new automobile suspension system the client offers.

Features	Benefits
(Stuff)	(What's In It For Me—WII-FM)
Reduced single wheel stiffness	Improves ride comfort
Near equal wheel loading	Improves traction and steering
Increased suspension travel	Superior off-road handling ability
Stabilization control	Reduces rollover risk

It's interesting to note that the brochure lists both features and benefits side by side in a chart. This listing of both is due to the mix of target audiences at automobile manufacturers. The benefit column is intended for the marketing managers, whose focus is primarily on marketing to end consumers. The feature column speaks directly to the engineering managers at client companies

Scientists, engineers and others who work on technology are prone to focus on features instead of benefits. Features are the things they get to invent, design, tool and build. They live with the technology day to day. Thus, the translation from features to benefits is obvious to them.

In technology-driven companies it's common for management to lose focus. Instead of communicating what's in it for customers, managers can fall into the trap of communicating their technology discoveries as the big news. Transforming the "joy of technology" into true customer benefits can be a challenge, especially if the person in charge is exceptionally rational. Dan, VP for technology for a major manufacturer of kitchen appliances, is a good case in point. Dan was the proud papa of a number of patents for incredible technologies. In fact, his promotion to VP had been in large part due to his incredible skill at inventing technological breakthroughs. For two frustrating years, Dan and his company had been unable to transform their patents into high-potential products. They had written a collection of concepts for new products; however, in each case, quantitative research found poor customer interest. That's what prompted them to visit us at the Eureka! Ranch.

A review of their previous efforts made it clear that their visions for new products violated the first law of Marketing Physics. They lacked benefits. Their concepts proclaimed amazing technologies but the benefit to a customer was obscure at best.

I suggested that we focus our time on finding ways to transform the technologies into benefits. At first Dan did not see the value in my assessment. "What you're proposing sounds trivial. It's obvious why these technologies are important. An idiot can understand them."

So I declared myself the village idiot. I proceeded to relentlessly ask the why questions.

Why should I care about this technology? *Why* did you create this technology? *Why* is this technology important? *Why* is this technology necessary? *Why* doesn't competition have this technology?

Slowly the concepts evolved. At first, Dan held tight to his techno speak wanting to make sure we provided full and complete explanations. I pulled equally hard to make it customer relevant by declaring overt benefits. "I'm not trivializing your great work." I explained. "I'm just trying to translate it into the benefit language so customers will want to buy it."

Dan started to understand the differences between technology features and true customer benefits. As the technology features were repositioned as customer benefits, he saw it didn't trivialize the technology as he had feared but rather it celebrated the core reason for the technology.

Dan's transformation was complete when he declared, "It seems we have to think differently. We need to start our development efforts by stepping back and focusing on what's really important—the customer's needs—if we are to make a real impact on the company." He even agreed to discard some of the new technologies because they offered little customer benefit.

Small business people can also fall into the feature trap. Having gone through the challenge of developing a vision into a tangible product or service, business owners want to explain all the technology and effort that went into creation. Don't. Customers don't care how much work you had to do. All they want to know is what's in it for them.

The conclusion isn't very complicated. Turn technology features into customer benefits if you want to realize a real return on your investment.

Practical Tactic: Turning Features Into Benefits

Your task is to learn how to translate features into customer-focused benefits.

Step 1 Make a list of all of the defining features associated with your service or product offering.
- List the attributes, ingredients and dimensions that define why you are as you are.
- Focus on both *what* you offer and *how* you deliver it to customers.

- List the obvious points of difference between you and your competition.
- List the less obvious but still significant points of difference versus competition.

Step 2 Transform each feature into a benefit. Follow the system I used in the story above about Dan the technology expert. Relentlessly ask the why questions of each feature.
- Why should I care about this feature?
- Why did you create this feature?
- Why is this feature important?
- Why is this feature necessary?
- Why doesn't competition have this feature?

Step 3 Review your current marketing materials for features and benefits. Each time a feature is listed, modify it to communicate the benefit that results from that feature. Now step back and review the piece again. Most likely, it will now be much more exciting and persuasive to customers.

The New News Is Overtness

For years, marketing textbooks have emphasized communicating customer benefits. The new news from our analysis is the importance of overtness. Customers don't have the time, energy or attention span to decipher implied or obscure benefit communications.

The average customer is overwhelmed with marketing messages. He bumps up against thousands of advertising messages each day. Millions of Web sites scream for his attention. He has fractions of seconds to evaluate your idea and determine if it could provide real value to his life. He has to "get it" immediately. The value to him needs to be self-evident.

Today because of the hurricane of marketing messages customers are exposed to, there is a need to be brash, bold and in-your-face *overt* about your customer benefit and point of difference. It's estimated that customers use only 2% of the available information they are exposed to. Net, this is no time to be humble or shy. Being brash and overt with your benefit is the path to genuine growth.

The average supermarket has over forty thousand different items in it. The total of all printed knowledge is estimated to double every five years. In 1993, *The New York Times* estimated that humanity publishes as many words each week as it did in all of human history up to 1800. A report by 3M corporation indicated that the average consumer is exposed to some three thousand advertisements a day!

Years ago you didn't need to declare your Overt Benefit. In a small town, you could hang a sign showing a picture of a loaf of bread and communicate baker, a mug of beer and communicate tavern, or a needle and thread and communicate seamstress. Merchants had virtual monopolies for their respective trades in their towns. Customers had no choice because there were simply no other options. Business rose or fell based on the number of customers who came through town looking for your goods.

In rural towns, this situation still exists. Simply being open and doing what you say is enough. As a monopoly, it also means greater flexibility in pricing and thus the potential for higher profit margins.

As a business grows, eventually competition enters the market seeking to steal some of the pioneer's success. Now it's not enough to say "baker." Now you must define and declare what customers can get from your bakery they can't get anywhere else. In effect, by making an overt statement of benefit you are restoring the perception of monopoly uniqueness in the marketplace. And thus, you are able to retain reasonable profit margins.

If no Overt Benefit is offered, pricing becomes the key decision criterion for your customers. The long-term result of this is a lowering of profits and eventual ruin of one or more of the businesses. It doesn't have to be this way. By carving out an Overt Benefit you and you alone stand for, you can thrive without continuous discount pricing.

Today, competition for customers is intense. In Cincinnati, Ohio, the phone book lists 100 bug exterminators, 51 window cleaners, 72 martial arts schools, 186 antique dealers, 129 funeral directors and 1,739 lawyers. In short, consumers today are overwhelmed with options. They don't have the time to interview each and every pest exterminator to determine what its unique offering is. Thus, they review ads, talk to friends and make their selections. If you offer an Overt Benefit, the odds of someone selecting you from an advertisement or being recommended by a friend dramatically increases (e.g., "I'd call XYZ Pest Control. Its treatment kills pests yet is really safe for pets.")

Practical Tactic: Turning Benefits into Overt Benefits

A few pages back, you translated your features into benefits. Next, the challenge is to turn the benefits into Overt Benefits.

Step 1 Make a list of your potential benefits.

Step 2 Transform each benefit into an Overt Benefit. You do this by adding directness, bluntness and specifics to the generic promises. As an example, if you were in the shoeshine business, you might transform the following generic benefits into Overt Benefits like this.

Benefits	Overt Benefits
Fast Shoeshine	2 Minute Shoeshine
Durable Shoeshine	Armor Shoeshine Lasts 7 days
Protect Your Shoes	Salt Guard Protects From Winter Damage
All Shoes Shined	Gentle Shine for Delicate Women's Shoes
Whole Shoe Care	Special Anti-Slip Sole Treatment

In summary, the transition looks like this.

1. Start with service and product features.
2. Communicate the customer benefit that the feature enables.
3. Turn the generic benefit into an Overt Benefit.

It's Not Boasting When You Deliver

When marketing your company be blunt about the benefit you offer to customers.

Let a customer say no because what you offer doesn't apply to him. But never let a customer say no because he doesn't understand what you offer.

You've worked hard to create a great product or service. Stand proud and let the world know the good news of the Overt Benefits you offer for them to enjoy. It's not boasting when you deliver what you promise.

When your benefit is communicated in an overt manner, customers can make reliable decision about your ability to offer them something of value. In addition, when your message is overt, it also has the ability to "travel well." Specifically, it can be shared from one person to another creating that all-important word of mouth that is the sign of a healthy business.

The childhood game of telephone relay brings this concept alive. In this game, a story is whispered in a person's ear. That person then whispers the story to the next person. In time, the story comes around the circle. If the story is complicated or obscure, what comes out in the end is often times hilariously different from the original story. If the message is simple, clear and overt, the communication travels easily.

When customers make inquiries based on responses to an Overt Benefit message, you and your staff will be able to spend more time servicing the highest potential clients. It's common sense. When you generate customer interest with an Overt Benefit, those attracted have in effect prequalified themselves as having tangible interest in what you're selling. Contrast this approach with mass marketing of a generic offering. Those customers who express interest will vary widely in their core interests—some may be seeking a high-quality service, some a low-cost service, some a highly customized service, some a highly specialized service. You and your staff can end up wasting half your time on customers who are low potential.

Sometimes people feel they might insult their customers if they are too overt about their benefit. Don't worry. You can't.

Years ago I worked on a food product that required customers to do some assembly. As the product was very different from anything done before, it was decided we would go to extreme lengths to ensure customers didn't make a mistake.

I had just finished inventing a board game for children who are too young to read. I suggested we use children's games as our inspiration for a new way of handling instructions for the new food item. A comic strip format was created in which the entire process was visualized. Where two eggs were called for, two were shown being cracked into the bowl. Where a third of a cup of oil was called for, it was shown. The new format was a huge success. In testing, virtually everyone was successful with the food kit and not one person complained about it being insulting.

When talking about what a customer receives, it is not possible to insult them. There is nothing more important to a potential customer than to know what she will get and enjoy as a result of doing business with you.

When you have a clearly defined Overt Benefit, everyone at your organization will be more effective. When great ideas are pursued, a chain reaction of brilliance occurs: product development focuses on what really matters, packaging is clear, advertising is meaningful and persuasive.

You can succeed with a benefit that is not clear, direct and overt, just as you can fill a swimming pool with a garden hose with a nozzle that is only half open. Eventually the pool will fill; it'll just take a while. Similarly, an implied or obscure benefit will eventually get communicated to customers. However, when you open the hose and tell it straight and direct, everything is made more effective. The pool fills faster, and your message gets communicated faster.

Benefits Are Relative . . . Relative to a Specific Target Segment

All benefits are relative to a specific target audience or occasion. The goal of a target audience definition is to provide focus and clarity to your marketing message and product or service design.

The target audience is the group of people you seek to delight and excite the most with your offering. The folks who define the target will have a higher-than-average interest. They are also the foundation of your initial and continuing volume. It's important to note that though the target audience you select is the center of your business's bull's-eye. It is not the sole source of volume.

A client of mine has a saying that describes this concept exactly: "Delight the few to attract the many." When a clear target audience is defined, all product and service design has clarity and focus. This results in excitement is generated among customers far beyond the core target audience. Examples of this are numerous. Four-wheel-drive vehicles and hiking boots were originally designed for outdoor-oriented customers. Today, these kinds of products provide a sense of security to a much broader range of customers.

Another example is specialized television networks programmed for those viewers who do a lot of cooking, gardening or home repair. Having specific target audiences such as these provide guidance to the shows' producers and writers. The total audience for these programs is much larger. Many, if not most, of those who watch cooking shows on television never cook what is shown.

In some categories, it's not so much whom you want as a target as it is when your product is used. Beverages in particular often have "occasion" targets: coffee—morning; margaritas—Mexican food; champagne—celebrations; orange juice—morning; sports drinks—after and during exercise.

With a clear target occasion focus, you can focus your marketing communications as well as your product or service.

Here are some examples of nontraditional target audience definitions.

Auto Repair Shop's Potential Target Audiences
- Foreign cars
- Cars that have been in accidents
- Four-wheel-drive vehicles
- Vintage/classic cars
- Basic transportation cars—just keep it running
- Owner-modified cars

Small Business Accountant's Potential Target Audiences
- Businesses that are family owned and operated by multiple generations
- Businesses with high debt
- Fast growth businesses
- Service businesses
- Companies doing business internationally
- Professional services firms (lawyers, doctors, etc.)
- Accountants' accountants (servicing other accountants)

Whenever you focus on a specific target audience, you immediately enhance customer perception of you as an expert. And, you expect to pay an expert more for the same goods or services than you would a nonexpert.

On Prince Edward Island, there is a sports adventure company called Outside Expeditions. The company offers a variety of kayak and biking trips. For years I saw its brochure and thought about going on a trip, but for some reason I didn't. A year ago, the owners, Bryon Howard and Shirley Wright, were part of a small business coaching program I was running. Later when we gathered in the basement of their home, the command center for the business, I related my experience of having seen their brochure yet never taking advantage of their services. After discussing the situation, the challenge became clear: They had a target audience problem.

The brochure shows a photo of a woman kayaking on the ocean. Being an adventure enthusiast, it didn't appeal to me, as the waters seemed still, the adventure boring. My wife, who is not a water sports enthusiast, saw something different. "There's no land in sight," she complained when I showed it to her.

Two people. Each with a different level of category expertise and each with a different perspective on the advertisement.

The original brochure

We then set about crafting a new brochure that talked directly to each target audience. Excerpts from the new brochure copy are detailed below.

Welcome, EVERYONE, to the world of outdoor adventures.

Make your next vacation one to remember!

Whether it's learning how to kayak, cycling with the family down a quiet rail, or joining an unforgettable multi-day expedition, Outside Expeditions has a tour that's perfect for you. Designed to be accessible to EVERYONE, our tours are based on both participants' outdoor adventure experience and individual comfort levels. Accordingly, tours are designed as either suitable for "Newcomers" to outdoor adventure or those who are "Experienced" adventurers.

The photos for each section of the brochure matched what would attract each target audience. Special trips were also developed to appeal to each target and described to help bring alive the experiential benefits of going on the trip. Here's an example of one of my favorites.

PEI Preserve Company Kayak Tour—Full Day

Paddle down the scenic Clyde River to New Glasgow's famous Prince Edward Island Preserve Company. See (and taste!) Canada's finest preserves being prepared for market, then enjoy a picnic lunch overlooking the Clyde. On this gentle river paddle you'll experience the best of PEI—beautiful landscapes, natural and cultural history and great food.

Merwyn forecast a 72% probability of success for the new brochure versus 21% for the previous day trip posters. Marketplace results were equally strong. Despite a summer season that had record levels of rain, Outside Expedition's revenue for the year grew 40%!

Practical Tactic: Who Is or Could Be Your Target?

The purpose of this tactic is to define your core customer. Before we begin, I would ask that you open your mind. If you complete this task by simply force fitting today into all options, you will not grow. By letting your imagination run a little, you get the ability to prototype in your mind at low cost the potential of exploring different definitions of your core target audience.

Customers With Extreme Needs Identify and list customer segments with extreme or special needs. Hotels and resorts have found success by catering to senior citizens, families with young children or even vacationers traveling with pets.

Customers That No One Else Likes to Hassle With Waste Management Corporation has become a $12.9 billion giant by doing what no one else wished to do—pick up trash. I have a friend from college who's built a large company handling toxic waste cleanup. Think about your industry. Who are the toughest, most obnoxious customers? Make a list of them customers as potential targets.

Customers Who Control Spending Decisions Follow the money. Look closely at your product or service offering. If you are involved in commercial or industrial businesses, this may not be a simple task. Often, many folks are involved in the buying process. Focus your energy on the key decision makers and success is a near certainty. Which customers control the buying decision?

Customers With Varying Levels of Category Experience Think about what level of experience your core customers have relative to your product category. The benefits you focus on will vary greatly if you focus on customers new to the category versus those with great experience. Given a choice, my preference is to focus on those new to a category. Those who are new often have some very specific complaints or negative perceptions. By addressing these directly, you will often find great success while generating interest from those already in the category. By educating customers new to a category, you potentially win loyal friends for life. Fine wine merchants often follow this strategy. Educational wine tastings break down intimidation and generate long-term customers.

Customers new to the category can require lots of time to service. Thus, established companies often neglect them, focusing instead on the higher end "sophisticated" customer.

Review the categories of potential target audiences. List three to five that interest you most. Then create ideas for how you might modify your communications or offering to provide a true Overt Benefit. When completed, look at the alternatives and weigh them versus what you offer today.

A Story of How Target Audience Can Create Benefit Ideas

The village of Victoria-by-the-Sea lies on the south shore of Prince Edward Island. It's a quintessential island village complete with fishing harbor, historic buildings, artists and craftspeople. The village is also the home to the Victoria Playhouse, the longest running little theater on the island. For twenty summers, Erskine Smith has staged plays on the stage of the town hall.

My wife and I love the town and playhouse and make two or three visits each summer to enjoy dinner, the shops and a play. For many years, Victoria enjoyed great growth and business. In recent years, however, that growth has slowed. It's slowed in large part due to the addition of major golf courses and tourist developments on the other side of the island and an explosion of theater offerings all across the island.

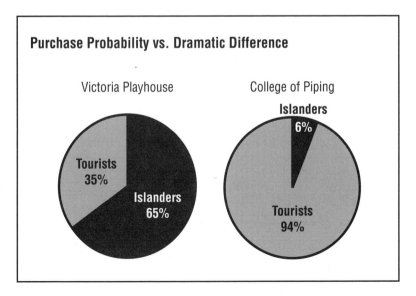

Last summer I volunteered to conduct a little research to identify opportunities for optimizing the village's marketing message. Surveys were passed out to those attending plays as well as to attendees of evening concerts at the College of Piping just thirty minutes away in Summerside.

The results showed clearly that even though both venues attracted about the same number of total visitors, proportionally Victoria attracted far fewer tourists than the College of Piping.

At first glance, this was discouraging as it meant that today the village wasn't attracting tourists at significant levels. This is especially important to the local merchants, as the data also indicated tourists spent much more money in the shops and restaurants than islanders did.

A Merwyn forecast was run on the marketing brochure from the playhouse's previous season. The results, like the season's sales, were not encouraging.

Overall Probability of Success: 23%

Returns on Effort Expended
(Percentiles calculated versus Merwyn's benchmark database of 4,000 concepts)

1. Overt Benefit   **30th percentile**
Specifically, obviously, directly—
What's in it for the customer?

2. Real Reason to Believe   **40th percentile**
Why should the customer believe you will
deliver on the promise made above?

3. Dramatic Difference   **10th percentile**
How revolutionary and new-to-the-world
is your benefit/reason to believe pair

After much discussion of what made Victoria and the playhouse unique, we made little progress coming to agreement. Upon reviewing the data again, an answer revealed itself. What if we turned the disadvantage of having so few tourists into a positive? Instead of looking at the high levels of islanders as a negative, use it as a positive. And thus was born a new marketing message.

Victoria-by-the-Sea

Where Islanders Go . . .

To Laugh . . .

When Islanders want to get away from the summer hustle and bustle, they head for Victoria-by-the-Sea. Located in the heart of the South Shore, Victoria is a 182-year-old picturesque village. Indeed, 65% of the visitors to Victoria Playhouse last year were Islanders.

"One of the prettiest towns in Canada"
—*Harrowsmith Magazine*

Victoria Playhouse Festival 2001
PEI's Longest Running Little Theater
Celebrating 20 Years of Genuine Entertainment

The new brochure then went on to describe the plays being offered.

The new concept went back into Merwyn. The results offer hope. Clearly the "where the islanders go" positioning dramatically enhances the persuasive power of the message.

Focus, Focus, Focus Your Overt Benefit

Benefit is one communication area where more is not necessarily better. Analysis of four thousand concepts indicates that the greater the number of benefits promised, the lower your chances of success.

One or Two Benefits = 44% Chance of Success

Three or More Benefits = 37% Chance of Success

The more you focus on doing one thing great, the greater your probability of success. Focus also elevates you from a mere merchant of goods or services to the level of becoming a brand. As a

Overall Probability of Success: 60%

Returns on Effort Expended
(Percentiles calculated versus Merwyn's benchmark database of 4,000 concepts)

1. Overt Benefit   90th percentile
   Specifically, obviously, directly—
   What's in it for the customer?

2. Real Reason to Believe   80th percentile
   Why should the customer believe you will
   deliver on the promise made above?

3. Dramatic Difference   50th percentile
   How revolutionary and new-to-the-world
   is your benefit/reason to believe pair

brand, you gain customers' respect for your expertise in a specific area. Because of your expertise, customers are more likely to try your new products and also more likely to repeat purchase your goods or services. Also important, as mentioned previously, customers are more willing to pay a premium price to an expert.

The value of your brand is ever changing. Each time a customer has a relationship with your company, his perception of your brand either goes up or goes down.

The more clear and distinct your benefit, the greater your potential to build a branded position in your customer's mind. In the world of automobiles, there are many nameplates; however, there are very few real brands that are associated with one benefit.

- BMW—driving
- Volvo—safety
- Mercedes—engineering
- Toyota and Honda—reliability
- Ferrari—speed

Contrast these nameplates with those of vehicles such as Ford, Chevrolet and Chrysler, which are all things to all people.

Look closely at your business. When customers hear your company's name, what is the one thing that comes to their minds? What one thing do you want to have come to mind? The answer to the second question is your Overt Benefit.

A quick way to confirm whether your organization has focus is to ask each employee the simple question: In your opinion, what does our company stand for in the eyes of customers? Don't be surprised if you get a variety of answers. And if you do get different answers, don't get angry. Rather, have them read this chapter, then sit down as a team and find common ground for what your collective Overt Benefit should be.

In Cincinnati, there's a fellow who understands focus. His name is Ken Eilers. He's "the screen man." He fixes screens for buildings. He doesn't do doors, windows or window boxes. Ken and his customized Screen Mobile fix screens. Ken says it's a simple concept: "I don't want to compare myself to a brain surgeon. But if you only do one thing, you tend to get good." Ken is booked months in advance because of his expertise.

Some businesspeople fear that by focusing on one thing they limit their customer bases. They assume that by promising everything to everyone, they broaden their business potential. The data doesn't confirm this assumption. What the data indicates is that the more you dilute what you offer, the lower your focus, credibility and customer appeal.

I've personally observed this same phenomenon in the market place. A client of mine named Deena introduced a line of innovative cookies into 25% of the United States as one single item. The message was clear and focused. The brand quickly became a huge success. Seeing this success, management got greedy and decided to expand the line with five other varieties. Deena explained, "The company was so desperate for sales growth that when we saw the regional success we figured more items would mean more sales." This is the same kind of thinking that salespeople often preach. They assume that the more different packages they can put on the shelf, the greater the overall volume will be. Sadly, this type of thinking is usually wrong.

In the case of Deena, the diffusion from one to six different subcategories of cookies seriously hurt her focus, as she now offered a "complete" line of cookies instead of one highly innovative type. Advertising that had been laser focused became diffused. Packaging that communicated one thought became confused. Manufacturing that had been producing one product with excellence became stretched, and three of the five new items suffered from product stability problems. The net result was a failure of spectacular proportions.

Senior management blamed the failure on poor execution. The real blame lay with the senior managers who in their greed lost focus.

Postscript: Deena's brand still exists today. The line has been reduced in size and the price has been dropped to the level of private label and generic products. The company doesn't make much money on it; it's used as a means for filling capacity at the company's plants.

When you proclaim and deliver excellence in one area, it gives credibility to your entire business. Rather than limit your customer base, you can actually grow it as a result of customer's perception of your excellence. Customers assume that if you do one thing great, you must have excellence across the board.

When I worked at Procter & Gamble, the Folgers coffee business was faced with the challenge of focusing. The question was, Should the company orient all marketing efforts toward the morning occasion? The challenge was while lots of coffee was consumed in the morning, more than 50% of coffee was drunk from lunchtime on.

After much debate, the leap was taken and Folgers was marketed as "The Best Part of Wakin' Up Is Folgers in Your Cup." The results were spectacular. By every business measure, Folgers grew. And, not only was it drunk more in the morning, it was also drunk more at lunch, during the afternoon and in the evening.

It grew in all occasions because the true torture test occasion for coffee had been selected. In effect, if it can wake you up in the morning, just think what it'll do for you in the middle of the afternoon!

Think about your business. What is the torture test occasion, torture test customer, torture test product or service? Can you show great expertise in this area and thus create a perception of excellence in all that you do?

Think for a minute about the last three full-service restaurants you had dinner at. Why did you go where you did? Oftentimes we select a restaurant because it has a reputation as being great at something. In Cincinnati it's Montgomery Inn for ribs, The Precinct for steak, Skyline for Cincinnati chili, The Grand Finale for dessert, The Heritage for genuinely innovative food. Each restaurant has a clear specialty it is famous for. That doesn't mean we don't visit these restaurants when we are not in the mood for their specialties. Rather, it sets in our mind a perception of excellence for each restaurant.

It is possible for the one thing that is marketed to customers to be what is called an "umbrella benefit." With an umbrella benefit, the customer is offered a singular benefit that is the cumulative effect of a collection of smaller benefits that are highly synergistic. A classic example of this is the cold medicine NyQuil. Its focused umbrella benefit is "so you can rest and have a good morning medicine." This umbrella benefit is the summation of a collection of smaller benefits articulated in its advertising line "The Nighttime, Sniffling, Sneezing, Coughing, Achy, Stuffy Head, Fever So You Can Rest Medicine."

Practical Tactic: Do One Thing Great

Step 1 Get out your list of Overt Benefits and write them on individual index cards.

Step 2 Deal your cards into three piles.
- Pile 1: Ideas that could stand alone as your singular benefit message
- Pile 2: Ideas that are strong but couldn't stand alone
- Pile 3: Ideas that are smaller and less relevant

Step 3 Evaluate each of the cards in pile 1. Arrange these from most to least motivational to customers. Evaluate the potential for combining benefits in pile 2 into pairs. Compare these options to those from pile 1.

CHAPTER 3

How to Find Your
Overt Benefit

*This chapter takes you through the process for defining your own bene-
fit and making it overt. For greatest effectiveness, you are advised to
work on refining your concept as you read. If you do, at the end of the
chapter you will realize an immediate improvement in your ability to win
more, lose less and make more money.*

The First Place to Look for Overt Benefits—
Why You Started the Business

The search for relevant Overt Benefits and how to communicate
them is a never-ending task. You can always enhance and improve
your message. In the second half of this book, multiple methods
that have great persuasion power will be discussed for helping
you inspire and articulate Overt Benefits. However, there are two
core strategies I want to highlight now.

   The first is that when it comes to an Overt Benefit, it's likely
you already know what you need to know. **Often the key Overt
Benefit for your company is the reason you got into the business
in the first place.** Your core Overt Benefit was the driving passion
that fueled your energy for going against the conformity of classic
employment to start your own enterprise. That passion could
have been a pet peeve, frustration or personal need.

   The stories of this kind of motivation for starting a business
are common. Walt Disney was disgusted at the dirtiness of amuse-
ment parks when he took his kids to one for a birthday party.
Thus Disneyland was born. Bill Bowerman needed faster shoes for
his University of Oregon track team and thus Nike was born.

Practical Tactic: Return to Your Roots

To discover your Overt Benefit, take a moment to respond to the
following thoughts. For best results, write down the first thing that

comes to mind. Then after thinking about it for day, rewrite your answer pushing deeper with fresh eyes.

1. Why did you get into the business in the first place?
   - first response
   - 24 hours later
2. What injustice, problem, pet peeve did you set out to address with your business?
   - first response
   - 24 hours later
3. What are you most proud of regarding what your company offers?
   - first response
   - 24 hours later
4. What would your most loyal customers boast most about regarding what you offer?
   - first response
   - 24 hours later
5. Complete this statement: We're the best/first/only company to offer. . .
   - first response
   - 24 hours later

The questions listed above are similar to the ones I ask top executives when working on projects for them. The challenge with many corporations today is that as a result of mergers and acquisitions, it's rare to find a manager who has a sense of history, understanding of customers or passion for the business. In these cases, I seek out old marketing materials, articles written about the company and brochures or ads from the beginning of the company. From these historical documents, the inner passion that was the reason for the brand's existence often reveals itself.

As a small business owner, you have a great advantage versus large corporations because you live and breathe the business every day.

The Second Place to Look for Overt Benefits—
Your Personal Passions

The second and related place to look for Overt Benefits is within your personal passions. If you are a true entrepreneur, you feel passionately about your business. If you're an accountant, you love spreadsheets. If you're a restaurant owner, you love good food. If you're a plumber, you love figuring out how to fix pipes.

Because of your personal involvement and understanding of your industry, you know the good, the bad and the ugly about your industry and competitors. By channeling your passion, you can oftentimes identify the insights necessary to define a provocative Overt Benefit.

Using your personal passion as a source for focusing your business has the added value of providing a source of continuing energy. It's just natural when you are working on what you love that you have more energy and do a better job. Conversely, when you are forced to spend time on that which doesn't interest you, your personal energy declines.

Challenge yourself right here. Right now.

What part of your product or service gets you most excited? How can you modify your marketing or product design to allow you to spend more time on that area? What target audiences would most appreciate excellence in the area you are most excited about?

When clients visit the Eureka! Ranch, I am very sensitive to supporting their brands. To give you a few examples, I carry an American Express Centurion Card, I use *Band-Aid* brand bandages, I eat Frito-Lay snacks, I serve only genuine HoneyBaked Ham during the holidays, I drive a Ford F-series pickup truck, and one day I will be buried in a Batesville casket. I do this because I believe in supporting my clients. I also do it because I am passionate about my clients' brands.

All of the companies listed above are run by managers with an equal level of passion for their brands. Sadly, not all executives have the same feelings of passion. For example, we once worked on a project for a company selling a leading brand of breakfast breads. When the managers visited the ranch, we had an overwhelming amount of the client's breads available in every room of the ranch. In addition, we had engaged the services of a leading local chef to create a wide range of variations of the client's base product. In the morning, we had transformed ordinary breads into a broad range of incredible breakfast and snack foods. Our thoughts were that these new culinary creations would stimulate fresh thinking.

The executives entered that morning and to our amazement

ignored their own product. "Is their anything else to eat?" they asked. It was all I could do to not blow my top. The mission was breads, yet this was clearly not a team that had a passion for their product. They were corporate mercenaries doing a job. It showed in their attitude. It showed in their lack of commitment to crafting bold ideas.

If you want to get customers excited, you yourself must be genuinely excited! Energy in equals energy out. The more energy and excitement you have about the benefit your company offers, the more your customers will respond.

Practical Tactic: Leverage Your Passions

Record yourself explaining what you offer. Have it typed. Then read the words. Do they match your brochure and your advertising? The key here is to let your passions run wild. This is not the time to be professional and calm. Let yourself get excited about what you do and what you can do for customers. By listening to these tapes, you can often learn what your Overt Benefit really is.

Creating and leading a small business takes a lot of work. If you're going to commit the energy to being your own boss, take advantage of freedom that small business ownership offers and spend as much time as possible on what you truly love.

It's a safe assumption that if you focus your energies on your true passion, you will develop an expertise your customers will recognize and you will generate genuine sales and profits.

Your Overt Benefit Is Your Mission

When you make a focused decision on what your Overt Benefit is, you dramatically increase your sales potential. In addition, defining your Overt Benefit provides benefits that go beyond marketing. Defining your Overt Benefit provides a clear sense of calling and mission to everyone involved in your business.

An Overt Benefit helps all employees focus their energies on what really matters. For example, if you work for Volvo, you know that you always select the product design that reinforces safety. If you work for BMW, you reinforce the driving experience. If you're Ken the Screen Man, at a trade show you focus your energy on the booths that sell products and services related to screens.

The power of having a clear definition of your direction is immense. A study published by the American Marketing

Association found that the greater your definition of your core message/idea at the start, the greater your probability of business success at the end.

Impact of Early Concept/Message Definition	Success Rate
Poor Definition	23%
Moderate Definition	64%
Strong Definition	85%

It just makes sense. If you're building a new house, the more exact and clear the definition you have at the start, the less costly it will be to complete construction.

When your employees and key suppliers know what is critical, they have a clear definition of what to do. Just as a boat cuts through the water more efficiently when it has a pointed bow, so, too, does your marketing message cut through the clutter with greater efficiency when it has clear clarity.

The most difficult yet important decision you make when focusing is deciding what you're not going to be. Saying no is difficult. With each no we feel we are giving up something that could be of value.

Say no. Say no with conviction. Say no because it gives you a greater chance of success. Say no for the good of the business. Say no in order to enhance your employees' effectiveness.

There is a natural passion that comes when employees are focused on what they believe is the right and just cause. It happens with political revolutions. Those who believe in a cause will pledge their lives, fortunes and sacred honor to win. The giving of one's life is generally not necessary for entrepreneurial success. However, the spirit that fuels this kind of attitude is the same. **When you say no to little ideas, big ideas happen!**

Benefits of the Heart Versus the Head

Customer benefits can satisfy the logical mind by having rational dimensions. They can also satisfy the heart through emotional components.

Rational benefits include tangible dimensions that can be quantitatively measured. In a laboratory, we can test and validate these dimensions.

Emotional benefits are also tangible dimensions. However, by their very nature, they are harder to quantitatively measure. Customers feel a difference, yet, like the emotion of love it is hard to quantify.

The greatest of emotions—love and fear of death—provide classic examples of emotional benefits. The gift of a diamond is seen as the ultimate statement of love between two adults. It wasn't always this way. This perception is the result of a smart marketing effort that started around 1900.

The life insurance industry provides a classic emotional benefit. In exchange for your payments, while you are living, you receive emotional peace of mind knowing that when you die, you are providing for loved ones.

Advertising gurus will tell you emotional benefits are far more important and valuable than rational ones. When probed on the facts to support their preaching, the gurus typically retreat, claiming that an emotional benefit can't be measured-it's just a feeling. I'm sorry, but feelings never filled a bank account. And in fact, the data says differently. Our analysis of some four thousand concepts indicates that there is no difference in effectiveness between rational and emotional benefits.

Primary Communication	Probability of Success
Rational benefit	45%
Emotional benefit	42%
Emotional and rational benefits	36%

The key learning is clear: Do one thing great! Both rational and emotional benefits have equal chances of success (45% and 42% are statistically equal). However, when the message is diffused, with combinations of emotional and rational, probability of success declines.

The issue is once again focus, focus, focus. If you are going to appeal to the customer's heart, do so, but do so with focus.

Emotional benefits can help with communications discipline. When benefits are emotional, there is often greater focus on true customer benefits. With a rational benefit, it's easier to become lazy and fall into the trap of communicating features instead of benefits.

Emotional benefits can be difficult to work with. I've found that it's easier if, rather than discussing emotions, I use the term "experiential." It's easier to discuss, manage and lead the creation of customer experiences.

Customer experiences are emotional transformations that take a customer from one state of feeling to another. When presented with focus and skill, they can be incredibly motivating.

One of my favorite stories about the power of experiential benefits involves the Indian River Festival of Fine Music on Prince Edward Island. The Indian River Festival is a summer concert series of classical music offered within the acoustic perfection of Saint Mary's Church. For years, the festival promoted its concerts with rational, feature-focused descriptions of who was performing what.

> July 23, the music of Bach, Chopin and Liszt by Peter Allen, piano, and Patricia Creighton, flute.

This type of marketing message is very common in the "high arts," for example, symphonies, art museums, ballet, opera. Institutions of high arts tend to utilize snobbish marketing focused on the microniche audience of arts fanatics. There is a feeling in the high arts that if you have to ask questions, you are not worthy of participating in the experience.

The challenge in today's market is there are often not enough cultural elite to fill the concert halls and pay the bills. Even more troubling is that many of the fine arts "club members" are old and slowly dying off.

If fine music and art programs are to survive, they are going to have to start communicating the emotional/experiential benefits of what they have to offer.

The Indian River Festival committee took just such a step. After attending a Marketing Physics training program, they repositioned all concerts to have overt experiential benefits. Here's the reworked announcement for the concert listed above.

An Evening of Romance
An evening of romance ... complete with flowers and candlelight. This one-of-a-kind evening will leave you relaxed and stress free. The music of Bach, Chopin and Liszt by Peter Allen, piano, and Patricia Creighton, flute.

For this specific concert, attendance nearly doubled versus

the year before by simply leveraging experiential benefits.

My wife and I were sitting in the church during the "Evening of Romance." Sitting next to us were a couple I would judge to be in their late sixties. Regarding the evening's concert, I overheard the gentleman remark cynically to his wife, "That's quite a sales gimmick to sell classical music as a way to create romance." His wife saw it differently. "I think it's a wonderful idea," she said and gave him a wink that communicated clearly her emotions. A smile came over the gentleman's face, and I do believe he even blushed a little. That, my friends, is an emotional benefit in action.

The overall Indian River Festival marketing message leveraged the experiential benefits of enjoying music within the unique acoustics of St. Mary's Church.

> The historic church of St. Mary's has a worldwide reputation among performers as one of the finest concert venues in the world. This architectural and acoustic treasure, with its rib-vaulted ceiling and all-wood construction, provides a purity of sound and musical richness like nowhere else.
>
> Music at St. Mary's is an experience to arouse the heart, enrich the mind, stir the soul and thrill the senses.
> - The sounds of the world's top musicians . . .
> - The tastes of tea and treats on the lawn overlooking Malpeque Bay . . .
> - The sights and feel of wood untouched for 100 years . . .
>
> The result is a once-in-a-lifetime concert experience that will shimmer in your memory long after the notes themselves have faded away.

In Merwyn, the new brochure generated a 72% probability of success, more than double the 30% probability of success the brochure from the year before had. And Merwyn's results were borne out in the marketplace. Festival attendance grew by nearly 50%, setting new records. Most importantly, the transformation energized the festival staff and volunteers as it gave them a clear focal point for all communications.

Experiential benefits are common in the world of food and

beverages. At a coffee cafe or neighborhood bar, beyond the liquid we consume, we receive camaraderie, a sense of belonging and comfort. The world of fashion also stresses experiential benefits. When we wear new clothes designed with great style, we feel good about ourselves.

Experiential and the closely related emotional benefits are not more powerful or less powerful; they are just another tool we can use to excite customers.

Visualization of Overt Benefits

Words often provide the starting place for defining overt benefits. However, pictures, are the most powerful means of communicating them to customers. By visualizing the moment of benefit, we can dramatically impact our communications.

When working with clients, we call this instant of benefit the Magic Moment. With birthday cakes, it's the moment just before the candles are blown out. With college tuition payments, it's the moment of graduation. With children's birthday gifts, it's the moment of tearing open the wrapping.

Tom Attea, a very creative and smart writer, once told me the story of how he created the commercials that introduced Mattel's Hot Wheels toy racing sets. "To bring the cars alive, I had them get the camera down real low to show the cars zooming buy and leaping in the air. With toys, it's critical that you show them as children see them."

Tom's advice holds true for all customers: **"Show it as customers see it."** When a customer purchases your goods or services, he is often buying a moment visualized in his mind.

A bride buys a gown for the moment she's walking down the aisle. A homeowner buys the new landscaping that will be the envy of the neighbors. Parents buy a computer for their children so they'll be ready for the future.

In each case, the thing being purchased is secondary to the moment the thing will make possible. As you craft your communications for customers, think about visuals. How could you visualize your end benefit? What is the defining moment of success for your product or service? The more you can visualize it, the easier it will be to get customers to visualize it and buy it.

Ben Franklin recommended to readers of his *Poor Richard's*

Almanack that they look before buying: "Believe none of what you hear and half of what you see."

Post Your Benefit in Your Most Important Place—Your Name

The singular most important marketing decision you will ever make is your brand name. Done properly, hearing just your brand name will cause your customers to have an immediate perception of what benefit you offer.

The power of benefit-focused naming is immense. It's not always possible, as names are often already established before you become involved with a business. However, when you can identify your benefit in your name, then every brand logo, business card, letterhead, truck sign, advertisement and Web site reinforces what makes you great! Review the following names that I just pulled from a phone book and, with nothing else, see if you can tell what the Overt Benefits are that these companies offer.

- Results Marketing
- Like New Auto Repair
- Best Buy Auto
- Catering With Elegance
- Classy Cuts Hair Salon
- Built-Rite Building Inspection Service
- The Uncommon Grocer—Gourmet and Natural Foods
- Prestige Kitchen Cabinets
- Hands-On Car Washing
- Purity Dairy
- Men-ergy Exotic Dancers
- Love-a-Lot Kindergarten

Legal note: It is important your name be suggestive yet not merely descriptive of the Overt Benefit you offer. The way U.S. trademark law works, names that are suggestive can be legally protected; however, names that are simply descriptive cannot. Thus, you cannot stop other companies from using descriptive terms associated with the category.

In my experience, when you know what your Overt Benefit is, then naming is a simple task. It's when you don't know what you want to stand for that naming is confusing and frustrating. When you get the Overt Benefit right, everything works: the name, the packaging, the marketing, the advertising and everything else.

Names can also be suggestive of emotional and experiential benefits.

- Chuckwagon Clem's Spicy Rattlesnake Salsa
  (rugged, Southwestern, dangerous)
- Country Kitchen Down Home Delicious Apple Pie
  (pure, honest, homemade)
- BeachBreeze Slow Sipper Coladas
  (relaxed, oceanside, soothing)

It's really important you get your brand name right. In the event you select a "fanciful name," it's especially important you provide a descriptive phrase that clearly describes what you have to offer.

Confusing customers is never a good strategy for winning their interest and patronage. Clever and obscure naming does not create customer curiosity. They simply reject you.

The Original Sign

The story of the sign in front of small business owner Stefan Czapalay's establishment is a classic.

What do you think Stefan's establishment offers customers?

a. A gourmet food store?

b. A specialty herb and health food store?

c. A gourmet restaurant?

d. A health food restaurant?

e. A luxury food store?

The answer was "c," a gourmet restaurant. When asked what his thinking was behind the sign, Stefan replied, "When I opened, I thought it was clever and classy. Looking at it now, I think I need a new sign." We spoke for a while about the experience he intended for his customers. A few weeks later a new subtitle sign was installed.

The New Sign

Stefan called me after the new sign went up and related that the impact of the change was immediate, "The first night after the new sign went up, I went out to the dining room visiting guests and asking them how they'd found out about us. The third table I visited said they learned about us from the sign out front." Stefan went on to explain this was a novel occurrence. "In all my years, I've never had anyone say they came in because of the sign."

Stefan's story is amusing but it's not uncommon. Look at your core name and description of your business. Is it clear? Is it overt? If not, why not?

Put It in Writing

Throughout this book, I will be pushing you to commit your thoughts to paper. If you're like most adults, you'll resist this, claiming you're not a writer, an author or a copywriter. You don't have to be.

I'm not asking you to write like Hemingway or even Stephen King. All you need to do is to document on paper the thoughts you think and speak associated with your business.

Writing is a process for organizing your thinking. When we give words to our ideas, they become real. You can think of writing or typing as a prototype marketing system. When you write an idea, the strengths shine through and the holes become glaringly obvious.

The great news about the kind of writing I'm encouraging you to do is you don't need to use any fancy words. In fact, analysis of customer reactions to written concepts shows that the optimum level of complexity in your writing is at about the fifth-grade level!

The findings above are not surprising when you realize that according to a 1992 survey by the U.S. Department of Education some 46% of adults lack a sufficient foundation of basic reading and writing skills.

Keeping writing clear and simple is also important for the potential customers with advanced reading skills. In today's cluttered, overcommunicated world, even those with great skill have little time to interpret or analyze your ideas. Say it straight, clear and overtly and you dramatically enhance your probability of success.

Practical Tactic: Giving Words to Your Overt Benefit

Your writing mission in this tactic, is to define your Overt Benefit in simple words.

Step 1 Speak onto the paper. You know in your head and heart what your Overt Benefit is. The challenge is to get it out of you and onto paper so others can understand it.

To overcome any barriers to writing, simply type or write what you speak. Speak your answers to the following questions and write them down. Use as many words as necessary. Tell the story of your business in your voice. Answer the questions as many times as necessary. If you can't speak and write simultaneously, then tape-record your voice and transcribe it.

Speak onto the paper your thoughts on some or all of the following:

My most important target audience is . . .

I am most proud of our ability to . . .

We're "famous with customers" for our ability to . . .

If the local newspaper was to do a story about us they would report we offer . . .

Unlike our competition, we offer our customers . . .

I'd like my customers to tell their friends that we provide the best . . .

My company enhances customers' lives by offering . . .

Be very specific. We offer customers the best . . .

Step 2 If you don't know the answers to these questions, go back to the front lines. Ask the questions of your people who work day to day with customers. Ask the questions of customers. When you've finished, you should have two to three pages of thoughts regarding your Overt Benefit.

The hard part of writing your Overt Benefit is generating the momentum to get the first words on paper. Once you have a draft, no matter how rough, you can then edit and revise. It's easier to edit then it is to create.

Step 3 After gathering a collection of thoughts, take a bit of a break for fifteen minutes or more to refresh your mind. When you return, take a pen and read what you've written. Circle any phrases or ideas that resonate with you. Put an X through any phrases that don't seem to be the essence of what your Overt Benefit should be.

At this point, I've found it helpful to take the words and phrases I've circled and rewrite them on another piece of paper. Then rewrite them again and again. Sometimes I fill five pages or more of alternative wordings, each line of writing being a complete prototype.

The best thing about writing prototypes is that they cost absolutely nothing to build. Writing thoughts makes them become more real and encourages personal honesty. I don't fully understand it, but often an idea that sounds great in my head loses its appeal when staring back from the computer screen.

If you have lots of benefits, look for new ways to combine them into bigger picture benefits. If you have lots of benefits and can't combine them, rate them from most to least important to customers. What benefits are unique to you? What benefits are simply the cost of doing business? Use your ratings to help you focus.

In the end, your goal should be to get your benefit down to

two to ten clear and focused words.

As you write, focus on the idea, not the words. Words are mere representations of ideas. What separates Overt Benefits that have real impact from those that don't is the ideas the words represent. **Ideas are what matters to customers, not the literary collections of letters selected.** Words are a means of communication. But they are of no value unless their meaning is relevant to those who receive them.

Never Ever, Ever Give Up . . .

Churchill said during World War II, "Never, ever, ever, ever give up." The same wisdom applies to your search for an Overt Benefit.

Articulating your Overt Benefit is a never-ending journey. You can always do it with greater relevance, interest and excitement. Depending on your line of business, the core benefit may stay the same. The way you execute it may then vary. In other industries, where change is more revolutionary, you may need to evolve your core benefit and execution with the changing marketplace.

At the Eureka! Ranch we worked on some categories of products for over twenty years. In many cases, the core issues have changed very little. Tide laundry detergent has been communicating clean clothes for over fifty years. Nike has been communicating winning since its inception. Coca-Cola has communicated refreshment since its start.

In my own business, defining the Overt Benefit is an annual affair. Each fall I personally craft our brochure and marketing message for the upcoming new year. The process involves looking at what competition is saying, talking to my core customers and combining these inputs by writing dozens and dozens of alternatives. From this process evolves a fresh way to say the Eureka! Ranch provides big ideas.

By personally evolving our message on an annual basis, I insure that I am in touch with the marketplace and that the organization is focused on what I, as the leader, feel is most important. With a focus properly set, all levels of the organization know where to focus their energies and, just as important, where not to focus their energies.

Note to leaders of large organizations: Setting the Overt Benefit is equivalent to setting the mission of the organization.

You can have staff members help you, but it is your responsibility to set the vision. It's your job to define what the Overt Benefit is, what your brand stands for, what your company stands for. You cannot and should not delegate mission setting to others. **The job of the leader is to lead. Do it.**

Beware of These Common Mistakes Made With Overt Benefit

When setting an Overt Benefit, there are many common mistakes. I know these mistakes well since I've made many of them myself. It's my hope that reading the next few pages will help you avoid these mistakes.

Beware of Solving a Problem That's Not a Problem: The number one Overt Benefit mistake is attempting to provide a solution to a nonexisting problem. For a benefit to have motivational power with customers, it must be relevant yet unexpected. It must be relevant to their true needs. It must also be unexpected in that it offers a new insight, perspective or approach to their needs.

A good indication that you're on the right track is if the problem you are solving causes a healthy level of tension for customers. The greater the feeling of anxiety, fear, frustration or concern that customers feel when thinking of the problem your benefit addresses, the greater the chances that they will come running to your solution. **The natural way of customers is to seek solutions and resolution to the tensions that they feel.**

The copy from a flyer for Life Line Health Screening shows the power of leveraging a problem that generates significant customer tension.

> **We Can Help You . . . Avoid a Stroke in Just 10 Minutes.**
>
> Stroke is America's third leading killer. It is also the #1 cause for nursing home admissions. Unfortunately half of all stroke victims have no warning signs before a stroke occurs.
>
> Three Ways We Can Help: We provide non-invasive, completely painless screenings for vascular disease using the most advanced Doppler ultrasound technology. The screenings will quickly detect arterial abnormalities, which can cause irregular blood flow. We offer three separate tests. . . .

By educating consumers on the facts associated with the problem of strokes, Life Line insures that potential customers understand the true benefits of Life Line's screening services. The education creates customer tension and anxiety that is resolved by using Life Line's services.

Think about your own business category. What are the true tensions that customers feel? What Overt Benefit could you offer that addresses customers' anxieties, uncertainties and frustrations? What little known or unspoken issues could you educate customers on, so to insure that they understand the importance of your Overt Benefit offering?

Beware of Selling the Absence of a Problem Instead of a Positive Benefit: Beware of focusing energy on selling the fact you don't have something. It is far more powerful to sell the presence of a positive then the absence of a negative. For example, instead of saying you don't have preservatives in your food, sell your natural wholesomeness. Instead of selling the benefit that your company's bumper stickers won't pull off car paint, sell that your bumper stickers come on and off easily. Instead of selling your lack of having any medical malpractice suits filed against you, sell your 98% client repeat rates.

There is far greater energy and power in selling the positive than the absence of a negative. Selling "we don't have a negative" requires customers to know that all others in the market have that negative. And, whenever customers have to do more work, you receive less sales.

Beware of Assuming Knowledge: Beware of assuming your customers are aware of anyone or anything. Consider your customers to be twelve- to fourteen-year-olds who have just immigrated to your country, and you will never be disappointed. I have a simple test for all my direct-mail materials. I have my children read them. If they can understand what I'm offering, then the odds are good that time-stressed executives and, importantly, their assistants in large corporations can understand the materials in an instant.

As you define your Overt Benefit, make it self-evident and avoid industry jargon.

Beware That Low Price Is a Benefit . . . . but a Hard One to Own: If at all possible, avoid price as your core benefit. The only time price can be a true sustainable basis for a brand is when you have a genuine systemic advantage in your cost of production. For example, if your product is made using a process that is cheaper to run, or you have a greater economy of scale or are vertically integrated, then you can use price as a benefit. Classic examples of U.S. companies with a tangible pricing advantage built into their systems include Southwest Airlines, Wal-Mart and Dell Computer.

It's rare, but every now and then you can make a simple investment in technology and because of societal pressures or stubbornness among competition keep a price advantage for a long time. My great-grandfather Will Holder is an example of this. He found a systemic price advantage about one hundred years ago when he was the first to bring sewing machines into his father's sail loft in Saint John, New Brunswick, Canada. With the aid of machines, men could produce the sails for a great ship three times faster then they could by hand. Normally, you would have assumed competitors would have immediately copied.

They didn't. In fact, young Will Holder and his dad were ridiculed as the "Petticoat Sailmakers." Sail making was considered a manly craft and the use of sewing machines to be feminine. The net result today is George E. Holder and Son (the son being my great-grandfather) remains in business on Water Street while its competition has long since gone out of business.

Beware of Oversimplifying: To be effective, you must distil your message into a clear and overt piece of communication. In the process, you need to be careful to not distill it to the point of nothingness.

I encourage distillation but not at the expense of communication. Given a choice, I'd rather you utilize twenty words to clearly define your benefit than say five words that don't communicate anything.

Never forget it's the ideas not the words that matter.

Just arriving at Newark Airport from Cincinnati, I went to to make a phone call. As I'm a curious type, I couldn't help but hear the young manager next to me explain some clearly simplistic thinking: "Let's stick our logo and Web site on a bunch of stuff-pens, notepads all kinds of stuff. People love free stuff. We'll create sort of a Pavlovian response: Every time they see our pen, they'll think of us." I don't think so. Pavlovian response? What does he think his customers are? Dogs?

Customers are thinking beings. When you recognize that fact, you are on the path to success. **Treat your customers with the same respect you wish to be treated with and success will be yours. Disrespect your customers and they will disrespect you.**

Beware of Charming Humbleness: Beware of being too humble. It's common among small business owners to not want to "toot their own horns." This is especially true among those living in small rural communities. Many small business owners feel it's inappropriate to shout on signs or marketing materials what makes them great. This humbleness is fine if they want to sell only to their neighbors and those in the immediate community.

The challenge in today's world is that to survive and thrive, we must sell beyond our communities to those who have not known us for our entire lives. In today's world, we must sell the tourists visiting for the summer, customers on the World Wide Web, even folks who are simply new to town. To do this, we must communicate an Overt Benefit.

The challenge with Overt Benefit is it must be overt and direct, and this can seem like boasting. And boasting has a feeling of dishonesty to it.

I am *not* advocating lying or any form of dishonesty. Lying about your Overt Benefit is a sure way to ruin. Rather, I'm simply recommending that you tell the truth. As mentioned earlier, **it's not boasting when you do what you say**. If you have a skill at painting, tell the world. If you've worked hard creating the best team of employees, tell the world. If your furniture lasts longer because you put three extra coats of sealer on it, tell the world.

Remember, customers want to be delighted. Customers are seeking benefits. Customers will never look upon you with shame if you are telling them what they honestly will receive.

Big companies often use what are called focus groups to review ideas. A focus group consists of eight to twelve customers who are brought together to talk for two hours about an idea. It's a forced viewing situation, with little distraction. As a result, customers often advise pulling back on the overtness of a benefit message: "You don't need to say that. We know that." Small business owners often get similar reactions when they show potential marketing materials to family and friends who are familiar with what they offer.

Beware: Comments from focus groups and close friends can send you in the wrong direction. The real world is chaotic and distracting. The real world is not familiar with your offering. The real world does not sit and talk with no distraction about your idea for two hours. Your business has two seconds, not two hours, to spark customer attention. Be overt.

Beware of Doing What Everyone Else Is Doing: When it comes to Overt Benefit, it's important you focus on what your Overt Benefit is. What is the unique, distinctive yet still relevant benefit you alone offer customers? Three chapters from here, uniqueness will be focused on with even greater intensity. The point is you need to beware of falling into the trap of simply offering the same old stuff as everyone else.

A client named Dwayne visited the Ranch looking to add freshness dating to the hundreds of millions of food packages his company sold. Freshness dating had become the rage in foods and beverages, and everyone was doing it. He came to the ranch and asked for help to figure out how to best leverage this change. In particular, he wanted to know what specific words to put on the package. We conducted a test among Dwayne's customers of a wide range of alternatives. From this, we learned by a measure of nearly 3 to 1 that customers preferred we tell them "For Best Taste, Eat Before *Date*." This finding shouldn't have been very surprising. Best taste is an Overt Benefit. The benefit of freshness is implied.

Dwayne was excited. He could see clearly the benefit of focusing on taste instead of freshness. Sadly, the CEO and advertising agency never understood the difference. A few months later, when advertising was aired explaining the new "freshness dating," consumers and the media were confused. They didn't understand why they should care about a freshness date. What was never communicated was they really should care because this food category declines in taste rapidly with age. In this case, an important Overt Benefit lost impact because instead of being a pioneer, the corporate system decided to "safely" follow the path of everyone else.

Quick Process Summary on Overt Benefit

1. All benefits are relative to a specific target audience. You can start with a target audience and then define a benefit,

or you can start with a benefit and then define a target. In either case, be sure to remember they are relative to one another.

2. To find your core benefit, look to the beginning. Look at your roots. Why did you start, or why was your company started? What was the burning issue that created it? What are your true passions?

3. Optimize your communication by following four simple steps.

   I. Define target audience.
   II. Detail your features.
   III. Turn features into benefits.
   IV. Turn benefits into Overt Benefits.

4. Do one thing great. Make your Overt Benefit as focused and specific as possible.

5. Visualize your benefit. What is the Magic Moment of truth?

6. Don't forget to consider experiential benefits as a genuine alternative to rational ones.

7. Never, ever, ever give up the search for fresher, more relevant ways of communicating your Overt Benefit.

Final Thoughts on Overt Benefit

You can create a business that will make people happier, healthier, more relaxed, more beautiful, more of just about anything. In exchange, those people will give you their support in time, effort and money.

The strongest brands and strongest companies each offer one focused benefit. And they do so with a relentless passion. It's time for you to take charge of your communications with your customers. Please understand there are millions, yes millions, of customers in the world seeking to be delighted. If you don't step forward and offer them an Overt Benefit, someone else will!

It's likely that in your day-to-day world, you are often too busy to think about Overt Benefit. The operational demands you face are so intense it's all you can do to simply survive.

Sorry, but you don't have a choice. If you want to grow, you are going to have to take responsibility for what your company stands for. It's up to you to determine where your team's attention and resources will be focused. Your competitors have limited time, talent and resources. So do you. How you deploy them is what makes all the difference.

Fundamentally, employees want to be successful. They want to help your company succeed. It's your job to tell them where to focus their energies so they can achieve that success. It's impossible for you to be involved in every decision every employee faces, but if you have articulated your Overt Benefit, your people will have a road map for making all important customer decisions.

When you have a clearly defined Overt Benefit, you attract the right customers for the right reasons, employees know where to focus and, most importantly, every piece of customer communications you present to the world is made that much more effective.

As one client said after a session at the Eureka! Ranch, "How rare it is to think at this level. We are implementers. . . . We spend way too little time thinking about the important stuff that really matters."

Implementation is of critical importance. Without excellence in execution, the greatest Overt Benefit in the world is wasted. However, implementation and operational excellence is not enough.

To survive and thrive in business, you must generate customer excitement. And the first step is through communication of a relevant yet unexpected Overt Benefit.

CHAPTER 4

The Secret to Doubling Effectiveness at "Closing the Sale"

*In the previous chapter, you learned how to use Overt Benefit to gener-
ate customer interest. In this chapter, you will learn how to convert that
interest into sales by providing customers a Real Reason to Believe that
you will deliver on your promise.*

Second Law of Marketing Physics: Real Reason to Believe

Customers withhold their final commitment to purchase until they perceive a Real Reason to Believe that
you will deliver on your Overt Benefit promise.

An Overt Benefit offers a promise to customers that you will
make their lives easier, more enjoyable, more exciting or more
rewarding. However, customers understand they are gullible to
promises of benefits. As a result, they are very cautious when it
comes to making a financial commitment to purchase. Before they
will act on their initial interest, they seek evidence the merchant
making the benefit promise can or will deliver on it.

Analysis of thousands of new business concepts shows that
enhancing Real Reason to Believe tangibly increases your odds for
success and correspondingly your return on effort expended.

Unfortunately, analysis also finds that only 20% of concepts
offer a significant reason to believe. That leaves 80% that don't. Is
it a coincidence that about 80% of all new products and services
fail?

**The benefit is what you're offering. The reason to believe is
how you're going to make good on your promise. To succeed,
you need both the what and the how.**

	Probability of Success
High Overt Benefit	42%
Medium Overt Benefit	29%
Low Overt Benefit	18%

Referring back to the progression from feature to Overt Benefit outlined in the previous chapter, let's see what happens as we add the Real Reason to Believe to our Overt Benefit promises of rational or experiential benefits.

Feature	Benefit	Overt Benefit	Real Reason to Believe
Rocks for sale	Historic rocks	Celtic treasures	Carved with Celtic symbols authenticated by experts at Edinburgh University
Boat for sale	Fast boat	Specialized racing boat for those with a passion for winning	Designed by America's Cup champion boat designer
Pizza for sale	Deep-dish pizza	Chicago-style deep-dish pizza	Winner of Best of Chicago Award
Real Estate Agent	Distressed property specialist	Real Estate for sale 20 to 50 cents on the dollar	Specialty alliances with bankruptcy attorneys, distressed sales possible
Fish for sale	Fresh fish	The freshest fish in town	When you sell more fish, it's fresher. We sell more fish than anyone.

Note how the addition of the Real Reason to Believe adds depth and substance to the Overt Benefit promise.

Customers' evaluation of Real Reason to Believe sometimes happens in a split second. Sometimes it's even decided before you make your offering. Think back to a time when you met vendors selling watches or jewelry at a county fair or on the streets of New York. The gold looked flashy, the watches looked impressive, the prices were clearly fantastic. What not to like? Probably somewhere in the back of your mind was a story that said it was too good to be true—they're probably fakes, copies or stolen.

Customers see your offering and make a decision. And the greater the Overt Benefit promise, the greater the level of Real Reason to Believe required.

Small Overt Benefit	→	Small Real Reason to Believe required
Big Overt Benefit	→	Big Real Reason to Believe required

Correspondingly, if your benefit offering is perceived to be exaggerated, customers discount your offering immediately as being overhyped.

The New News About Real Reason to Believe

In today's marketplace, Real Reason to Believe is the number one weakness of new business concepts.

Credibility and reason to believe have long been understood to be important in the world of marketing. The new news is credibility has risen to an unprecedented level of importance. In the early 1980s, when I worked at Procter & Gamble, reason to believe was thought to be probably only one-third as important as benefit. Today, reason to believe is of equal importance to benefit.

Customer confidence in marketing messages, and new product and service claims is at an all-time low. A 1999 study of four thousand Americans conducted by the respected research firm of Erdos and Morgan found extremely low confidence in advertising.

Advertising Medium	Americans' Distrust of Advertising Medium
Network television	58%
Cable television	85%
The Internet	90%

Customers' lack of confidence is not surprising given the explosion of hype and lies they have been subjected to. The lies are extreme. From dot com promises of great riches to politicians' campaign pledges, customers are subjected to lies and deceit.

The trustworthiness deficit between customers and merchants has accumulated over time. The deficit has been built from hundreds of disappointing customer experiences.

- "Great-tasting health foods" . . . that taste like cardboard
- "Simple-to-program VCRs" . . . that end up blinking 12:00 forever
- "Easy-to-assemble doll houses" . . . that take Santa eight hours to build
- "Low prices on the Internet" . . . with high prices for shipping and handling
- "Never shrinks clothes" . . . except when washed in lukewarm, warm or hot water
- "No-worry extended warranty" . . . except for regular maintenance, wear, tear and use

Real Reason to Believe is about credibility and trust. It's built through clear, direct communication. It's enhanced by a multitude of small acts that add and subtract from customers' perceptions of your trustworthiness. To paraphrase author Tom Peters, "Coffee stains on airline seat trays make you wonder about airplane engine maintenance."

When your staff wear neat uniforms and drive clean trucks, they evoke confidence. When your staff answer phone calls promptly and courteously, they build credibility for your business.

Think of credibility as a bank balance. Every time you do what you say you'll do, you add to your trust balance. Every time you overhype, overpromise or don't do what you promise, your account decreases. Today virtually all companies start with a negative credibility balance with customers. In time, the companies either earn customers' trust or go out of business.

When customers have trust, confidence or faith in your company, they're more likely to be willing to purchase. They will also drive farther to do business with you, are more loyal and are less likely to be tempted by competitive offerings of low prices.

The Challenge With Internet Credibility

Our research indicates that Internet-centered offerings face an even greater challenge when it comes to consumer confidence. There is good reason for this lack of confidence. Recent years have seen well-publicized failures of Internet companies to ship products on time as well as Internet start-ups going bankrupt and assorted other financial scandals.

The challenge Internet companies face instilling customer trust is not dissimilar to the challenge facing television infomercial merchants. In both cases, the customer has to trust someone or something on the end of a phone line. With the Internet, it's a phone line carrying a Web page. With an infomercial, it's a toll-free number phone bank.

For an infomercial to stay on the air, it must generate sales and profits in excess of the cost of the advertising time. For this reason, infomercials that stay on the air are some of the most effective advertising you'll ever view. Unlike most television advertising, whose effect is diffused as just one part of the marketing mix, infomercials are usually the entire marketing, distribution and sales effort all wrapped up into one thirty-minute pitch.

The infomercial offer, like the Internet offer, starts from a position of poor credibility with potential customers. For this reason, successful infomercials utilize over half their time communicating Real Reason to Believe. They do this by providing visual demonstrations, "skeptic conversion" testimonials and kitchen logic explanations of how the product works, as well as detailing the expert pedigree of the inventor of the product.

For Internet marketing to be successful, it must overcome the customer confidence gap. And there is no better place to learn this than via infomercial television.

Retail establishments have a significant advantage over Internet firms as the physical store provides customers a level of confidence and security. It provides a tangible place where the customer can present his problems to real people, face-to-face. If you don't get satisfaction, you can even ask to see the manager. With the Internet and infomercials, the customer has little recourse but to play phone or e-mail roulette looking for satisfaction. This does not enhance a feeling of confidence.

Long-term consumer confidence in Internet-delivered products and services is bound to increase. I do expect, though, that like their infomercial counterparts, Internet marketing will always face a credibility challenge. It's simply systemic to the concept of remote access to a merchant. I advise clients that if they are offering your goods or services via the Internet, they need to triple their levels of credibility communications to achieve the same impact as classic physical retailers.

Practical Tactic: Learn From the Masters of Real Reason to Believe

Tonight, let's learn from the masters.

Stay up late this evening and watch a few television infomercials. If you're not a night owl, set the VCR to record them. Newspaper television listings usually indicate "paid commercial programming" for the airtime when infomercials run.

Watch the infomercials with a conscious awareness of Overt Benefit and Real Reason to Believe. With paper and pencil, keep a scorecard of the Overt Benefit promises as well as the Real Reasons to Believe used to provide supporting credibility that the benefit will be delivered.

It doesn't require specialized training to identify Real Reasons to Believe. Simply list those elements, words, visuals and communications elements that increase your confidence that the company will deliver on its promises.

Pictures have a power that transcends words. Turn the sound down for a while and watch the pictures. Can you "see" the Overt Benefit? Can you "see" the Real Reason to Believe? Television is at its most persuasive when the words and the pictures both communicate.

For comparison, channel surf looking for "regular" thirty-second commercials. Do you see the same level of Real Reason to Believe? It's unlikely, as most advertising aired today is ineffective.

Now evaluate what impact each type of advertising had on you. Which of the two formats would make you most likely to make a purchase now? Which is the more memorable?

The more you watch, with consciousness, the greater your understanding and sensitivity toward Real Reason to Believe.

Real Reason to Believe Multiplies the
Effectiveness of All Marketing Efforts

The bottom line for business growth is closing the sale. Generating interest through an Overt Benefit and then not converting that interest into a sale is an inexcusable waste of effort. The good news is that through simply adding a Real Reason to Believe to your communications, you can multiply your marketing effectiveness.

A client of mine named Darla is marketing manager for an old and familiar brand in a well-established category. Five years ago, it was a distant number three. As a result of her lower sales, her budget was but 50% of the size of the number two brand's budget. Things looked hopeless. She didn't have enough sales to justify greater marketing spending, but without more marketing spending, she couldn't generate greater sales. Appeals to the corporate bankers received no support. They explained, "Darla, there are other investment priorities offering a greater potential return on investment."

Darla is not a woman who is content "milking a brand for profits." She believes in growth. If her budget was a fixed amount, she decided her only chance for growth lay in making her advertising more effective than the competition's.

To maximize the impact of every dollar she spent, she set up a program of intensive pretesting to insure that each element of her advertising was optimized. If a testimonial was offered by a consumer in a commercial, she would test ten different people to identify who was the most convincing. She had her technical people develop five different demonstrations showing her product's effectiveness. She tested each demonstration to identify the most persuasive.

The net effect of Darla's development effort was advertising that initially had double the persuasion power of either the number one or the number two brand's advertising. She put it on air with her limited funds. The effect was slow but steady. Just like constant dripping wears away the stone, so, too, advertising that's twice as effective slowly wears away at your competition's market share.

As sales grew, Darla received proportionally more money. With her success she has not forgotten what generated her success. In time, she has led the creation and testing of advertising that now has nearly triple the persuasion power of the number one brand's ads. It's been five years since she started on this quest. Darla has been promoted yet still has responsibility for the brand. It continues to experience double-digit sales growth in a category growing only 2% a year. She's closing in on the number two brand and has visions of one day being number one.

Darla's story clearly shows how by committing to Overt Benefit and Real Reason to Believe, it's possible to make small dollars generate a big impact for your business.

The Overt Benefit to You of Communicating Real Reason to Believe

In most small businesses, you, the owner, are the primary reason to believe. When you are in the store, on the phone, with customers, sales happen. As the founder, chief and boss you provide customers a level of confidence that you will take care of their needs. The buck stops with you. Your employees don't have that same air of authority or credibility. The result is that it takes greater effort for them to close sales. When you articulate a tangible Real Reason to Believe—be it a demonstration, a guarantee or a book full of testimonial letters—you dramatically enhance your employees' credibility and thus selling effectiveness with customers.

The bottom line is simple: When you define why customers should believe that your company's promised benefit will be delivered, you improve the effectiveness of all advertising, promotions and employees. And when employees and advertising can generate sales, by themselves, you are more able to make money without being physically present. This means you have the potential to actually take a vacation. And you can have more than one retail store—and make money at each. Net, with a clear Real Reason to Believe, you can grow your sales without growing your personal working hours.

Practical Tactic: Score Your Real Reason to Believe Versus the Competition

Before we set to work on enhancing your Real Reason to Believe, it's important that you get a solid understanding of where you stand now. To do this, we're going to create a list of your points of credibility and those of your competition. We're then going to compare and contrast until we discover who has the edge when it comes to credibility with customers who are totally new to your industry.

Step 1 Gather the materials that detail your brand, business or concept, as you did in the last chapter. Also gather similar materials on your competition.

Step 2 Make a list of each element of overt communications that enhances credibility for you and your competition.

Step 3 Add to your list and that of your key competitor the unstated things that should give customers confidence.

Step 4 Match and compare. Cross out the first item on your list. Then find a credibility item on the competitor's list that is of equal impact and cross it out as well. If it takes two from one list to equal the credibility of one on the other list, then cross out two for one. Continue to cross items off each list until only you or your competitor is left standing with items still on the list.

What you have just done is close to what goes through customers' minds when they are trying to make a decision between you and your competition in a head-to-head decision situation.

Real Reason to Believe Is Relative

Just as you can't have an Overt Benefit without a target audience, you can't have a Real Reason to Believe without an Overt Benefit. **Real Reason to Believe is relative to an Overt Benefit that is relative to a target audience.** It's a chain reaction with each piece working together. And it's a good thing, as this interaction provides the educated businessperson a tremendous marketing advantage. When your sales increase as a result of following the laws outlined on these pages, your competitors will react. However, it's likely that they will react by claiming they offer the same Overt Benefit. In most cases, this copycat effort will fail. It will fail because they will miss the importance of addressing the target audience and providing supporting credibility.

Last summer Stefan, owner of the previously mentioned Seasons in Thyme restaurant had a great evening business but lunchtime was slow. To address this, Stefan developed a focused offer of lobster lunches. Stefan had a quick banner made up announcing the offer.

It was an immediate hit.

The original sign

The competitior's sign

The new sign with Reason to Believe

Seeing Stefan's parking lot filled with cars at lunchtime, another restaurant just down the street decided to make a similar offering.

Stefan called asking what he should do with the new competition. "The banner is good," I replied, "but it doesn't offer a Real Reason to Believe. Let's be more overt about the experiential benefit and provide a Real Reason to Believe on the banner." The banner was redone for the rest of the summer.

The experiential benefit of Stefan's lobster lunches was that they were truly a gourmet taste experience. The credibility for gourmet came directly from the medals he and his assistant chefs had won in world cooking competitions.

With the new banner, Stefan's lunch business remained at about ninety guests versus the twenty lunch guests he had averaged the year before. This was done despite having a direct competitor offering a generic version of the benefit just down the street.

Author note: As a result of a variety of new marketing efforts, Stefan significantly increased operating profits that summer. However, he also dramatically increased his debt load by buying the bar that was attached to his restaurant. In the end, the growth of debt was greater than the growth of profits and Stefan went out of business the following January.

This is an important reality check. The discipline of the laws of Marketing Physics can dramatically increase your sales, but they are not a miracle cure. To be a profitable business, you must also have discipline with your debt management.

The Need for Real Reason to Believe Keeps Business Fair

Customers' natural skepticism prevents unfounded boasting of nonexistent benefits.

The need to provide supporting evidence behind Overt Benefit claims acts as a system of checks and balances. You can't simply promise anything you wish to promise to win customers. To be effective, your claim must be substantiated by clear supporting evidence.

Every time you make a claim of benefit, you challenge the established thinking and habits of customers. Overt Benefits offer them the hope that if they change their current behaviors, they will receive a reward. However, change is not without risk. Before leaving their current choices, customers have to be convinced that you will really deliver.

If an Overt Benefit offer seems to good too be true, it can be a challenge to get customers to not consider it unfounded boasting. This credibility gap can result in a poor conversion ratio of leads generated to sales closed.

The greater damage, however, is when a customer actually makes a purchase based on an exaggerated promise. A study reported in *Car and Driver* magazine found that a customer who has a great experience with a new car tells eight other people; however, a customer who has had a bad experience tells sixteen people.

Unfounded boasting causes damage that is far greater than loss of marketing efficiency. It ruins your reputation. To quote Ben Franklin, "Glass, china and reputations are easily broken and never well-mended."

The Most Powerful Source of Credibility Is the Real Truth

The most powerful means to provide credibility is to tell customers the honest truth regarding how you are able to accomplish delivery of the promised benefit. Nothing is more powerful than truth when communicating credibility. The real truth has a natural vitality that customers can feel and sense like no amount of boasting, hype or marketing speak can ever create.

My conviction regarding the power of telling the real truth is so great that I put the word *Real* in front of *Reason to Believe* to serve as a constant reminder to you about being real and honest as you craft your message to customers.

To quote my spiritual mentor Ben Franklin again, "What you would seem to be, be really."

A clear test of Real Reason to Believe is that it's so honest, so true that you wouldn't blink signing your name to it . . . or telling your mother about it . . . or telling your child about it. With real truth there is no room for hedges of any kind, no "sort of," "mostly," "in certain cases," or "kinda's" allowed. The message is just the straight at you truth and nothing but the truth.

Sometimes the most real thing is to understate with genuine humbleness. Ivory bar soap became number one in America by promising to be 99 44/100ths% pure. Environmentally conscious products have been extremely successful making the honest and understated claim: "It's not going to save the whole world, but it's a step in the right direction."

When consumers do business with you for the first time, they face risk. They can lose time and money. The risk is even bigger if the customer is purchasing on behalf of a company. A wrong decision could result in damaging the buyer's reputation inside the company—if what she purchases causes production problems for the company, they could hurt the company's reputation. A bad purchase could even cause the buyer to lose her job. When you fully understand what's at stake, you will be on the path to understanding the importance of Real Reason to Believe.

CHAPTER 5

Proven Strategies for Real Reason to Believe

In the last chapter you gained an understanding of why Real Reason to Believe is critical to success. This chapter explains the five proven strategies available for enhancing credibility. Your mission is to create a Real Reason to Believe in support of your Overt Benefit promise using each of the five proven strategies outlined. That's right. At the end of this chapter, you should have at least five distinct reasons to believe that support your promise. The net result will be a dramatic increase in your probability of business success.

The Five Proven Strategies for Communicating Real Reason to Believe

There are five proven Real Reason to Believe strategies you can use. They all can be effective. The decision as to the proper one or ones for you to use rests on which is most relevant and effective considering the Overt Benefit you are promising

The following chart details your probability of success for each strategy when other key dimensions are held at average values.

Strategy	Probability of Success
Kitchen logic	42%
Personal experience	45%
Pedigree	41%
Testimonial	41%
Guarantee	60%

Statistically, aside from guarantee, all five strategies are equally effective.

Real Reason to Believe Strategy 1: Kitchen Logic

Old-fashioned common sense continues to have enduring value. This approach is called kitchen logic because it takes the form of a simple story everyday people can understand and explain to friends and family around the kitchen. **Kitchen logic conveys to customers how the benefit is delivered, using language that they can easily understand and quickly relate to.**

When a Real Reason to Believe uses kitchen logic, it has a quality about it that "seems" like it would work. It just makes sense. Kitchen logic is a matter of explaining in a direct and straightforward manner how and why a product works.

- Lower Interest Rates, because we have access to more capital
- Extra Comfortable Shoes, because an air cushion is inside each sole
- The Freshest Flowers, because the greenhouse is out back
- The Most Durable Blue Jeans, because they're made from triple-thick denim
- Double-Sweet Donuts, because we use twice as much sugar

The key with kitchen logic is to be clear and direct. It's not uncommon for business owners to become so comfortable with how they do what they do, they forget to explain the obvious. Often business owners know in their minds why a benefit is possible but they neglect to explain it to customers.

The classic commodity category is beef. Prices for beef are set by the forces of the marketplace at stockyard auctions. The P.W. Supply Company of Ontario Canada doesn't accept that it is in a commodity business. Managers there believe they can add value to the hamburger they sell by promoting a benefit of safety supported by the kitchen logic behind their process. Their brochure promotes this benefit.

[Benefit Statement]
Simply put, STEAM PASTEURIZATION significantly reduces the risk of disease-causing bacteria on a side of beef. The process results in 99.9% reduction in disease-causing (pathologenic) bacteria and 90% reduction of food spoilage bacteria without changing the great flavor of our all Canadian beef.

[Real Reason to Believe]

Explain the Process

Steam pasteurization is used after a side of beef has passed Agriculture Canada's final inspection and wash station. A side of beef passes through an in-line closed cabinet where it is subjected to three simple steps:

1. DEWATERING—removal of water left on the surface by the final wash.
2. PASTEURIZATION—exposure of the beef surface to a steam blanket for a minimum of six seconds in a pressurized chamber raising the surface temperature to a minimum of 185 degrees.
3. CHILLING—chilling the side of beef with a cold water shower.

Other steps taken to prevent bacteria growth

1. We store all our beef at 30 degrees.
2. Freshly ground chuck is always processed daily.
3. All equipment is sanitized daily.
4. We never regrind or reprocess beef.
5. We grind at 42 degrees.
6. Our basic minimum turnover of patties is 95% each day.
7. Hamburgers are cooked to an internal temperature of 160 degrees (the recommended level for killing any potential bacteria).

I will admit that I don't fully understand all they're saying from a technical perspective. However, it is clear that they are very serious about health. When I eat their burgers, I can feel very confident that the meat is healthy and safe. As it turns out, the burgers they serve also taste fantastic.

Another way to gain support is through an overt kitchen logic claim relative to your competition, as in these claims about a new blueberry muffin.

- Our muffins contain twice the number of blueberries of the leading national brand.
- Our muffins are made with natural butter instead of processed oils.
- Our muffins are baked up fresh from the oven every hour on the hour.

Kitchen Logic—Now It's Your Turn

Take your optimized Overt Benefit statement from the previous chapter, and define a kitchen logic Real Reason to Believe for it. The following prompts will get you started.
- Tell the truth. Why can you deliver on the promise?
- What do you do that makes it possible for that benefit to be delivered?
- If you changed one thing, what would cause your benefit to not be delivered?
- What is the key to your success at delivering the benefit?
- Think people.
- Think process.
- Think what makes how you operate different from your competition.

Real Reason to Believe Strategy 2: Personal Experience

Personal experience is about providing your customers with an opportunity to see, feel and experience your product benefit. There are three types of personal experiences: (1) sampling, (2) demonstration and (3) sensory feedback. In each case, the goal is to provide the customer with a first-person experience of the effectiveness of your product or service. Through first-person experience, customers gain faith in your delivery of the benefit you promise.

1. Sampling: The most fundamental approach to personal experience is providing a free sample to customers. Having experienced the wonder of your Overt Benefit, they are destined to be long-term customers. America Online (AOL) focused single-mindedly on this strategy to become the number one Internet service provider in the USA. Tens of millions of free trial membership and CD-ROMs have been distributed via magazines, stores, newspapers and direct-mail packages. AOL knows from experience that once customers experience how easy AOL is to use, they will likely stay with it.

Sampling may be the most worthwhile customer promotion there is. If you have a truly great product or service, once people have experienced it, they'll buy it again. And they'll tell their friends, which is the most powerful of all marketing tools. To make sampling financially viable, your product has to be outstanding. It also helps if you can produce a smaller or limited-use version of your product or service.

2. Demonstration: Sometimes, it's impractical to sample your product or service. In this case, a targeted demonstration in action can make your product or service come alive. **A demonstration allows customers to see and experience the transformational power of your benefit firsthand.**

In Tacoma, Washington, a company called J.L. Darling Corporation makes a line of notebooks called Rite in the Rain. They're specially designed for uses where field notes can be destroyed due to rain, humidity and other outdoor hazards. If it worked, it seemed to me to be the perfect solution for keeping journal notes when on outdoor adventure trips.

I sent the company an e-mail requesting information and in the mail received a brochure along with a couple of test sheets. These Dunk n' Doodle test forms featured Rite in the Rain paper on one half and normal paper on the other half. Following their instructions, I wrote on both pages, dunked both in water and was sold on Rite in the Rain in seconds. Now whenever I need to take and record notes in the outdoors, I use Rite in the Rain.

At Procter & Gamble, I led the national introduction of Spic and Span Pine cleaner. This hard-surface cleaner was specially designed to clean bathroom dirt—the gunk you see on shower walls, sinks and tubs. We used a demonstration to show our effectiveness.

P&G's research scientists developed a formula that replicated bathroom gunk. The gunk was baked onto bathroom tiles, in accordance with detailed protocols that replicated what it's like in the average bathroom. In advertising, a hidden camera was used to videotape real customers pouring Spic and Span Pine and its leading competitor, Pine-Sol, on prepared tiles and spraying both tiles with a water bottle. Like magic, the Spic and Span tile literally dissolved the dirt in seconds.

The demonstration was so powerful, the sales staff repeated it live in presentations to buyers. As a result, Spic and Span Pine had a record introductory year and was one of the top three new products in the company that year.

A demonstration is particularly effective when it's set in a situation that seems nearly hopeless. These can be done live as described above, or they can be documented and used as evidence in brochures or advertising. If your landscaping company converted a backyard that usually floods into a vegetable garden, photos of the before and after would serve as testimony of your effectiveness. Similarly, a fitness trainer can use photos of customers before and after as a torture test demonstration of efficacy. In touting its track record of victories in the heat and extreme pressure of the Indianapolis 500, a tire manufacturer invites customers to imagine how well its tires can perform for them under ordinary driving circumstances.

3. Sensory Feedback: This is about providing your customers with signals that reinforce your effectiveness. At its simplest, this means help them see, feel, smell, taste or touch the experience.

The "psssst" when you open a can of coffee or a carbonated beverage tells you it's fresh. The bubbles in an aerosol tub-and-tile cleanser reinforce the product's cleaning action. The meter that makes a clicking sound as it detects airborne dust particles reinforces the value of advanced HVAC hepa air filtration.

Banks use sensory feedback to reinforce customers' confidence regarding the safety of their money. Banks station armed guards at their doors, have imposing government-style buildings and very thick and impressive vault doors.

Plastic lunch bags have used sensory feedback to help reinforce the promise that they close tight. One brand promotes the fact that one side of the bag opening is blue, the other yellow and when they are closed together you get green. Another promotes the feeling of it locking. Another promotes the "zzzzzip" sound when it closes.

Sensory feedback doesn't always have to be pretty or positive to be effective. The Eureka! Ranch worked with the Andrew Jergens company on the development of the Bioré beauty care brand. The hot item in the product line was the first "deep-cleansing pore strip." This special strip is applied to oily areas of the face, then peeled off, revealing chunks of gunk pulled from deep inside pores.

It's ugly and somewhat stomach churning—and the most powerful tool imaginable for showing the product's effectiveness. To the client's credit, it had the courage to use less somewhat nasty sensory feedback element and showed it in advertising, encouraged demonstrations and even leveraged it in PR. The media loved it.

As a result, Bioré became the top beauty care brand at the market-leading Wal-Mart chain.

A good friend of mine, Bruce MacNaughton, also uses sensory feedback to convince customers of the quality of the jams he sells through his Prince Edward Island Preserve Company. Bruce's production and retail facility is located in the tiny village of New Glasgow. The place is always bustling with people, even though it's well off the main road, away from the oceanside where the tourists on this Canadian island tend to gather. Still, Bruce's sales are ten times greater than those of the average island summer business. When I asked him how he does it, he took me on a tour, beginning on the front porch.

"Listen," he said. The sounds of Celtic music played on the front porch, setting the tone. Then we stepped inside his gift shop.

"Look," he said. The floor, walls and cabinets were of a natural, warm wood. The merchandise was attractively displayed.

"Smell that?" Bruce said. The aroma of fresh preserves can be smelled as they are cooked and packaged behind a glass window to the right as you enter the shop.

Then he led me to a counter, where more than a dozen different jams were arrayed for free sampling. "Taste," Bruce said.

I was sold. The mystery of the PEI Preserve Company's success is no mystery at all. It's a result of a multisensory celebration of the spirit inside the jars. Listen. Look. Smell. Taste. How could you not make a purchase?

The best part is that when you get home, the taste of Bruce's preserves lives up to the memory. Each morning when I spread one of his preserves on my breakfast toast, I'm transported to Bruce's place on the River Clyde in New Glasgow.

Postscript: Not only does Bruce have revenues ten times greater than the average island store, he sells his jam at $6.75 a bottle versus $2.25 for the national brand of jam in local stores. That is the power of sensory feedback.

Services can also leverage the power of sensory feedback. When you place an order with a company online and you get an e-mail confirming the placement of the order, that's sensory feedback. When you get another e-mail indicating that the product has shipped, that's sensory feedback. It's also sensory feedback when a car dealer calls you a month after you bought a car to check to see how you like it. In some cases, the sensory feedback builds credibility for making your next purchase as well as reinforcing your first decision.

Personal Experience—Now It's Your Turn

Take your Overt Benefit and seek a way to use one or more of the personal experience approaches as a means to provide credibility that your Overt Benefit will be delivered. The following prompts will help get you started.

1. Sampling:
- How can we help customers experience the benefit?
- What types of limited-use sampling could we do?
- How could we invent a way to provide a limited use version of our benefit?
- What portions of our product or service could we provide?

2. Demonstration
- How can we visualize the impact of our benefit?
- What impossible situation can we use to "show our stuff"?
- What types of before and after situations can we document?

3. Sensory Feedback
- How can we show customers our product/service is working?
- What signals of sights, sounds, smells can we build into the experience?
- How can we provide feedback to the customer that we are doing our job?

Real Reason to Believe 3: Pedigree

Pedigree is about providing confidence to potential customers as a result of detailing the heritage behind your product or service.

There are three different types of pedigrees: (1) development pedigree, (2) marketing pedigree, and (3) trademark pedigree. Before I review the three types, read a short story that features the power of pedigree.

Don Maxfield and Jeannette Arsenault are the founders of a

small company called Cavendish Figurines on Prince Edward Island. Twelve years ago, they traded in their regular jobs and decided to create their own business. Their mission was to make fine quality figurines of scenes from the *Anne of Green Gables* stories by Lucy Maud Montgomery. The stories were set on the North Shore of the island, where the author was born and lived.

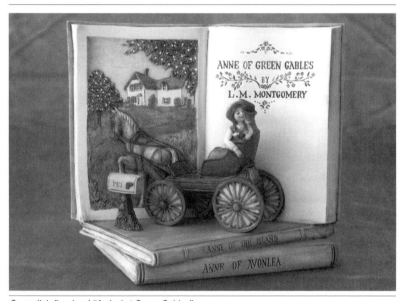

Cavendish figurines' "Arrival at Green Gables"

Don and Jeannette have been successful; however, it has been a lot of work. They put in long hours producing the figurines, but given the high costs associated with molds and equipment, profits are slow in coming. As Don said when I first spoke with him, "To date we've focused our time nearly exclusively on production. We now understand that to generate the sales we need, we have to start focusing our time on marketing."

They participated in a Marketing Physics and Capitalist Creativity training program sponsored by the Prince Edward Island Business Development group. The coaching process began with information gathering regarding what made their figurines great: how they made them, how they built them, why they did what they did, what the pedigree and history behind the development of their process were.

Next we turned to their current brochure.

Cavendish Figurines Ltd.

Free factory tours: See the making of a figurine from the Anne Collection and the Cavendish characters. Guided tours every hour from 9:00 a.m. to 4:00 p.m.

Gift shop: Quality souvenirs and gifts at reasonable prices! Many original items not found anywhere else. Large Annetastic section. Year round Christmas section-lots of stocking stuffers!

Dress up as Anne: We supply the costume. Bring your camera.

Whimsy Garden: Flower beds like you've never seen.

"The Spirit of Anne" statue: The world's only! This landmark statue is an excellent photo opportunity.

- Wheelchair accessible
- RV and motor coach parking
- Letter drop

You might notice from the above that Don and Jeannette had lost a little focus. In their desire to entice customers to visit their shop, they had lost the focus on their reason for being in the first place. Instead of promoting their figurines, they promoted tons of borrowed interest "gimmicks" from dress-ups, to gardens to cheap souvenirs. Clearly they had lost the focus.

Merwyn provided a forecast of their probability of success based on their current brochure. We used the brochure, as it was the primary piece of communications that island visitors had to learn about Cavendish Figurines. As expected, Merwyn indicated a low probability of success.

Overall Probability of Success: 13%
Returns on Effort Expended

Overt Benefit	5th percentile versus database
Real Reason to Believe	10th percentile versus database
Dramatic Difference	25th percentile versus database

Having attended training in the importance of Overt Benefit and Real Reason to Believe the day before, Don and Jeannette were not surprised. We then set out to rewrite their brochure telling the true story behind their fine figurines.

Cavendish Figurines

At the Cavendish Figurine studio, we craft heirloom-quality collectibles destined to become family treasures, handed down from one generation to the next. We offer fine earthenware figures inspired by Lucy Montgomery's timeless childhood classic, "Anne of Green Gables"—beautifully detailed figures that capture the spirit of the Anne novels through a commitment to the facial expressions and body language of the characters, as well as the genuine colors of the times.

Jeannette Arsenault and Don Maxfield, cofounders of Cavendish Figurines, have studied throughout Europe the art of crafting fine art figurines. In fact, Cavendish Figurines is the only place in North America to feature the genuine old world European craftsmanship, methods and materials made famous by such European production houses as Hummel, Wedgewood and Royal Doulton.

The new brochure went on to describe the various figurines and the fact that each piece is hand-signed by the artists who cast, craft and paint it.

Note how this brochure copy focuses on the core drama inherent in the product. The experiential benefits of these figurines becoming "a family treasure" are articulated clearly. Real Reason to Believe is provided through detailing the pedigree behind their creation. The copy doesn't boast. It doesn't lie. Rather, it tells the truth behind Don and Jeannette's fine figurines.

The concept was resubmitted to Merwyn. The results were very encouraging.

Jeannette and Don were excited. They felt they had a new way of thinking about their business that offered great hope. In an interview with the CBC television show *Venture*, Jeannette articulated her feelings on the new marketing focus: "It's a little bit of work but it's not like it's changing the whole operation around. It's really just about returning our focus to how and why we started."

Overall Probability of Success: 51%
Returns on Effort Expended

Overt Benefit	60th percentile versus database
Real Reason to Believe	65th percentile versus database
Dramatic Difference	65th percentile versus database

Jeannette and Don's story of discovery of Real Reason to Believe is a common one. Behind virtually all new products and services, there lies a pedigree that can be leveraged.

Now back to the explanation of the three kinds of pedigrees.

1. Development Pedigree: Development pedigree involves providing credibility of delivery of a benefit as a result of the design, creation, formulation or production process behind a product or service. It was this approach that we used with Don and Jeannette.

For example, if we were selling a better tasting blueberry muffin we could make the following offers.

- Made with only State of Maine blueberries
- Made with blueberries that have been picked and packed the same day
- Made using a patented flash cooking process that seals in all the blueberry flavor
- Made from blueberries grown on family-owned and -operated farms
- Made with blueberries genetically engineered by a Nobel Prize winner
- Made from blueberries grown in the same field that produced the winning pie at the State of Maine blueberry festival

Anything you do during your development or production that is unique or different offers potential as a reason to believe that you will deliver on your promises.

One of the most powerful development pedigrees is a patent. A patent is a government endorsement of originality and a Real Reason to Believe. It's also the only legal monopoly a nonregulated entity can enjoy. The discussion of patents helps reinforce understanding of the relationship between Overt Benefit and Real Reason to Believe.

If you ask your customers if it's important that you tell them you have a patent, most will answer no. And they're right, given the way the question is phrased. Patents are not benefits. However, if you ask them if having a patent makes them more confident that a product or service will really do what it says it can do, the answer is much more likely to be yes.

The distinction is very important. Don't confuse benefits with reasons to believe. Patents, pedigrees and the like are not benefits. They're simply reasons to believe.

One of the cleverest uses of development superiority claims is utilized in the U.S. battery industry. In order to legally support a claim of superiority, a battery maker makes claims against its former formulas: "Today's alkaline lasts three times longer (than our old battery)." In the process, the company implies it has superiority versus competition. As the companies are always improving their batteries, they have a steady source of claims they can make versus old formulas.

2. Marketing Pedigree: Marketing-focused pedigrees have an added advantage of being something you can actually create. By entering a contest, reviewing sales histories or conducting customer research you can often craft yourself a piece of powerful credibility.
- The number one best-selling blueberry muffins in America.
- Taste tests show that Americans prefer our muffins 2 to 1.
- The original super giant blueberry muffin.
- For over 50 years the number one blueberry muffin baker in America
- Winner of the Great American Blueberry Festival Muffin contest 5 years in a row!

The good news about marketing pedigree is you can define the field of competition that your claim is based on. For example, if your unique chocolate chip blueberry muffin is a huge hit with kids, conduct your test with them. "Kids prefer our muffins 2 to 1 versus cereal." When you narrow your claim like this, be honest and clear about how you are defining your "win."

Contests and awards are a great form of marketing pedigree.

In Naples, Florida, there's an eatery called Michelbob's Championship Ribs. The place is decorated from floor to ceiling with accolades and trophies from local, regional and national rib contests across America.

I went to Michelbob's on the advice of my good friend Tom Ackerman. Tom had raved about how great the ribs were and how Michelbob's had won every rib award there is. The hype was almost too much. But Tom was insistent and I trust Tom's judgment, so we went.

In a word, wow! The ribs actually lived up to the awards they'd won. The place is a little out of the way, but the ribs are well worth the trip and the wait.

That's the power of a great product or service. Great benefit and powerful Real Reasons to Believe. They're worth the trip, the wait, the cost. Customers get really excited when they find products or services that are truly worthwhile. They get so excited they tell everyone they can of their great finds.

Stop for a moment and reflect on your business. Is it worth it, too? If not, why not? How about doing something about it? How about doing it now?

3. Trademark Pedigree: One of the most common means for generating credibility is to use a trademarked brand name that has a pedigree of trust.

One of the oldest utilizations of trademark pedigree is the practice of British royalty to provide royal warrants to goods and services—as in "By appointment to her Majesty the Queen," this product or that product has been given a special commission. Such products are allowed to display the queen's coat of arms as evidence of their quality.

Trademark pedigree can utilize the name of a company, a person or even an organization as the source of quality.
- Julia Child's Blueberry Muffins
- Duncan Hines Blueberry Muffins
- State of Maine County Fair Association Blueberry Muffins

The use of an established brand name on a new product or service is very powerful if the established brand name has a pedigree of excellence in the Overt Benefit area being articulated.

How far you can stretch a name from what it currently

stands for to a new product or service must be evaluated on a case-by-case basis. Review of our concept database indicates that when other key factors are controlled, the use of a name has widely varying results, ranging from 15 to 51% probability of success. The low potential is caused by companies trying to stretch their names further than then they should. When a trademark is used on a product or service that is inconsistent or wildly different from the existing business it can have negative results. Here are some hypothetical good and bad uses of established brand names.

Good Use	Bad Use
American Express Airport Lounges	American Express Trash Collection
Walt Disney Preschools	Walt Disney Alcoholic Rehab Clinic
Nike Sports Performance Medicine Centers	Nike Ballet Slippers
Ford Truck Construction Trailers	Ford Demolition Derby

Another way of using an established brand name is as a source mark. Here, the new item has a name of its own. The established trademark is used as a modifier or as a company source mark.

- Duncan Hines presents Big Blue Blueberry Muffins
- Gooey Gourmet from the Kitchens of Chef Jon Paul
- True Decadence Blueberry Muffins with Godiva Chocolate Chips

The most common way that a new small business acquires a trademark pedigree is through franchising an entire business concept, such as Subway, McDonald's or Jiffy Lube. One of the greatest values of a franchise is that, if it is successful, it provides instant Real Reason to Believe to potential customers.

Short of franchising a full business concept, you can leverage trademark credibility by focusing your efforts on one brand of goods and services. You can market your retail store as specializing in Sony brand electronics. You can market your computer education service as specializing in Microsoft Windows training.

Pedigree—Now It's Your Turn

Now it's your turn to build one or more Real Reasons to Believe using pedigree. Use the following prompts to get you going.

Development Pedigree
- What ingredients or components come from a special source?
- What elements of your production process are unique to you?
- Do the designers or creators of your business offering hold any awards or certificates?
- Can you apply for a patent?
- Do you ship, service or deliver in a uniquely excellent way?
- What can we document as better today versus three years, five years, ten years ago?

Marketing Pedigree
- What group of customers could we test with and get a big win?
- Who could we compare versus and get a big win?
- What segment of the market do we hold a number one position with?
- Can we leverage the age of our company, our formula, our founder's experience?
- What awards have we won or could we apply for?

Trademark Pedigree
- What name in our corporate history could we leverage?
- Whose name could we license to provide leverage?
- What name could we use as a source mark to provide leverage?

Real Reason to Believe 4: Testimonials

Testimonials can be provided by customers, experts or independent third parties.

Customer Testimonials: The overt satisfaction of current customers can be used to convince others of your credibility. The satisfaction of a listing of repeat clients can also provide credibility.

- "Beware: You won't be able to eat just one muffin." John Sampson, Boston
- "In my ninety-two years, I've never tasted as fine a blueberry muffin." Jane Islay, Vermont

Expert Testimonials: Here an expert provides independent authentication of your performance.
- "This is the quintessential blueberry muffin." James Jones, Head Chef, Culinary Institute of America
- "The American Society of Doctors has found that the antioxidants in blueberries can help prevent some forms of cancer."

Remember to get signed permission when using someone's name, be it a customer or an expert.

Nike provides Real Reason to Believe that its footwear performs at the highest level every time one of its athletes goes on the field or court. Nike also goes to extraordinary lengths to ensure the footwear you buy in the store is exactly the same used to win championships in professional sports.

In Cincinnati, Dr. Gary Varley offers laser surgery to eliminate the need for glasses. In his waiting room is a montage of photographs of seven other doctors in town. They're shown without glasses. Each is identified, along with his or her medical specialty. And there is this banner: "Dr. Varley . . . the Doctors' Surgeon."

What better testimonial than to have doctors endorse your surgery by having you operate on them?

Celebrities are a mixed bag when it comes to expert testimonials. In most cases, they don't work. For celebrities to add credibility, they must have clearly acknowledged expertise in the benefit areas they've been hired to pitch.

For instance, Paul Schurke is an explorer who has completed more dog sledding expeditions to the North Pole than anyone in the world. Paul adds credibility to his wife Susan's line of Wintergreen outdoor gear. Having worn Susan's gear on a trip with Paul to the North Pole, I can vouch for the fact that when Paul and Sue say something works at 20 below zero, you can count on it.

Likewise, chefs can vouch for the quality of produce, meat or herbs; swimmers can vouch for the quality of swim goggles; photographers can vouch for the quality of a certain camera.

Most television or sports celebrities can't vouch for the quality of tires, financial services or automotive repair shops. All a celebrity can do in such cases is be an expensive pitchman. Because people are well known doesn't mean they are believable.

As a small business, don't overlook the potential for using a local celebrity to help promote your credibility. If you do, however, be sure the person has a level of expertise that is either readily known or can be communicated easily.

Media Quotes: A powerful system for gathering independent testimonials is to use excerpts from media stories. Obviously the more well known the media outlet is, the better. However, don't ignore local publications. In some cases, they are more credible, as they offer a feeling of local expertise.

- "The number one Blueberry Muffin in America." *USA Today*
- "Spring Brook's number one bakery ten years in a row." *Spring Brook Post*
- "This is one blueberry muffin that's worth the trip. But get there early as they often sell out by 11:00 in the morning." *Off the Beaten Path* radio show

Testimonials-Now It's Your Turn

Build one or more Real Reasons to Believe using testimonials. Use the following prompts to get you going.

- What quotes do you have from customers?
- How could you start gathering quotes?
- Who of your customers is best known? Would they give you quotes?
- Who are your current clients?

Expert Endorsement

- Who is the most trusted person in the field?
- Who is the most well known person in the field?
- What expert would you trust to judge quality in your business area?

Media Endorsement

- Do any articles written about you contain a quote you can use for credibility?
- Has your business been featured in any magazines, guides or review services?

Real Reason to Believe 5: Guarantee

The last of the five Real Reason to Believe strategies can be the most powerful, if—and it's a big if—you keep the fine print, the qualifiers and exceptions to a minimum.

For a guarantee to have impact, you must maximize customer confidence, rather than reduce legal risk. **The power of your guarantee is directly linked to the level of risk you and your company are perceived to be taking.**

At the Eureka! Ranch, we "guarantee to exceed your expectations or we'll work for no fee until we do. There is no fine print."

Note the claim "exceed your expectations." We don't promise you'll be happy. We promise you'll be happier than you expect to be. Doing what you say you'll do is good service. Exceeding customer expectations is great service.

Also, check out the overt mention of no qualifiers: "There is no fine print."

Read the guarantee again. "We guarantee to exceed your expectations or we'll work for no fee until we do. There is no fine print." Does it give you a feeling of boldness, confidence, peace of mind?

Is there a risk in a guarantee like this? I don't think so. As CEO, if the Eureka! Ranch doesn't wow customers, I want to know about it. When the business was launched years ago, we worked hard to make sure clients were satisfied. One day, I realized that, without saying it, we were already guaranteeing everything. Today we declare our guarantee openly, thus gaining the full marketing value of what has been a long-standing policy.

Perhaps the grandpappy of all great guarantees is the one L.L. Bean offers. Back in 1912, Leon Leonwood Bean grew tired of coming home from hunting with wet, sore feet from the heavy leather woodsman's boots that were common then. Leon invented a new boot with waterproof rubber bottoms and lightweight leather uppers. The boots kept feet dry, but they still "breathed." Leon sold one hundred pairs through the mail. As it turned out, there was a problem with the stitching and ninety pairs were returned. He refunded all the money and started over. Soon the company's legendary guarantee was posted in every store and in every catalog. It reads like this:

> Our products are guaranteed to give 100% satisfaction
> in every way. Return anything purchased from us at any

time if it proves otherwise. We will replace it, refund your purchase price or credit your credit card.

We do not want you to have anything from L.L. Bean that is not completely satisfactory.

Note again how the wording gives you a sense of genuine confidence. Someone selling junk would not make a guarantee of this nature. Contrast L.L. Bean's guarantee with the following guarantee's fine print: "money back, if not on sale, if packaged in original packaging, if still in saleable condition and if within seven days of purchase."

Guarantee—Now It's Your Turn

Now it's your turn to build one or more Real Reasons to Believe using guarantee. Use the following prompts to get you going.

Guarantee
- What do you guarantee now as a matter of course yet don't claim?
- What part or portion of your product or service could you guarantee?
- What would be the most daring guarantee you could make?
- What type of guarantee would most scare competition?

Common Mistakes Made With Real Reason to Believe

From experience, the following are common mistakes businesspeople make when defining their reasons to believe.

Not Offering Enough Reason to Believe: The most common mistake is companies not providing enough reason to believe. Real Reason to Believe is not like Overt Benefit where focusing gives you an advantage. We've never been able to find a relationship between the number of reasons to believe presented and probability of success. My advice to you is if in doubt add more. You can't have too much Real Reason to Believe.

Offering Irrelevant Reason to Believe: For a Real Reason to Believe to be effective, it must speak directly to the promise made in the Overt Benefit. The two must be relevantly linked to be effective. Here's an example of a good and bad linkage for a potential radio station.

> Overt Benefit: "Skip the same old, same old music jukebox and experience the originality of tomorrow's superstars on Rising Star Radio 820."

> **Bad** Reason to Believe: Winner of the silver hog award for early morning farm reports.

> **Good** Reason to Believe: Playing only artists who've signed with the top three recording labels within the past twelve months.

Synergy between Overt Benefit and Real Reason to Believe is itself a strong contributing element to credibility. Synergy is also important with regards to the message you tell through various channels of communication. Take a close look at all of your customer communications. Are they articulating the same or different messages? Aligning messages amplifies the impact of every dollar you spend on marketing. When the messages are different, you lower your credibility with potential customers.

In today's world, the number of vehicles used to communicate is far broader than yesterday's. Marketing today includes Web sites, trade show booths, the message printed on your trucks, invoices, and business cards. And most importantly, it also includes the first words spoken by employees when asked about the company on the phone, at trade shows or when on site with customers.

Seeking Crediblity From a Declining Brand-Name Trademark: Brand names only provide credibility if they are healthy and respected businesses in their own rights. A business that's been in a long decline will do little to grow your credibility. This doesn't mean you can't use the name, but don't depend on the name for credibility. Be sure to include an extra dose of credibility from other areas.

Following the Industry: A great mistake business owners often make is to follow their industry. They only consider whatever method of credibility is accepted and commonly used in their category.

There are many categories like this. Scotch whiskeys talk primarily of pedigree. Movies use "expert testimonials" from movie reviews in their newspaper ads. Mail-order companies offer money-back guarantees.

The more a strategy is used, the less credible it becomes because customers conclude, "They always say that." The repetition causes them to reduce their confidence. By using a unique and unexpected strategy, you can break the cycle of cynicism.

Failing to Support Emotional/Experiential Benefits: When promoting an emotional or experiential benefit, be sure to communicate a Real Reason to Believe. The data from our archives indicates that for an emotional or experiential benefit to be effective, it must be supported with relevant credibility elements.

Primary Communication	Benefit Only	Benefit and Real Reason to Believe
Rational Benefit	35%	45%
Emotional/Experiential Benefit	25%	42%

Net, if you're going to present a benefit that plays with people's emotions, you'd better back it up. Recognize, too, that if an emotional benefit is used, the Real Reason to Believe must be synergistic. If your benefit is emotional, for example, you should make sure your reason to believe is relevant to the business. An emotional benefit can't be abruptly supported by a scientist in a lab coat explaining your technology pedigree.

Voluntarily Destroying Your Own Credibility: It's amazing how often companies damage their own credibility. Often it's the lawyers who are the cause. For instance, an early Internet bank/investment house offered customers this bit of kitchen logic Real Reason to Believe: "It works because it was built from the Internet up. Not from a bureaucracy down." In small print, they also included this startling admission: "Investments not FDIC insured. May lose value. No bank guarantee."

This disclaimer probably wasn't a real confidence builder for customers who were considering putting their assets in a virtual

Internet bank. In fairness, the legal department required the admission because the company was selling stocks in addition to taking bank deposits. Later the company separated its banking group from its stock sales group and instead of a negative, the fine print became a positive: "Deposits FDIC insured. Guaranteed by the U.S. Government."

Here's another example of overt negative credibility. I recently purchased some market share data from one of the largest companies in the industry. I was shocked to read in boldface, all caps the following statement in the purchase agreement.

> DATA COMPANY MAKES NO REPRESENTATION OR WARRANTY AS TO THE VALUE, MERCHANTABILITY, DESIGN OR FITNESS FOR USE FOR A PARTICULAR PURPOSE OF THE DATA TO BE PROVIDED HEREUNDER.

Say what?

I guess that's what you get when you let lawyers call the shots.

Forgetting to Refresh Your Credibility: Companies often start out providing strong reasons to believe. Then as the companies grow they stop reinforcing credibility because they feel everyone already knows about them. This attitude is reinforced because the staff spends so much of its time servicing existing clients. Existing clients already have faith in you. If you are to convince new customers of your merit you need to be relentless looking for new, more exciting and convincing options for Real Reason to Believe.

Quick Process Summary on Real Reason to Believe

1. Remember the linkages between target audience, Overt Benefit and Real Reason to Believe: Real Reason to Believe is relative to an Overt Benefit that is relative to a target audience.
2. The most powerful source of credibility is to tell the real truth about what makes your service or product perform the way it does.
3. There are five proven strategies for communicating Real Reason to Believe.
    I. Kitchen Logic: Offer commonsense explanations.
    II. Personal Experience: Have clients see, feel, touch and experience your benefit.

- Sampling—the ultimate proof.
- Demonstration—extreme conditions where you've proven yourself.
- Sensory feedback—sights, sounds and other feedback that it works.
III. Pedigree: Detail the heritage behind your product or service.
  - Development pedigree—how and why you make it as you do.
  - Marketing pedigree—using claims, contest wins and customer results.
  - Trademark pedigree—borrowing credibility from another brand.
IV. Testimonials: Have others speak to your quality.
  - Customer testimonials—real-world testimony to your ability.
  - Expert testimonials—specialists' testimony that enhances credibility.
  - Media quotes—excerpts that provide evidence of your skill.
V. Guarantee: Put yourself at personal risk if you don't deliver as you say.

4. If in doubt, add more Real Reason to Believe.

5. Never ever, ever, ever give up the search for new, fresh ways to communicate credibility. These messages are not as important for existing customers, but if you are to win new customers, you must continuously seek new ways to convince them of your efficacy.

Final Thoughts on Real Reason to Believe

In an ideal world, there would be no need for Real Reason to Believe. All products and services would do what they claim to do. Honesty would rule and customers would trust all. In a world of total trust, a merchant would offer a solution to a problem and customers with that problem would make a purchase.

Today that's not the case. Cheats, crooks and exaggerated marketing hype are the rule. Thus, we must offer our customers a Real Reason to Believe that our solution will solve their problem.

When probed on their primary marketing system, many small business owners will claim that most of their business comes from referrals. Clearly it's a powerful system. But think for a minute. The reason referrals are so powerful is because your customers are providing one-on-one, first-person testimonials on your efficacy.

It's an effective system. But it is also a slow system for growth. Plus, if the chain reaction of confidence building is broken by a competitor using mass-marketing tactics, then your momentum and sales growth die.

Without communicating a Real Reason to Believe, you can still generate some business. There are always a few brave and bold souls who will buy most anything. Academics call them early adopters. The challenge with early adopters is that they are the first to try your product or service and also the first to leave to try the next new thing. It's hard to build a stable long-term business on early adopters.

The results of having a Real Reason to Believe are well worth the effort. When customers believe you'll do what you say, they're more likely to buy your product or service and try it. When they don't believe, you have to spend more money on advertising, marketing, discounts just to get them to consider it.

The power of offering an Overt Benefit and Real Reason to Believe pair is unquestionable. However, with this power comes a responsibility to be honest and truthful.

Sadly, examples of the gap between promise and truth are everywhere. Not long ago on a Saturday morning, I walked into my local convenience mart to pick up some eggs, bacon and milk for breakfast. As I walked out the door, I noticed a declaration on the side of the bag: "Extra Heavy Duty Paper. No Double Bagging Needed."

I smiled inwardly, happy to see an Overt Benefit and Real Reason to Believe so clearly stated. Ten steps out the door, the bacon package slit the bag, and I was juggling eggs, milk and bacon.

"@?#%$!!!" I screamed. "What the *#&@ is wrong with this country? Why can't we do what we say we're going to do? How hard can it be to be honest?"

The secret to success is simple. Promise your customers an Overt Benefit. Then deliver on that promise.

How to Design Your New Product, Service or Business for Power Profits

We have optimized the Overt Benefit and Real Reason to Believe of your current business proposition. For most businesses, marketplace experience has shown that this alone can generate a 5 to 50% growth in sales. Continued growth in sales and most importantly profits margins requires enhancing Dramatic Difference, the focus of chapters six and seven.

Third Law of Marketing Physics: Dramatic Difference

Sales and profits explode when an Overt Benefit and Real Reason to Believe pair is offered with a Dramatic Difference.

You supercharge your growth in both sales and profits when you bravely offer customers an Overt Benefit and a Real Reason to Believe pair that has a Dramatic Difference.

Offering a Dramatic Difference gets you noticed, remembered and acted on by customers. Customers are creatures of habit. To change purchasing behavior, you must offer a meaningful perceptible difference versus the status quo. The data indicates enhanced Dramatic Difference levels increase probability of success from 15 to 53%! This means that you have a 353% greater chance of success when you have a high level of Dramatic Difference. These results confirm an earlier study by J.H. Davidson reported in the *Harvard Business Review* (April-May 1976). Davidson found a 370% greater chance of marketplace success for ideas that are dramatically different.

When you are unique, you stand out in the marketplace. Think back to your drive to work or home yesterday. What did you see?

	Probability of Success
High Dramatic Difference	53%
Medium Dramatic Difference	40%
Low Dramatic Difference	15%

What do you remember? Probably not much. Now if for some reason an African elephant crossed the road in front of you, the odds are you would have remembered it. Seeing elephants is a novelty that while noticeable doesn't cause much more than interesting dinner conversation. Now imagine if, on your drive home, you saw the sign for a new bakery named Muffin Madness, home of the Monster—the World's First Stuffed and Frosted Muffin! There is a decent chance you'd be thinking of stopping the following morning on your way to work. I don't know what the Monster is, but with its stuffing and frosting, I have reason to believe it could be one fantastic taste experience.

With customers, the Dramatic Difference associated with incredible muffins is very different from that of seeing African elephants. Muffins are more relevant to their needs.

The Big Picture on Dramatic Difference

The interrelationship of the laws looks like this when Dramatic Difference is added: **Real Reason to Believe is relative to an Overt Benefit that is relative to a target audience that evaluates the Dramatic Difference relative to meaningfulness of differences and pricing versus existing options.**

Dramatic Difference is a two-step evaluation criteria customers use to evaluate your proposition. First, they evaluate whether you offer meaningful uniqueness versus existing options. Second, they evaluate your price versus existing options.

If the first evaluation is favorable, you will likely generate healthy sales and healthy profits. If the second evaluation is favorable, you will likely generate healthy sales and low profits. If both evaluations are unfavorable, you are likely to generate low sales and low profits.

Evaluation of Dramatic Difference is how customers decide

if their purchase decisions should be based on value or price. When there is no perceived meaningful difference, then price becomes the primary if not exclusive decision criterion.

When you don't articulate your true Overt Benefit and Real Reason to Believe, customers simply skip step one and move directly to step two-evaluation based on price. This is why it is so important that you clearly articulate your Overt Benefit and Real Reason to Believe.

To generate sales, we must offer customers either a meaningful point of difference or a great price. There are no other known methods for success in a capitalist marketplace.

How to Win With a Commodity

Success with total commodities, such as pork, beef, potatoes and soybeans, is determined based on marketplace pricing. Your control over your destiny is your ability to manage your costs and thus sell at a price lower than your competition.

The following story is an unconfirmed legend of how Ben Franklin dealt with a pesky competitor who insisted on undercutting the prices Franklin charged for printing. He invited the other printer over for dinner. On the table was set a bowl of broth and a piece of bread. Beside the fireplace lay a blanket. Franklin explained to the gentleman, "I can live on this bread and broth and have no trouble sleeping by the fire wrapped in that blanket. If you can live on less, then you can starve me out. If you can't, you had best reconsider your pricing."

In today's world, Franklin's actions would be considered price fixing. The learning is clear, however. **Do not market your goods or services based on low price unless you can truly live on less than your competitor can.**

Your Mission Is to Create a Monopoly

Your mission should be to create a business that is as close as possible to being a monopoly. As a monopoly, you hold a 100% market share and have the potential for high profit margins. When you offer a Dramatic Difference versus all other competitors, you hold a monopoly-like position in the marketplace.

All businesses exist on a continuum between 100% commodity and 100% monopoly.

100% Commodity ....100% Monopoly	
Many equal alternatives	No similar alternative
Low profit margin	High profit margin
Market share based on how low you will price	100% market share

When your Overt Benefit and Real Reason to Believe pair is *dramatically different* from everyone else's on the market, you lie closer to the monopoly side of the continuum. When it is easy for customers to find alternatives that are "just about the same" as what you are offering, you are closer to the commodity end of the continuum.

Most successful small businesses start out closer to the monopoly side. This occurs because entrepreneurs found them with a passion for offering something unique, different and better than is currently available. With success, the new business attracts competitors without brains enough to be original. In time, the original company's level of monopoly decreases and it finds itself in a price-driven commodity marketplace.

The natural gravitational pull of business is from distinctive monopoly to price-driven commodity.

The mere word *monopoly* brings with it visions of illegal activity. A monopoly can wield its incredible power improperly. It can flex its power unfairly to destroy potential competitors through artificially low pricing or other strong-arm tactics. It's for this reason governments monitor the actions of monopolies very closely.

However, most monopolies are not illegal. A patent is a legal monopoly. A commitment to building an advanced distribution

Total COMMODITY ◄ ◄ ◄ ◄ ◄ ◄ ◄Total MONOPOLY

system is effectively a legal monopoly. A commitment to spend more on training your staff so they provide better service than all competitors is effectively a legal monopoly. A willingness to build a more advanced manufacturing plant than anyone in the market is effectively a legal monopoly.

Most monopolies are about a businessperson making a commitment to deliver dramatically different benefits to customers.

The New News About Dramatic Difference

Dramatic Difference has a long-standing heritage as being critical to helping companies avoid commodity pricing pressures. The new news is uniqueness is significantly more important than ever imagined. As a rule of thumb, I tell clients to take whatever they think new and different is and multiply times ten!

The word *Dramatic* in front of *Difference* was specifically chosen to help reinforce and define the level of uniqueness you must seek. Dramatic as in bold. Dramatic as in having a bit of theatrical wow. Dramatic as in engaging, involving and motivating to customers.

In my experience, corporate executives give a 0 to 5% weighting to uniqueness when evaluating new business ideas. Managers of large companies conduct quantitative tests of new business ideas by asking two key questions to up to four hundred customers.

• How likely are you to purchase the new product or service?
• How unique is the new product or service?

When evaluating the data, management gives near 100% weight to the purchase intent question and uses the uniqueness question only as a means for breaking ties. In twenty years of work with corporations, I am yet to see an executive give anything more than token acknowledgment to uniqueness.

This decision-making approach has always bothered me. I have long felt new and different had a greater impact than it was being given credit for. To help determine the truth, the Eureka! Ranch R & D team conducted an analysis. The team took a collection of five dozen products and correlated customer reactions to the products prior to introduction with how the products did in the marketplace. The team explored various weightings of purchase and uniqueness to find the best fit descriptor of actual behavior. As the chart below shows, a 60/40 blend of customers' purchase intent and perception of Dramatic Difference had the highest correlation with actual marketplace results.

What this means is that when evaluating the potential for marketplace success, Dramatic Difference must be a primary consideration.

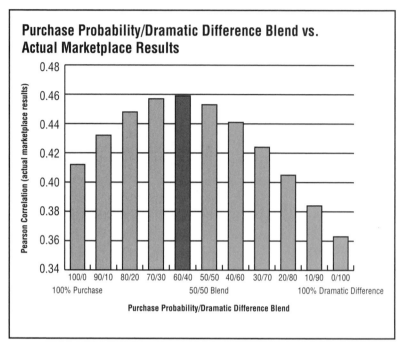

Purchase Probability/Dramatic Difference Blend vs. Actual Marketplace Results

More Reasons Why Dramatically Different Ideas Have a Greater Chance of Success

Dramatically different ideas provide your sales force with genuine news to tell customers.

Dramatically different ideas provide your trade customers with something exciting to sell and merchandise in their outlets.

Dramatically different ideas generate free publicity as they represent "real news."

Dramatically different ideas result in "talk" and "buzz" among users.

Dramatically different ideas provide motivation to new customers to make a purchase in the category, thus generating true net extra volume and growth.

Dramatically different ideas provide a true story to tell via advertising and marketing.

The president of one of New York City's largest advertising agencies recently told me, "I'll let you in on a secret. Great advertising comes from great products. Find me a product with great drama and news, and I can guarantee you great advertising." I agree.

A dramatically different idea provides a sense of mission and calling to your company and its employees. Working on a business that is uniquely great at something is a source of pride for all those who work with you. Everyone involved with the production, distribution and marketing of your product or service gets more excited, motivated and excited when working on something that offers genuine uniqueness.

A client took a product to market that had outstanding levels of Dramatic Difference. When word got out the product was coming to market, members of the retail trade actually called the company asking when they could get it. Most importantly, the new item was stocked without paying any slotting or listing fees for carrying the product as is the normal custom in that industry. It was also placed on the shelves without reducing any of the space allocated to the company's existing items. That is the power of Dramatic Difference.

It makes sense. If a new item is simply a variation of the same old stuff, it holds little opportunity to grow net extra customers and sales—for the retailer and for you.

Dramatic Difference represents the small business person's most important weapon in competing with larger competitors. When a company gets large, its courage tends to get small. By simply being courageous in the pursuit of dramatically different ideas, you can multiply the impact of your small company in the marketplace.

A Story of How Dramatic Difference Can Be Lost and Found Once Again

The following is the story of Peter Baker of Island Winds chimes. It's a story of a business offering a dramatically different product and finding incredible success. It's also the story of competitors flooding the marketplace and nearly driving him out of business. Lastly, it's the story of bringing the business back to life through focusing his marketing message on his true Dramatic Difference plus focusing once again on innovation.

Peter established Island Winds twenty years ago to make tubular wind chimes. For nearly ten years, he had a virtual monopoly as he was the only producer. Volume grew until at its peak, his chimes were featured in over four hundred outlets. As he explained to me, "We had ten years of continuous growth. Then competition came in with prettier looking chimes. Since then, we've had ten years of compounded sales declines."

After reviewing his history and production process, I suggested we review the Merwyn forecast on his current marketing brochure to see where he stood. Here's the copy from inside his brochure.

Island Winds' Chimes

Our handcrafted wind chimes have been ringing all over North America since 1980.

Mellow and compelling harmonies will ring out from your house because each of our bells is tuned by ear using a silver flute, rather than being tuned electronically.

This pleasing, natural scale of notes gives a sound that is superior in quality to electronically tuned bells.

We make our chimes in two converted hilltop 19th century barns overlooking the rolling hills of Queen's County, Prince Edward Island.

The tubes or bells of our chimes are finished from a steel alloy designed to resist rust. We also offer the chimes in a rust resistant aluminum alloy, and in copper. The striker is made from the same wood as the support. The bells, striker and hangers are hung with fine braided steel wire.

The Merwyn success forecast made it clear that Peter's concept had a decent level of Real Reason to Believe as a result of his twenty-year pedigree and construction materials; however, it lacked uniqueness.

Peter's reaction to the low new and different score was a classic, "Twenty years ago they were unique," he protested. And, yes, he was right. Twenty years ago Peter was the pioneer of wind chimes. Orders came in faster than he could make the chimes. Today, however, he was but one of many. And the majority of the

Overall Probability of Success: 23%

Returns on Effort Expended
(Percentiles calculated versus Merwyn's benchmark database of 4,000 concepts)

1. Overt Benefit   **35th percentile**
Specifically, obviously, directly—
What's in it for the customer?

2. Real Reason to Believe   **65th percentile**
Why should the customer believe you will
deliver on the promise made above?

3. Dramatic Difference   **30th percentile**
How revolutionary and new-to-the-world
is your benefit/reason to believe pair

sales in a category he had pioneered had been lost to competition.

I asked Peter if he had had any thoughts regarding changes to his chimes. He explained he was considering making his chimes look prettier. It seems the current market leader had taken Peter's original design and reworked it to make it cosmetically more attractive.

Where Peter used braided wire and bolts to hang his chimes, the competitor used nylon fish line. Where Peter used industrial-strength steel alloy tubing the competition used thin-gauge aluminum. He felt that these were the kinds of changes he had to make if he were to be successful.

The more Peter described the potential changes and how he would match the competition the more I started to boil. Finally I burst, "No, no, no, no . . . Don't do it! Peter, you have a Dramatic Difference. You just need to communicate it."

Peter's chimes were different for a reason. They were made strong and durable because of where he lived on a wind-swept hill . . . on an island . . . in the North Atlantic. The problem was, in the absence of communicating the Overt Benefits behind Peter's design philosophy, price and cosmetics were ruling purchase decisions.

We set to work crafting a new marketing message that clearly communicated Peter's Overt Benefit and Real Reason to Believe. We even gave the product line a new name that suggested the fundamental benefits of Peter's approach to wind chime design.

Nor'easter Chimes from Island Winds
Wind Chimes Designed for Real Wind—365 Days a Year

Most wind chimes are designed to make soft tinkling sounds in a summer breeze; to sound pretty, delicate, ethereal, and almost fragile. But they aren't built to handle real wind.

Nor'easter Chimes are unconditionally guaranteed to last a lifetime plus one, no matter how hard the wind blows. If they ever break—for any reason—return them for a free repair or replacement.

Nor'easter Chimes are gale-force chimes, built in Prince Edward Island, Canada, in the North Atlantic, where we live with serious wind, weather and storms 12 months a year.

Our chimes are built from industrial-strength steel alloy tubing with an average weight three times greater than the thin-gauge aluminum the competition uses. Instead of nylon string and plastic, we use steel wire and Canadian birch hardwood. To see test photos and independent test reports on the differences in strength and durability, check out our Web site.

Nor'easter Chimes are also the world's first wind chimes that you can "turn off" if you wish. A simple adjustment with a clip on the central wire lets you slide the clapper below the tubes, in effect creating an "on-off" switch.

As expected, the Merwyn forecast indicated a dramatic increase in probability of success.

Peter now had a simple and distinctive Overt Benefit message backed up by tangible Real Reasons to Believe.

You should have seen the look of joy on Peter's face when he saw the results. He was excited about improving his potential return on sales effort. However, what really made him happy was that he could remain true to his personal passion of making

Overall Probability of Success: 69%

Returns on Effort Expended
(Percentiles calculated versus Merwyn's benchmark database of 4,000 concepts)

1. Overt Benefit   **70th percentile**
Specifically, obviously, directly—
What's in it for the customer?

2. Real Reason to Believe   **75th percentile**
Why should the customer believe you will
deliver on the promise made above?

3. Dramatic Difference   **75th percentile**
How revolutionary and new-to-the-world
is your benefit/reason to believe pair

hearty, durable wind chimes. He admitted to me afterward, "Doug, I really never wanted to make cheap and flimsy chimes like the competition. I just couldn't figure out anything else to do."

In the case of Peter, the existing product had Dramatic Differences that could be leveraged through simply enhancing communication. Importantly, by communicating Peter's benefit, the competitor's "advantage" with regard to cosmetics was turned into a negative.

In addition, the concept added new news to the category, an on-off switch.

In addition to the switch, two other revolutionary designs for wind chimes were created that day. The specifics of these new ideas can't be revealed as Peter is seeking patent protection on them.

Today, Peter has a renewed sense of mission. He is once again taking the leadership role in the category. He has a message that can enhance communications effectiveness in the short term. And he has a long-term plan to add even greater Dramatic Differences to his product line.

It's still early, but when we checked with Peter five months later, for the first time in ten years his sales were up significantly versus the previous year.

The Moment of Judgment

In chapters two through five, we optimized your current marketing message. We made your benefit more overt and added credibility support behind your benefit with a Real Reason to Believe. Now comes the critical moment of judgment. We must evaluate your Overt Benefit and Real Reason to Believe pair to determine how dramatically different it is versus competition. Based on that evaluation, you will have an understanding of how urgent it is for you to embark on a program of development for greater Dramatic Differences.

Note, continuous development of Dramatic Differences is not optional. Every business has a need for enhancing uniqueness. In today's market, if you are successful, you will eventually have a copycat competitor. The only difference is how urgent is the need.

If you are an established business, with a healthy level of uniqueness today, then you have some time to develop your next Dramatic Difference. However, now is the time to allocate a portion of your resources on "the next big idea." If you don't, then one day you'll look up and realize your uniqueness and profitability have disappeared.

If you are an established business without a healthy level of uniqueness, your need for defining and discovering a Dramatic Difference is urgent. Your challenge will be reinventing your business simultaneously with maintaining your core business.

If you are not yet in business, you have the greatest control over your destiny. Use your planning time wisely, enhancing your uniqueness as much as possible.

I feel strongly about this issue. When potential entrepreneurs come to me with new business concepts that lack uniqueness, I advise them to think again. It is easy to do what others do. **Finding the courage to blaze a unique path takes energy. And it is easier to find that energy before you've started your business.** Once the business is opened, the day-to-day chaos of operations will consume your energy.

Beware, ideas rarely become more unique. The path of least resistance in business is to reduce uniqueness in favor of faster speed to market, enhanced feasibility and lower cost of development. I'm not saying this is right, just that it's the natural way. This is why it is so important that your concept start toward market with as much uniqueness as possible.

Development of Dramatic Difference is a never-ending journey. Competition is never static. Marketplaces are always moving and adjusting to those who have an advantage. And, as stated earlier, if you are successful, what starts as a monopoly soon becomes a commodity.

Practical Tactic: How to Know a Dramatic Difference When You See One

Being honest with yourself regarding the true uniqueness of your business concept is one of the greatest challenges in the world of business. **The natural tendency is to exaggerate differences based on minor distinctions that are irrelevant to customers.** The more insider knowledge we have regarding a business category, the more we tend to amplify the importance of small differences. Instead of seeing the bigger picture associated with the overall category, we subcategorize into micro differences.

Comparing one idea versus another, it's relatively easy to

determine which idea offers the greater uniqueness. The challenge is determining what level of Dramatic Difference is needed to be successful.

When I was at Procter & Gamble, I had a conversation with Ross Love, VP of Advertising, regarding a television commercial I was working on with the advertising agency. The production had not gone well. After the first edit of the videotape it was clear the commercial wasn't very good. The advertising agency went back to reedit it in an attempt to save the idea. Ross saw me in the hall way the morning after I'd been to New York to view the new edit. He asked how the newly edited commercial looked. "It's a lot better," I replied. He then surprised me with another question "Is it now good?" That was tougher. I stopped and admitted, "No, I'm afraid it isn't."

This is a common occurrence. We head to market with an idea that is a virtual clone of the competition hoping that an executional miracle will transform S.O.S. (the Same Old Stuff) into something spectacular. Get over it. It doesn't happen. Dramatic Difference must be built into your product or service. Uniqueness must come from within.

There is no easy way to define Dramatic Difference. Each case is individual and relative to the set of competitors available. However, the following five dimensions can help you more honestly asses your level of uniqueness.

1. How relevant is your point of difference? For a Dramatic Difference to be successful, it must be based on a combination of Overt Benefit and Real Reason to Believe that is relevant yet unexpected—relevant in that it has meaning, purpose and applicability to customer needs; unexpected in that it is novel, unusual, original, unique, new and different.

We must be always conscious of the relevance of our point of difference. The graph below shows the bipolar nature of Dramatic Difference. Each point on the graph represents a new product or service. As the uniqueness becomes greater, the customer probability of success becomes either strong or weak. Conversely, as the ideas becomes less dramatically different, the more the probability of success regresses to becoming average and with a 25% average success rate for new businesses, averageness equals a loss.

The lesson is clear. We must push for Dramatic Differences that make a real difference for customers. Dramatic Difference without an Overt Benefit asks consumers to change behaviors for no good reason. Consider Peter Baker's original claim that "each of our bells is tuned by ear using a silver flute, rather than being tuned electronically." While charming, it is not a relevant claim. It implies that the competition has a bad sound. However, to the untrained ear, a simple ring of the competitors' chimes finds Peter's claim to be irrelevant as all chimes seem to sound about the same.

To maximize relevance, your Dramatic Difference must flow

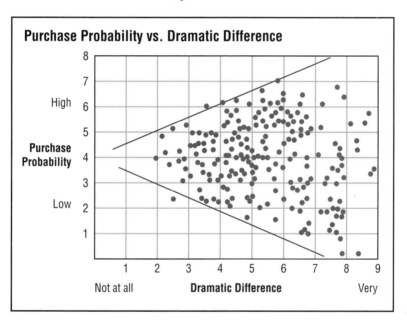

directly from your Overt Benefit and Real Reason to Believe pair. The only difference that is important to customers is one that impacts the experience they receive. Thus, relevance is linked directly to the connection between Dramatic Difference and Overt Benefit/Real Reason to Believe.

To get customers to change their existing behaviors, that is, their existing brand choice, they must be offered a difference that really makes a difference for them.

Ask yourself these key questions when evaluating relevance.

- Is the difference relevant or is it more of a shallow gimmick?
- Is the difference based on customer needs?
- Does the difference offer a relevant Overt Benefit for customers?

2. Do you have clear news to tell your customers? Ideas that offer true Dramatic Differences provide clear news to tell customers.

Several of my clients spend advertising money only on brands that have "news" to tell. This standard is driven by internal corporate analyses that show news to be the number one driver of advertising success. It's a harsh standard, but it does have the effect of forcing product development and marketing people to focus their energies on creating customer propositions that offer real differences.

News provides customers with hope that better, more effective options are now available.

News, like new and different, is in the eye of the beholder. A test to determine the news value of an idea is to evaluate it on the following increasing standards of uniqueness.

Is your idea new to your company?	Yes or No
Is your idea new to your region of the country?	Yes or No
Is your idea new to your industry?	Yes or No
Is your idea new to your country?	Yes or No
Is your idea new to the world?	Yes or No

Compare the difference. No one cares if an idea is new to your company. Rather, your goal should be to make an offering that is truly new to the world. If your idea is simply new to you but not the industry, it is a copycat. Robert Cooper, professor of marketing at McMaster University in Hamilton, Ontario, reports in his remarkable book, *Winning at New Products*, that 80% of all copycat efforts fail.

Another way to check for news is to see if you can explain it in simple words to someone who is not knowledgeable in the field. The more you need to have an "education" to understand the point of difference, the less unique it is.

Challenge yourself to explain your uniqueness to a child, a relative or friend who is not involved in your industry. When you can explain your uniqueness easily, you are on your way to success.

3. Is your idea evolutionary or revolutionary? Ideas that offer an evolutionary enhancement to existing options are called "er" ideas. By "er" I mean they're faster, quicker, cheaper or more of whatever dimension has been enhanced. Ideas that are revolutionary make a total transformation in how the Overt Benefit is delivered or make never-before-possible benefits possible.

Status Quo	Evolutionary	Revolutionary
Typewriter	Electric Typewriter	Computer word processing
Horse	Stage Coach	Train or Plane
Potato Chips	Low-fat baked chips	Fat-Free Chips with Olean
Eyeglasses	Contact Lenses	Laser Eye Surgery
Off-the-shelf blue jeans	Jeans with length adjusted	Made-to-order jeans

Not every idea can be totally revolutionary. The day-to-day needs of the marketplace require us to ship evolutionary changes to remain competitive. That's OK. Just be sure and set your expectations appropriately. Don't expect a little evolutionary change to make a transformational impact on sales. Little changes are simply that. To create a revolutionary improvement in sales, you need revolutionary ideas.

For a dramatically different idea to fly, it must have enough energy to break free of the natural gravitational pull of conformity. Ideas often start as revolutions; however, as the costs associated with new tooling, new methods, new systems, new packaging, and so on are quantified, the pressures build against revolution. Before you know it, you're pursuing carbon copy conformity.

To quantify how revolutionary your idea is, review how much work it has taken to develop it or that it will take to make it feasible. Research indicates that time and money are a reasonable measure of level of originality. Abbie Griffin reported in the *Journal of Product Innovation Management* (10:112-115; 1993) that on average, development time increased by seven months for every 20% change required versus established company practices.

Change in Product Versus Existing Practices	Average Development Time Required
20%	13 months
40%	20 months
60%	27 months
80%	34 months
100%	41 months

Griffin's report is based on large corporations. It's fair to estimate these times are shorter for more nimble, entrepreneurial organizations. However, it's probably true that even for small companies the greater a concept's uniqueness, the greater the time it takes to develop and execute it.

I am not encouraging you to be purposely slow when developing your ideas. I'm pointing out the simple fact that dramatically different ideas require dramatic differences in how you design, develop and produce your product or service.

The popular press promotes hyperspeed development as the path to instant riches. I, too, believe in speed to market but not in place of old-fashioned, original research and development.

Many fast-to-market initiatives are more expenditures of effort than accomplishment of real work. It's a fundamental truth. **If you can develop an idea quickly and easily, it's probably just as easy for your competitor to copy it.**

To succeed long term, ideas must offer sustainable points of difference. The greater the amount of time, money, intelligence and energy required to execute, the greater the barrier to competitive copying. So the energy you put in equals the sustainable difference you get out.

Check how revolutionary your idea is by answering the following questions.

- How much time and money has it taken for you to develop your product or service?
- If competition made a decision to copy you, how long would it take them?
- What percent of your concept is different from the competition—10%, 30%, 80%?

4. How crazy is your idea? Big, bold, dramatically different ideas break the rules of "business as normal" in your market segment.

Ted Turner, inventor and founder of CNN, does not shy away from crazy ideas. In an interview in the *The Atlanta Journal-Constitution*, he remarked on the importance of being a touch crazy when creating big, bold ideas:

In college there was no reason that I should end up winning the America's Cup more than any of the other good sailors. But I went out and made it to the top. I worked 18 hours a day. I moved with speed. I plotted, schemed, and planned, and did crazy things. . . .When you're little you have to do crazy things, you can't just copy the big guys.

Any idea worth pursuing contradicts established history. One of the simplest acknowledgments of a Dramatic Difference is the granting of a patent. When you file for a patent at the U.S. Patent and Trademark Office, one of the first questions asked is, "How does your approach compare to standard industry practices?" If it follows established protocols, is politically correct and is historically proven, then your request for a patent is denied. You don't have an original idea.

If, however, your idea breaks the rules and contradicts established ways of thinking you are on your way to a patent. It's important to remember patents are given only to crazy rebels and revolutionaries. Patents require that your idea go against the historical wisdom and knowledge of the industry. And going against everyone in the industry generally requires a touch of inspired craziness.

Ben Franklin spoke of how pursuing the impossible provided a valuable element of competitive surprise: "In war, attempts thought to be impossible do often for that very reason become possible and practicable, because nobody expects them and no precautions are taken to guard against them."

Here's the bottom line. **Dramatically different ideas *always* cause chaos for one or more areas of your company.** There is no way to avoid it. If your idea can be executed with little to no changes to the various functional areas of your company, it's simply not dramatically different.

Fame and fortune come to unreasonable people who continue onward, long past when reasonable people would give up. The pessimist sees the chaos of uniqueness as a negative. The optimist sees it as an opportunity to show how great they can be.

Dramatically different ideas cause the people working for you and your suppliers to change what they do on an operational basis and how they do it. Take this quick check on how dramatically different your idea is.

- How many "rules" of established industry thinking does your idea break?
- How dramatically do you break industry rules?

- How much operational disruption will your idea cause in order to execute it?
- How much chaos from employees and suppliers does your idea generate?
- How much resistance have you faced with your concept?

Net, as you pursue your idea, resistance from others is a sign that you are on the right track. If the people working for you and with you simply nod their heads at your idea and see it as a sure thing, it's time to get worried. You are probably not stretching yourself enough. Brilliant ideas are crazy ideas that look obvious only after the fact.

The graph on page 145 defines the options you have before you.

Quadrant 1 These ideas are hard to execute yet offer customers the same old stuff. These are an expensive waste of time and effort. Many high-technology research and development efforts end up as quadrant one ideas.

Quadrant 2 These ideas are easy to execute yet offer customers the same old stuff. Some executives call these "low, hanging fruit." The reality is these are commodity efforts that become huge organizational distractions. In addition, they are often "pitched" to the organization as something more than what they truly are, resulting in dramatic failures versus expectations.

Quadrant 3 These ideas are easy to execute yet offer customers a Dramatic Difference. These are great ways to make quick money; however, they must be pursued with great efficiency as they are usually short-term opportunities. As soon as you realize strong results, the competition will copy.

Quadrant 4 These are the ideas that offer the potential for sustainable growth. They are difficult to execute yet offer Dramatic Differences. They provide benefits to customers and barriers to

Hard to Execute

	1. Expensive Waste of Effort	4. Sustainable Growth
	2. Cheap Waste of Effort	3. Make money fast . . . before you get copied

Same Old Stuff   **Dramatically Different**

competition copying. If you have a vision for long-term growth, this is where your vision should be focused.

Taking the same graph and drawing the commodity-monopoly dimension, we see that the key to business success lies in how far toward the upper right (quadrant four) we can move our idea.

Quadrants one and three are short-term locations. Eventually the cost of executing something of little benefit to customers causes quadrant one concepts to be discontinued. Marketplace success eventually causes quadrant three concepts to be copied in the marketplace. Quandrant two is the land of no profits.

Draw a graph similar to the one below, and from your judgment alone, locate where each of your key competitors would be located. Consider the following as you are thinking about where to locate each company.

- The pricing and profit margins of each company
- The distinctiveness of each company's offerings
- The volatility of each company to pricing changes

Having mapped your industry, now evaluate whether you're happy with your location. If you're not, now is the time to pursue enhancing your level of Dramatic Difference.

5. Does your idea offer a value ratio that generates spontaneous excitement?
When customers assess a dramatically different offering, they

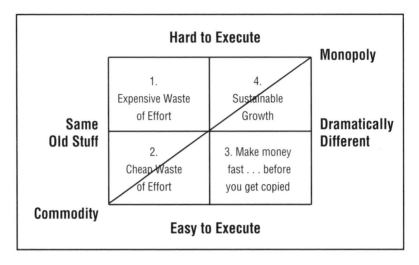

weigh the value ratio of what you give them divided by what it costs. The ratio for you is then compared with a similar ratio for your competition.

Your Offering	Competitive Offering
What customers get divided by what it costs	What customers get divided by what it costs

In the real world, what your customer receives and what it costs vary for both you and the competition. This is an important point to recognize because it is common that Dramatic Differences end up costing more than existing options. This is not a problem as long as the benefit increment is greater than the price increment.

The price increment is a result of relentless cost savings that have been pursued in recent years. Today, most products have little room for additional savings in order to counterbalance enhancements. The one exception to this is the high-technology area where chip costs, processing power and software design costs continue to drop as new efficiencies are realized.

Your goal is to make your value equation tip more in favor of customers then your competition's value equation. This is most profitably accomplished by providing a more relevant Dramatic Difference.

The more your equation tilts in favor of customers, the greater the excitement, buzz and interest you will develop. When the value received by customers is greater than the cost of purchasing, customers flock to buy. When the value received by customers is less than the cost of purchasing, customers say no thanks.

Setting the value at a fair level, that is, having what customers receive equal to what they pay, doesn't work either. Customers don't make a change from their current behavior unless they see an advantage. **To win with customers, you must tilt the value equation in their favor.**

Let's develop versions of these equations for you and your competition.

Step 1 Make a list of your relevant points of difference and the cost to customers in terms of price and time and trouble required when using the product or service.

Step 2 points of difference and the cost to customers in terms of price and time and trouble required when using the product or service.

Step 3 As we did earlier, cross out one relevant difference you have for each equivalent one (or two if appropriate) your competition offers.

Step 4 When you are finished, look at what's left. Compare what customers get from you versus what they get from your competition. Next compare your costs versus the competition's. Which would you choose if you were a customer?

Some stubborn types will look at the equation listed here and perceive that they can win by simply lowering their prices. Don't count on it. Robert Cooper found that low price as a strategy is only half as effective as strategies that add value.

In many respects, your pricing is a direct measure of your level of uniqueness. If you have a profit margin that's dramatically higher than the competition's, you probably have a Dramatic Difference. If your margin is the same or lower, you probably are marketing a commodity. And, for a commodity, price rules buyer decisions.

My nine-year-old son, Brad, and I used a lack of relevant differences to get some good prices recently when on vacation in the Bahamas. We were touring a straw market looking for a "boy" necklace as my son called them. At the first stand we came to, they had necklaces that cost $12. As we were out for a walk, we decided to hold off purchasing and see what other options existed. In time, we realized that all the street vendors sold basically the same thing. It became a game to see how low they would go. In the end we paid $10 for three necklaces.

On the same walk, we also purchased a wood carving of a dolphin for $20. This was quite a discount from the original offering price of $75. Again, many vendors offering similar wood carvings resulted in heavy discounting and reduced profit margins.

At the straw market, pricing moves down quickly as there is little time in which to make the transaction. In your marketplace, the movement may be slower but the end result is the same when no point of difference is offered.

In the future, pricing pressures will be even greater. Web sites and Internet agents provide comparison shopping with the click of a mouse. When no meaningful differences can be found between services or products, free market forces turn toward what is being charged. Soon the marketplace sets the profit margins, and it's a matter of survival of the fittest—or in this scenario, the low-cost producer.

CHAPTER 7

How to Craft a Dramatic Difference

The practical tactics for inspiring Dramatic Differences will be left to the upcoming Capitalist Creativity section of this book. In this chapter, we will review three guiding principles you need to understand as you journey to craft a Dramatic Difference.

The Three Guiding Principles

1. Provide Leadership and Take Responsibility: It is your job to provide the leadership for identifying the Dramatic Difference for your business. Companies, committees and teams don't invent. People invent. It's for this reason that the U.S. Patent office only issues patents in the names of individuals not corporations. Individuals can assign their rights to a company, but companies can't and don't invent anything.

For the same reason, you cannot rely on asking customers what they want in order to discover your Dramatic Difference. Customers can only describe *the world that is.* They have great difficulty describing *the world that could be.*

When asked what they want, most customers will regress to their existing experiences. Plus, some customers are initially scared at the thought of revolutionary change. As one client whose customers were Fortune 100 corporations said to me, "Our customers are cowards. It's up to us to give them the courage to be great."

It is your responsibility to lead the journey to Dramatic Difference. The following two quotes from Dr. W. Edwards Deming sum up this point quite well:

> A customer can seldom say today what new product or new service would be desirable to him three years from now, or a decade from now. New products and new types

of services are generated, not by asking the consumer, but by knowledge, imagination, innovation, risk, trial and error on the part of the producer, backed by enough capital to develop the product or service and to stay in business during the lean months of introduction.

Did customers ask for the electric light? No. They never asked for it, the producer produced it. No one asked for a car, nor a telephone. No one asked for a copy machine or a fax machine. Innovation does not come from the customers. Innovation comes from the producer, from people who are responsible for themselves and have only themselves to satisfy.

It's not enough to ask customers what they want. Our responsibility as the leaders of our businesses is to take our customers to new places—and to open our imaginations to what could be, not to simply relive what's already out there.

Pursuing dramatically different ideas takes courage, as the unbeaten path is not nearly as comfortable to travel on as the highway of conformity.

A CEO of one of the ten largest companies in America told a product development team I was working with, "Your product will be great, if you have the courage to really do it." The team was focused on developing a totally new type of product for the company. As of this writing, the answer to the CEO's challenge is not certain. As the team moves forward, the gravitational forces of conformity weigh heavily on the team. It will require great leadership from the team leader to keep the team focused on the vision.

The leadership challenge with existing businesses is often even more difficult.

Frequently, a company has a strategy that generates sales increases. Yet it's clear to all involved that the strategy is flawed in the long term. The challenge is to find the courage to turn away from a flawed yet relatively certain strategy to a potentially more powerful approach despite it having a higher level of uncertainty and risk.

Davidson is a vice-president at a major brewery that regularly introduces new flavors of beers. The first new flavor generated 70% net extra volume, with 30% of the volume being sourced from his existing brands. The next flavor was 55% net extra and so on until today he's lucky if a new flavor provides a 10% increase in sales. The challenge is how to break the cycle. The "corporate system" has learned how to create and execute a new flavor every year. It will take great leadership from Davidson to stop the madness and move toward ideas that are more dramatically different then simply a new flavor.

Think.

What have you done to provide leadership?

What are you planning to do tomorrow to help lead the effort?

Approach the task with an attitude of adventurousness, of exploration, of pioneering, and you will find the momentum necessary to make Dramatic Differences reality.

2. Put It in Writing: For a Dramatic Difference to become real, it must be definable, and that means putting it in writing.

When I work with businesspeople, I oftentimes ask them the direct question, "What makes your business unique?"

Most times I get dribbles of this, that and whatever they can mumble out. I then condense their five minutes of jabbering into a one-sentence statement of uniqueness using one of these two forms.

_____ (business name) is the first to
offer _____ (Overt Benefit) that's because of
_____ (Real Reason to Believe)

or

What makes _____ (business name) dramatically different is that it's the only company to offer _____ (Dramatic Difference)

It's amazing but when your Dramatic Difference is distilled to a short phrase it either glows with vitality or is quickly exposed as a mirage. The written word has a way of exposing a lack of Dramatic Difference that the spoken word can hide.

The writing I'm talking about doesn't involve fancy words. It's about the ideas the words represent. Words describe. Ideas lead.

In turning your thoughts to words, don't overthink. Just do it.

Sit down with paper, pencil or computer. Take a deep breath. Then dive in headfirst.

Let your ideas free-flow. Let the words come out. Don't edit at first.

Later, go back and review, revise and reorder them. Find the best points, the most exact and precise descriptions of your true ideas.

Then rewrite and rewrite until you have an honest statement of who and what your company is about today. Or will be about tomorrow.

Writing and defining your thoughts on paper is also important if you are seeking to transform or revitalize an established business. If you can define clearly what will be different in the future versus the past, then your chances of a new reality are good. If, however, you can't define with great clarity what will be done differently your chances of true change are near nil.

Some years ago I read the following quote from Don Hewitt, creator and executive producer of the television show *60 Minutes,* in Frank Coffey's book *60 Minutes: 25 Years of Television's Finest Hour* (General Publishing Group, 1993):

> When all is said and done, telling stories is what it's all about. It is your ear as much as your eye that keeps you in front of a television set. It's what you hear more often than what you see that holds your interest. The words you hear and not the pictures you see are essentially what *60 Minutes* is all about. People always ask me for the formula for our success, and I tell them it's simple-four words every kid in the world knows: "Tell me a story."

Crafting your story for customers is easy. Tell me a story.

Stop reading and write your story. Tell your story with honesty and truthfulness and success will be yours.

3. Remember Dramatic Difference Flows From Overt Benefit and Real Reason to Believe: Dramatic Differences must flow from the product or service itself.

Dramatic Differences are only relevant when related to the Overt Benefit the customer will receive or to Real Reasons to Believe in the benefit offering.

In general you will find that Overt Benefit is the more fertile area for leveraging. It is possible, however, to craft your Dramatic Difference from your Real Reason to Believe. This is especially true when working in a category that for one reason or another has but one fundamental benefit. It also works in categories where there is a high degree of hype and extremely low levels of customer trust.

Vodka is an example of a category that is five hundred years old and that the U.S. Bureau of Alcohol, Tobacco and Firearms has by official regulation defined to be "neutral spirits . . . without distinctive character, aroma, taste or color." Based on that definition, a generic price brand should by law taste the same as the most expensive brand.

Thus, without the ability to market based on taste, the vodka producers leverage dramatically different Real Reasons to Believe along with distinctive graphics and bottle shapes.

Check out these Real Reasons to Believe for vodka.

- Made from Polish rye; distilled four times.
- Made from Polish stobrawa potatoes; distilled four times.
- Made from American grain using four-column distillation.
- Distilled four times, charcoal-filtered "carefully crafted" in Belgium's oldest distillery.
- Handmade in small batches; produced by a family distillery.
- Distilled five times; "created from meticulously selected grains of the highest quality."
- Quadruple distilled from organically grown grain.
- Triple distilled and filtered four times.
- Made with water filtered through Champagne limestone; distilled in small batches.

By law, the vodka has to deliver a neutral taste. However, through the use of unique reasons to believe, they enhance their marketplace points of difference.

Common Mistakes Made With Dramatic Difference

From experience here are some common mistakes made when seeking a Dramatic Difference.

Conformity Cancer: Business enterprises often start with a vision to be dramatically different. Then the harsh grit of reality sands

away the uniqueness. The movement to conformity rarely happens in one dramatic change. The movement is more like a slow cancer. One small change is made that has no significant impact on uniqueness. Then another and another and another. Soon you look back and realize a dramatically different idea has become the same old stuff.

Lorenzo Delpani, chief e-Business officer at Reckitt-Benckiser, once defined the movement to commodity this way: "Ideas start as a sparkling star. Then one by one the sparkles and points are taken away until all you have left is an egg. And only chickens market eggs."

There is no sure cure for conformity cancer. All you can do is maintain a vigorous vigilance against it. It is your job as leader to protect and defend the Dramatic Difference so it can survive and thrive in the marketplace.

Looking for a Magic Bullet: When creating entirely new concepts, there is a tendency to want to focus energies on one magic idea. I feel this is wrong.

When you can tell me the one stock to invest all my savings in, I will accept the selection of one magic bullet of an idea. With stocks, you invest using a portfolio approach. So, too, should you invest your long-term innovation efforts utilizing a portfolio approach.

My advice is to initially select three concepts for basic exploratory work. Often just a little work quickly identifies new opportunities or barriers that you were unaware of. I'm not advocating keeping all ideas alive forever. Do some initial exploratory development of the three concepts. Then, at a specific time in the future, review what you've learned and make an educated decision on which concept to pursue complete development on.

Focusing Exclusively on Reviewing the Possible: When looking for Dramatic Differences, the tendency is to simply review the possible, to explore that which is done now. I call this reorganizing the obvious. And it is not thinking big.

Innovation is not about taking everything you know how to do and rearranging the order. Like rearranging the deck chairs on the *Titanic*, it's a lost cause. What you do today will one day sink like the boat, overtaken by competition.

The execution of truly dramatically different means pursuing areas where there is some level of uncertainty regarding how to execute. Your ability to accept and manage this uncertainty is what will determine your success.

Solving Yesterday's Problems: You must stay current with the challenges facing today's customers. Often a company will stubbornly hold onto a vision of the marketplace that is simply outdated. For example, no amount of improvement to the Pony Express would have ever helped it overcome the transformational change known as the transcontinental railroad.

Not Facing the Facts With Honesty: You cannot change dramatically until you have fully faced the facts of who you are and where you are going. True change only happens when a healthy disrespect and dissatisfaction exist regarding your true level of Dramatic Difference.

A recent Eureka! Ranch client had a business that was declining 25% a year. Now with declines like that, it's no time to be tweaking the business; it's time for rapid revolutionary change! As the session progressed, it became clear that the client and I saw things differently. I kept pushing a set of revolutionary ideas. He kept rejecting them as being too radical. Finally, I restated the facts, as I knew them, regarding the business and how without dramatic action, the company's decline would simply continue. His response was so shocking I wrote it down verbatim on the spot: "You're right, Doug, you're 100% right about our situation, but I just don't want to talk about it." Interestingly, the company was acquired about six months later at a bargain-basement price.

Quick Process Summary on Dramatic Difference

1. Don't forget the interrelationship between the three laws: Real Reason to Believe is relative to an Overt Benefit that is relative to a target audience that evaluates the Dramatic Difference

relative to meaningfulness of differences and pricing versus existing options.

2. Make your Dramatic Difference ten times bigger than you
think you need.

3. Assess your Dramatic Difference.
- Is your difference relevant?
- Does your difference generate real news?
- Is your difference evolutionary or revolutionary?
- How crazy is your idea versus established ways of opera-
tion?
- What is the value ratio of what customers receive versus
cost?

4. Create dramatically different ideas.
- Provide leadership and take responsibility.
- Put it in writing.
- Remember Dramatic Difference flows from Overt Benefit
and Real Reason to Believe.

Final Thoughts on Dramatic Difference

Dramatic Differences offer **revolutionary news** that is **relevant** to
customer needs and offers great **value**. To create them, it helps if
you're a touch **crazy**.

A direct client requested, "We need to look for 5 to 10%
growth ideas. Our category is a stagnant category . . . we have to
be realistic."

If I was that lady's boss, I'd have fired her on the spot.

**You must always believe that the ability to enhance,
improve and differentiate everything is infinite. If you don't
believe, then get out of the business.** Get out before you get run
over by a competitor who still believes in growth.

I don't mean to say that there are easy miracle cures.
Articulating a dramatically different Overt Benefit and Real Reason
to Believe is hard work. Big, bold ideas usually require significant
R and D (meaning Research and Development, not the more common approach of large companies to "Rob and Duplicate").

The natural order of business and life is one of growth. To
thrive long term, we must always have a portion of resources
focused on true research and development of the innovations of
the future.

Fortunately, even if a low-cost producer wins in the short

term, it's difficult for the low-cost producer to win in the long term. The short-term win of business shackles him with low profit margins, leaving him no means for investing in R and D or plant expansion. In many cases, the short-term winner is destined for a slow, lingering death.

I will say, however, that with diligent work and effort and a total immersion into your challenge, when you least expect it a seeming miracle can occur. The reading you are doing at this very moment is preparing your mind and opening it to opportunities and answers that were always there but never had a voice.

It's important to start as unique as possible because the sad truth is that all ideas become more "normal or same" as time progresses, no matter how hard you defend them. Thus, the greater the stretch at the start, the greater your potential to end up with an idea that offers a true Dramatic Difference at the end.

A client friend defined the ultimate success for him as having an idea that someone sees and says to him, "Wow, how did you ever come up with that!"

CHAPTER 8

Frequently Asked Questions About Marketing Physics

You have now learned the three laws of Marketing Physics. These are the fundamental dimensions that have the greatest impact on the success of your business ideas. This last chapter answers common questions asked by participants at Marketing Physics training programs.

If I follow the three laws, am I guaranteed to succeed?

No. There is no such thing as guaranteed success. Marketing Physics is about probability. If you follow the three laws, you will dramatically increase your probability of winning in the marketplace. As was said in the introduction, by following these laws, you will be playing blackjack instead of low-odds slot machines.

The first step toward winning is to stop hurting yourself. You must first understand and address all the ways you can hurt your chances of success: lack of focus, implied benefits, no credibility, commodity offering. Addressing these critical dimensions does not guarantee you're going to succeed, but if you don't address them, you're probably going to lose.

Are the three laws the ultimate truths?

The laws of Marketing Physics are similar to Sir Isaac Newton's laws of motion. Newton defined a set of beautifully simple equations that describe the motion of physical bodies. Newton's equations have provided great value to scientists in understanding the world around us.

Einstein built on the work of Newton and defined a new set of equations, which included relativistic effects. Newton's work is still valuable, though we now know it's not perfect in all situations.

Defining the interactions between customers and producers is highly complex. In fact, we may never be able to fully understand or know reality in an absolute sense. However, the laws as detailed here are adequate, close-fitting analogs of reality. Using them as a benchmark allows us to better understand-and not just think that we understand-what is going on with customers in an objective sense.

Net, the laws of Marketing Physics are but a first step toward what I hope will be a revolution in business understanding. We continue to conduct research, and we encourage others to do the same.

How high should my probability of success be before going forward?

The probability of success level you should achieve before taking action is relative to the risk involved with the decision. As with financial investments, each person's risk tolerance varies. The value of estimating probability of success is that it provides an estimate of true risk.

With my business, I insist that all new business concepts, advertisements and marketing efforts have a probability of success of 51% or greater. Recall a 51% probability of success means we'll win more than we lose. It also means our chances of success are double the average for new products, services or businesses. With business decisions involving large investments of time or money, I require a probability of success greater than 75%.

If I don't have an advertising budget, why should I care about Marketing Physics?

If you are a business that is not a total monopoly, then you need Marketing Physics. The laws of Marketing Physics are important no matter how you make contact with potential customers. By defining and articulating your message with clarity, you can increase the effectiveness of in-person sales pitches, brochures, trade shows and even in-store signage.

Successful selling requires only two very low-cost tasks: (1) Making the effort to contact potential customers and (2)

Delivering the proper message.

The laws of Marketing Physics can help you with item two. It's up to you to make the effort—knock on customers' doors, make phone calls, mail brochures, etc. The greatest message in the world is worthless if you don't make the effort to deliver the message.

What about imagery? I've read that image is the most important dimension for success.

A great question. Imagery has been "sold" to marketers as a magic marketing solution when they don't have something "real" to sell customers.

Here are the facts: With all other factors held equal, an idea that offers features only—"it comes in blue" or "available in smooth or crunchy"—has a 10% chance of success. If the idea is filled with imagery and personality, the probability of success is 18%. If you are overt about just one of the core strategic elements —benefit or reason to believe (RTB)—and imply the other, your probability of success moves to 28%, evidence once again of the equal importance of RTB relative to benefit.

Interestingly, when flashy imagery is added to the mix, it has virtually no ability to improve odds of success for Overt Benefit and Real Reason to Believe. The biggest increase in probability of success comes when an integrated story is communicated involving Overt Benefit, Real Reason to Believe and Dramatic Difference. The chart below summarizes results.

Probability of Success (Other Variables Controlled to Average)	
Features only (implied benefit and RTB)	10%
Features and image only (implied benefit and RTB)	18%
Overt Benefit only (implied RTB)	28%
Real RTB only (implied benefit)	28%
Overt Benefit and image (implied RTB)	29%
Real RTB and image (implied benefit)	28%
Overt Benefit and Real RTB	41%
Overt Benefit, Real RTB and Dramatic Difference	51%

The numbers above are for an average level of each of the three dimensions. When you hit the maximum on each, your probability of success rises to 90%.

Image is not a benefit. But the image, style and personality of how you package your customer message can provide synergistic support for your Real Reason to Believe.

We rated four thousand concepts on their style and imagery. Holding all other dimensions constant, we learned that when the image overtly enhances credibility through a tone of genuineness, honesty, straight talk, sincerity, authenticity or competence, the probability of success is greater than when image is aimed at entertaining by being, say, funny, charming, romantic or exciting.

The following chart details our findings.

Probability of Success Assuming Constant Benefit and RTB Levels	
Genuineness: emotions and perceptions such as authenticity, honesty, sincerity, straight talk	55%
Competence: serious, intelligent	42%
Excitement: surprising, fun, lively, adventurous	23%
Sophistication: glamorous, romantic, charming	18%

It may surprise you to see that fun doesn't help sales. It shouldn't. Advertising's mission is not to entertain; it's to sell. Think of each of the four categories above as styles of salespeople calling on customers. Whom would you buy from? Whom would you trust the most? Whom would you be most likely to risk your companies money with?

When you communicate with genuineness and authenticity, you are taking a stand for something that matters. Interestingly, this same concept applies when it comes to what adults perceive to be the most important personal value. *Forbes ASAP*'s October 2, 2000, issue reported that authenticity is the most appealing trait for Americans.

Which of the following would you most like to be known for?	
(Survey of 1,021 Americans)	
Being authentic	49.8%
Being intelligent	22.2%
Having a sense of humor	22.0%
Being good looking	1.6%

This is good news. It indicates that you don't have to be a genius, tell funny jokes or look like a fashion model to succeed.

Simply present to your customers an authentic, genuine offer and they will respond.

In being authentic, there are times when a specific image can help with credibility. For example, if a natural bread is presented in a rustic brown paper bag with a straightforward homespun label, it has more authenticity than, say, a bread product packaged in a high-gloss, brightly colored plastic bag. Likewise, a product designed especially for children is more authentic if its look and feel is childlike.

Do I have to follow the order you described—Overt Benefit then Real Reason to Believe then Dramatic Difference?

No. You can start at any of the three. The key is to make sure that all three dimensions get fulfilled. Making them work together with synergy is often a great challenge.

The task is similar to the arcade game called Whack-a-Mole. Individual moles stick their heads up and your task is to whack them with a soft mallet. Just as you get one down another pokes up its head. It's the same with the three laws and target audience. Just as you get Overt Benefit fixed, Real Reason to Believe becomes a problem. Solve both benefit and reason to believe and you face a challenge with Dramatic Difference. Fix Dramatic Difference and you're back to working on Overt Benefit.

Concept synergy is when all four elements interact and work together.

- Target audience is *who* are your customers.
- Overt Benefit is *what* you're offering.
- Real Reason to Believe is *how* you're going to make good on your promise.
- Dramatic Difference is *why* customers should get excited.

When developing synergy, the relationships between dimensions are as critical as the dimensions themselves. Synergy involves the communications as well as all of the elements of the marketing mix. The following chart shows the power of overt synergy.

Probability of Success Assuming Constant Benefit and RTB Levels	
Overt synergy	45%
No synergy	36%

It's sad to note that synergy between concept elements is not common. New product marketing expert Wally Marx once told me that in his work he found that 80% of the time products featured different claims on their packages versus the advertising.

It's easy to understand why packaging and advertising are different. Lead times for ordering packaging are far longer than for advertising. However, it doesn't make it right. If ideas are clearly defined before taking action, then synergy can become a real reality.

Does the learning apply equally to products and services?

Those who work on services tend to believe what they do is a world apart from working with products. I generally agree. In my experience, services are significantly more difficult to invent, design and develop because they are by nature less tangible, more elusive. I have personally found it much more difficult to articulate the Overt Benefits and Real Reasons to Believe of services.

To explore the issue quantitatively, we tabulated a collection of products and services. The data shows that, at the same level of benefit and RTB, services get an even bigger increase in probability of success by following the three laws. The data indicates that having a less tangible customer benefit makes it more important to follow the laws of Marketing Physics.

Probability of Success Assuming Constant Benefit and RTB Levels	
Products	42%
Services	51%

Net, when working on less tangible services or even less tangible products, such as soft drinks or cosmetics, it's more important that with other products that you follow the laws of Marketing Physics. Granted, it can be difficult to do. But if you can't articulate your message, how do you expect your customers to figure it out for themselves? It's your responsibility to educate your customers as to what you're offering. They won't buy it if you can't explain it. And they can't read your mind.

Aren't you ignoring the importance of size of market when projecting success?

When marketing dramatically different products and services, market size is not a critical variable. Dramatically different concepts have the ability to take volume from multiple categories as well as bring new customers to the category.

One of the grand illusions in the world of business is the importance of market size. Executives have the illusion that if they just show up and market the same offering as everyone else they have a divine right to taking a proportional share of an existing category. The reality is if your concept brings "zero newness" to a large category, then zero times any size category is still zero. You lose.

Reporting in "Selecting Winning New Product Projects" (*The Journal of Product Innovation Management*, 2:34-44, 1985), Robert Cooper found, from modeling the success and failures of two hundred new products, that unique benefit is significantly more important than fit with company, market size or growth rate.

Factor Importance		
	(Regression Weight)	*Index vs. Market Size*
Superior benefit/uniqueness	1.744	(218)
Fit with company's overall skills	1.138	(142)
Market size and growth rate	.801	(100)
Fit with company technical skills	.342	(43)

What makes the three laws different from venture capital scoring models?

Venture capital models are primarily business plan models. They're designed to control all factors associated with the start of a business.

Our data indicates that none of these factors is important if you don't have a killer idea. And a killer idea is defined by the three laws. When the idea is right, everything else seems to take care of itself.

That said, it doesn't mean you can be incompetent at execution. Rather, it means that with the right idea and reasonable attention to detail and quality of execution, your odds of success increase dramatically.

I have lots of ideas but no money to execute. What can you do for me?

If I were meeting with you, I would first ask to see a written description of your ideas. If you haven't written them down, which is likely, I would have you describe them and I would write them down. The odds are you have lots of ideas for activities but few concepts that can make a tangible impact with customers in the marketplace.

I have repeatedly found that by simply optimizing your core marketing message through enhancement of Overt Benefit and Real Reason to Believe, you can realize dramatic sales gains. From these gains come the funds that allow you to make the improvements necessary to offer an even greater Dramatic Difference.

Spending more money is rarely the answer to growth. The first wave of Internet companies proved without a doubt that hundreds of millions in advertising could not buy success. Pouring an extra 30% into a flawed product or service is not nearly as impactful as thinking smarter and more creatively about how you spend the first 100% of your resources.

The U.S. Census Bureau confirms that a shortage of money is rarely the cause of business failure. A survey of 5,055,129 failed businesses found that only 11% of failures could be attributed to a lack of funding. But 72% failed because of poor sales. And sales failure is directly related to the genuine quality of your idea and the communication of your idea to potential customers.

You probably have noticed a pattern to my thinking.

It's the idea that matters.

The idea.

The idea.

The idea.

Who in my organization needs to know about Marketing Physics?

Anyone in the organization involved with creating, producing or marketing products to customers needs to understand the fundamental drivers of your business. And these drivers are your application of the three laws of Marketing Physics. In brief, virtually all your employees.

The leader of a new truck development project at one of the major automotive companies told me recently, "My greatest fear is that some junior buyer, far down in the organization, is going to save 40 cents on bolts that are critical to the delivery of our unique customer experience. I'll introduce the vehicle and within six months face a recall that never should have happened."

If all key employees understand your application of the laws of Marketing Physics then mistakes like cheap bolts will be less likely to occur.

I believe that employees want to do the right thing. Plus, employees generally want one thing to focus on. When you clearly define your business "story line" with its target audience, Overt Benefit, Real Reason to Believe and Dramatic Difference, you provide your employees and suppliers that singular point of focus they all crave.

Deming said that only 5% of quality problems are worker related. Some 95% are the responsibility of management. So, too, when it comes to setting the vision for your business. It is you the leader's responsibility to set the vision. It is your responsibility to ensure each employee understands the vital importance of each dimension of the vision.

When you run your business based on the customer-focused laws of Marketing Physics, decision-making efficiency and effectiveness will be enhanced dramatically.

Lacking principles, decision making becomes either hyperactively fast or constipatedly slow. A hyperactive orientation results in random decisions made quickly and changed quickly. The result is a revolving door of change that leaves employees dizzy and confused.

A constipated orientation results in a total shutdown of operations. Here decisions are avoided at all cost. Managers without principles send employees searching endlessly for the data that will "tell" them the answer to the decision they can't make themselves. The result is a test, retest and continuous fiddling environment that demoralizes everyone.

With a common foundation for evaluating ideas, the level of discussion and debate is elevated to a higher level. Diversity of opinions still exists. However, sound customer-focused decisions are arrived at faster and with greater strategic intelligence.

A Few Final Thoughts on the Laws of Marketing Physics

As I said at the opening, I bring you good news. Business success is not random. There are reproducible principles that when applied with diligence can help you win more, lose less and make more money with your business ideas.

Trust in the power of customers to respond to authentic offerings. Focus your energy and resources on the customers' true needs, and success will be yours.

Having defined clearly what success looks like we next embark on a journey to help you inspire and invent the high-probability ideas for your growth today and tomorrow.

PART II

The Three
Laws of

CHAPTER 9

The Science Behind Capitalist Creativity

In the first half of this book, you learned what a successful idea looks like. With this vision carved in your cranium, you're ready to create more ideas. This chapter provides an overview of the three laws of Capitalist Creativity and how they were identified.

Increasing the Power of Your Mind

The three laws of Marketing Physics define the kinds of business ideas that win more, lose less and thus can make you more money. The three laws of Capitalist Creativity teach you how to win more and lose less in your efforts to create ideas with a high probability of success.

As with Marketing Physics, experimentation and quantitative data are the basis for the three laws of Capitalist Creativity. However, the challenge of measurement and validation was significantly greater. Experts have maintained for decades that creativity is impossible to quantify. A special council of scholars, convened by the Library of Congress, studied the subject in 1981. They concluded: "There is very little that can be done institutionally . . . (to) foster creativity." The council's chairman reported, "I am very skeptical about the notion of organizing creativity and propounding stateable and reproducible rules by which we can promote it."

Alex Osborn, the inventor of group brainstorming, argued that a true definition of the creative process could never be achieved. "As an art," he said, "creative effort can never be formulated."

Researchers Wendy Williams and Lana Yang in the 1999 book, *Handbook of Creativity* (Robert J. Sterberg, ed., Cambridge University Press) maintained that any attempts at creativity measurement would hurt productivity. Their conclusion was that "organizations that so heavily emphasize control have had the effect of minimizing employee creativity."

Measuring and quantifying scientific laws of what drives creativity is against the established and educated way of thinking. Our Eureka! Ranch team understood this fully. However, as you learned in chapter six, the fact that an idea is crazy or impossible should never stop you. By definition, it means that you just might be onto something dramatically different and thus worth pursuing.

We started our research by conducting a dozen small experiments to check our probability of success. We asked clients a series of questions regarding the effectiveness of their groups' creative efforts. These results were correlated with the number of high-quality ideas each group had produced as judged by an independent observer. Early measurements from these experiments were encouraging.

Now some six years and thousands of groups later, we have quantified that business creativity is not random. There are reproducible laws that when applied with diligence can dramatically increase everyone's ability to invent, design and develop business ideas with a high probability of success.

Our Creativity Research Laboratory

The laboratories for our research were clients' inventing sessions at the Eureka! Ranch. Clients were measured while engaged in urgent quests to generate ideas to grow their businesses.

A valuable resource the Eureka! Ranch environment provided was a clear definition of creative success. As a hired gun think tank, the number of high-quality ideas our clients take away from a Eureka! brainstorming effort is a quantified and factual measure of success. To use the language of Marketing Physics, the Overt Benefit of hiring the Eureka! Ranch is the number of outstanding ideas you receive. Driving this bottom-line number was established as our clear research objective.

Research and Validation of Creativity Measurement System

The late Bob Goldstein, former vice president of advertising for Procter & Gamble, once said, "In many fields of human endeavor, improved measurement has been a precursor and a necessary requirement for improved solutions." Before we could discover laws of creativity success, we had to invent and validate a system for measuring creative effectiveness at the moment of actual creation.

After experimenting with many approaches, we settled on a survey approach for data collection. Eureka! session participants were asked to indicate their perceptions of the quality and quantity of ideas that had been created in the small groups they had participated in. The same basic survey was administered six to eight times during a day-long idea inventing-session.

A number of small base experiments were conducted using various questions. Early questions were focused on how pleased/unpleased or how satisfied/dissatisfied participants were with what they had just done. But as it turned out, their answers consistently failed to correlate with independent assessments of the quality of their ideas.

After much experimentation, it was found that the measure that correlated the strongest with the number of truly great ideas was a direct and to-the-point question of overall group effectiveness.

The scale provided for answering the question is known in mathematical circles as a fuzzy logic scale. It allows participants to express degrees of effectiveness. A group can be very effective, not at all effective or any point in between. By averaging client

---

With this exercise, how effective was *your group*, as a whole, in gernerating quality ideas? (Circle one number)

Not at all effective   Very Effective

0   10   20   30   40   50   60   70   80   90   100

---

responses, we're left with what is called a "center of mass" that turns out to be a quite effective predictor for a complex concept such as creativity productivity. Calculating the score for a specific creative exercise involves simply averaging client scores. Calculating a score for a complete day involves averaging the scores from all exercises.

Small base studies involving sixty inventing groups were very encouraging. Based on these results, we let the system run for a number of months to collect the data required to validate versus the final number of high-quality ideas resulting from a Eureka!

brainstorming effort.

For this study, a total of 728 inventing groups were measured over a total of twenty-eight client projects. Results from the client surveys taken at the moment of creation were then correlated with the number of actual ideas. Statistical analysis found a relationship at the 99.9% confidence level (r = .6) between the group effectiveness score at the moment of creation and the actual number of quality ideas generated. (Note that in social sciences research, such as this, values above .3 are usually considered important.) When the project groups are broken into three equal sets, the ability of the client measures to predict actual number of high-quality ideas can be seen clearly.

	Group Effectiveness Scores	Actual Number of Quality Ideas
Low effectiveness	66.2	22.6
Medium effectiveness	72.9	29.9
High effectiveness	77.8	34.7

Additional technical information regarding the research process and validations is available at the DougHall.com Web site.

Identification of the Three Laws of Capitalist Creativity

Once we'd validated a predictive measure of idea quality, we then initiated a separate set of research experiments to discover what variables drove success.

Hundreds of variables were tested with client groups. In time, some patterns emerged. Regardless of the nature of the ideas, product category, industry or customer segment, the same three overriding factors emerged. And all three factors consistently interacted to form a sort of 3-D picture of what most impacts idea-creation effectiveness.

The three fundamental laws are detailed below. For each law, the group effectiveness measurement is translated into equivalent number of high-quality ideas that would be created from a full-day brainstorming session.

The Three Laws of Capitalist Creativity

1. Explore Stimuli: Stimuli are the fuel that feeds business-growth thinking-or any creative thinking, for that matter. Feed your brain with multisensory stimuli that are both related and unrelated to your challenge.

Participants were asked their agreement or disagreement with the following statement: The stimuli content and process were

Number of Practical Ideas Invented	
High Stimulus	47.0
Medium Stimulus	38.4
Low Stimulus	22.3

instrumental in sparking new ideas by our group. Analysis of the data found the following relationships between stimuli and the number of bottom-line ideas created.

2. Leverage Diversity: Stimuli are the catalysts that spark the reaction that creates ideas. Diversity is the fuel that turns the spark into a chain reaction of continuous idea creation. The greater the diversity of opinions and perspectives you gather, the more effective you will be in creating ideas that can truly grow your business.

Number of Practical Ideas Invented	
High Stimulus	46.0
Medium Stimulus	29.9
Low Stimulus	18.5

Participants were asked their agreement or disagreement with the following statement: I felt the participants in my group provided and offered diverse viewpoints in the generation of new ideas. Analysis of the data found the following relationships between diversity and the number of bottom-line ideas created.

3. Face Fears: The depth of stimuli and the breadth of diversity fuel your ability to imagine new ideas. But they come alive only in proportion to the extent that you are able to face your fears. Fear directly destroys your ability to create and craft new ideas.

Number of Practical Ideas Invented	
High Stimulus	30.9
Medium Stimulus	33.7
Low Stimulus	42.2

Participants were asked their agreement or disagreement with the following statement: For whatever reasons, I didn't say all the ideas that came to me during this group. Analysis of the data found the following relationships between fear and the number of bottom-line ideas created.

Students of creativity will note similarity in these laws with the work of others, in particular, Theresa Amabile of Harvard's excellent research on culture, fear and its impact on productivity.

Readers of my first book, *Jump Start Your Brain*, will notice a similarity yet a significant difference between this work and the "theory" I offered on those pages. My first book was based on instincts. Now with real data, many of those instincts have been found to be true. More importantly, some instincts have been found to be wrong and are here corrected.

Bringing the Three Laws Together

The most striking discovery from our research was how the three laws interact. My lead researcher, Dr. Chris Stormann, modeled the various dimensions and discovered what we have named The Universal Theory of Creativity.

Utilizing the variables as measured, and taking the natural log of the exponential function, Chris found that the three variables of stimuli, diversity and fear could predict the number of quality ideas at the 99.99% confidence level ($r = .68$)

$$\text{\# of Quality Ideas} = \frac{\text{Stimuli}^{\text{Diversity}}}{\text{Fear}}$$

This is good news. It means the world of ideas can be defined! If you're stumped for an idea, you have three distinct options.

1. Use some stimuli as a catalyst for your cranium.
2. Look at the stimuli from different viewpoints, shifting your perspective or borrowing perspectives from others.
3. Challenge the fears that would keep you from saying what you really believe and really know should be done.

Quality Control Charting

Validation of a system of creative measurement allowed us to manage the productivity of our brainstorming sessions using tools and techniques from the world of manufacturing plants. Specifically we could use the quality control charting methodology made famous by Dr. Deming to quantify overall system quality levels as well as to validate systemic improvements to our process.

The graph on the following page charts our initial creativity system. Each point on the graph represents a singular client inventing project. The graph is bound by two horizontal lines defining the upper control limit and the lower control limit. These limits are calculated based on mathematical equations developed by quality control experts.

The dramatic "step change" improvement in results, halfway into the chart, is a result of instituting 100% training of clients in the laws of Marketing Physics and Capitalist Creativity.

As the chart shows, when clients were trained before participating in Eureka! brainstorming, overall process productivity increased significantly. Most importantly, not only did the average effectiveness improve, but the control limits, or variation in results, also tightened.

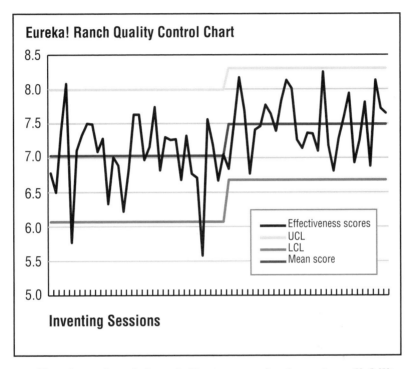

Eureka! Ranch Quality Control Chart

Inventing Sessions

Net, through training of clients, we gained greater reliability and effectiveness from our creative process. Most importantly, you are receiving these same benefits from reading and taking action on the content of this book.

Additional Research on Capitalist Creativity

With an understanding of the three laws and a quality control charting system, we then asked clients and other innovation experts to complete an in-depth study on what helped and hindered their creative development. The study was extensive with over five hundred questions probing every dimension we could think of. This research provides helpful perspective on how to best Explore Stimuli, Leverage Diversity and Face Fears.

What This Means for You

The creative process has long been shrouded in near mysticism. Quantitative research shows this isn't the case. Indeed, the mind can be managed like a factory. Creative productivity can be measured and systems put in place to improve quality.

You have the power to control your destiny.

The laws of Capitalist Creativity are simple. The potential for what you can create hinges on the stimuli you use and on the range of perspectives you use to explore those stimuli. Lastly, to realize that potential, the fears of your participants must be minimized. By following these laws you can invent your future. Now is the time to take action. To quote Ben Franklin: "Do you love life? Then do not waste time, as that is the stuff life is made of."

CHAPTER 10

How to Fuel Your Brain for Maximum Productivity

This chapter details how to use stimuli to expand your creativity. It explains how the use of stimuli is similar to how the brain functions, and it provides a step-by-step method for processing stimuli most effectively. Lastly, the two core types of stimuli are explained (related and unrelated) and lists of specific suggestions provided for how to gather them to fuel successful idea generation.

First Law of Capitalist Creativity: Explore Stimuli

Stimuli fuel the brain, setting off a chain reaction of idea associations and creations.

Stimuli are the fuel that feeds business-growth thinking—or any creative thinking, for that matter. Stimuli can take many forms—from sights, sounds and scents to customer data and firsthand experiences.

Feed your brain with multisensory stimuli that are both related and unrelated to your challenge. **The process of exploring stimuli sets off a chain reaction in your brain that brings new thoughts and ideas to life.**

Contrast this with the classic approach to idea generation, where you sit in a room and attempt to suck ideas from your mind. Participants sit in a room and poke, prod and push their brains in search of ideas. This process is often called brainstorming. The effect is more like braindraining. I call it the Suck Method of creativity.

Braindraining is neither effective nor efficient. With braindraining, the brain is considered the source of all ideas, a sort of idea library ready at all times for any withdrawals its owner may wish to make.

On the other hand, when you bring external stimuli into the

process, you're helping your brain work more like a processing computer; that is, you're programming your brain with stimuli in whatever form. The mind is then used to associate, connect and piece together the stimuli into ideas that are at once relevant yet unexpected.

The following chart shows how varying levels of stimuli impact results. The data is based on participants' responses to a question regarding the extent to which they agreed or disagreed that the stimulus provided during actual creative exercises was helpful in creating ideas.

	Number of Practical Ideas Invented
High Stimulus	47.0
Medium Stimulus	38.4
Low Stimulus	22.3

This is good news! It means that you don't have to be a storehouse of all the answers to new idea quests. Instead, you must simply gather outside stimuli and use your brain to process them. In time, as you gain more and more experiences, your brain archives multiply, making it possible for you to even explore the stimulus that resides in your own cranium.

A Brief Explanation of How the Brain Works

At its most basic, creating new ideas is a matter of association. It's about making unexpected connections between two or more thoughts. The pattern of creation is similar in many respects to how the brain itself works.

Most of us are walking around with twelve trillion neurons or brain cells, which is about the same number as stars in the Milky Way galaxy. Recent research by Elizabeth Gould of Princeton and Dr. Fred Gage of The Salk Institute indicates that, in fact, humans can grow new brain cells. However, the power of a human brain is thought to be less determined by the number of brain cells than by the number of connections between the brain cells.

Brain cells are interconnected by dendrites that make connections over what are called synapses. The greater the number of connections between your brain cells, the quicker and more effectively your brain works. As you feed and challenge your brain with stimuli, you create more connections between your brain cells.

The power of stimuli to increase our ability to think smarter and more creatively is well documented. Dr. Mark Rosenzweig of the University of California at Berkeley proved the point in a famous experiment involving rats. One set of rats was placed in what he called "impoverished environments," each containing a food dish and water supply. A second set of rats were given "enriched environments." Their cages were filled with an abundance of stimuli-ladders, running wheels, Ping-Pong balls and an assortment of other items.

The rats that grew up in the stimulus-rich environment were found to be clearly better at solving problems, finding their way through mazes and so on. In his report, Rosenzweig noted the following:

> Later, we took cross-sections from the brain and measured the thickness of the cerebral cortex, which controls memory storage and information processing. We found the cortex was thicker because, in the enriched environment, the nerve cells had branched out and made more connections. We concluded . . . that complex interaction with the environment leads to a significant increase in the development of the brain and a significant improvement in the ability to solve problems.

Interestingly, another of Rosenzweig's studies found that when rats were allowed to watch other rats in an enriched environment but were not allowed to interact with them, the first group derived no benefit. **Seeing isn't doing.** For a stimulus to work its magic, it appears we must have first-person interaction with it.

Think about it. Reading reports and hearing others talk about their experiences does not compare to having the experiences yourself.

Use It or Lose It

If you don't regularly send thoughts flashing between your synapses, your brain gradually loses its ability to function. The lack of mental acuity in many older people isn't due to dead brain cells, at least at first. It's because of nonuse. The brain is like a muscle in that regard: If you don't use it, it soon grows flabby.

A few years ago, I conducted a series of experiments with senior citizens. They were asked to spend an hour a day for one week working with creative stimuli to generate ideas for everything from new uses for whoopee cushions to new activities to try at their senior center. Their progress was measured with the Torrance Test of Creative Thinking, the most widely accepted standardized test of creativity. The test grades five dimensions of creativity, from creative fluency, or how many ideas a person can create, to originality, or how different a person's ideas are from what already exists.

Our subjects showed improvement in all five dimensions. Perhaps most importantly, the stimulus work helped increase the fluency of their ideas by 14% and the originality of those ideas by 41%.

No age was too old to benefit from daily mental exercises. In fact, those who were ninety and older showed the most improvement—an average increase of 73% in fluency and 125% in originality.

Not only did the seniors reawaken their powers of creativity, they found themselves becoming more willing to be active and more inclined to challenge their thinking. Jan Brate, activity director of the senior citizen center where the tests were conducted, was the first to notice a change: "The first day, they were like, 'This is hard, we can't do this.' But by the end of the week, they'd learned they could. And they were enjoying it, actually playing with it."

In my opinion, **we don't lose the ability to think as we grow older—we simply voluntarily surrender it**.

It's a good bet that as a child you were involved in all kinds of activities on a regular basis. As adults, we too often settle into ruts. We get together with the same friends, go to the same restaurants, eat the same food and then go to a movie that's a sequel to something we've already seen. We tend to maintain our same old, same old lives.

Engaging your brain provides a virtual fountain of youth. In his book *Brain Builders*, Richard Leviton reported that 40% of the middle-aged participants in a simple five-hour brain-growing seminar improved their thinking to levels of thinkers fourteen years younger. Imagine what an hour a day, 365 days a year would do.

Leviton also reports that most people use a mere 4 to 10% of their brain capacities. The good news is that by engaging your brain in new activities, you're making it easier for your mind to process stimuli and create new ideas.

Top Scientists Confirm the Power of Stimulating the Brain

The power of the brain grows in proportion to the breadth and diversity of experience. This conclusion comes from a 1958-1988 study initiated by Bernice T. Eiduson and continued by Robert S. Root-Bernstein, Maurine Bernstein and Helen Garnier that tracked forty male scientists, including four who eventually won the Nobel Prize. The study, "Correlations Between Vocations, Scientific Style, Work Habits, and Professional Impact of Scientists," sought to understand what relationships might exist between a scientist's success in his field and his participation in hobbies, sports and other leisure activities. Results were reported in the *Creativity Research Journal* (vol. 8, no 2, 1995).

Each subject's success was based on the number of citations other scientists made of his work in their papers, as reported in the Science Citation Index.

Each scientist was surveyed as to his degree of involvement in one hobby or another-photography, painting, poetry, music and so on. A clear relationship, at the 99.9% confidence level ($r = .42$), was found between the success of each scientist and the number of hobbies he had.

Each scientist was also asked to detail his involvement with athletic activities such as running, walking, sailing, skiing, swimming, biking, team sports, tennis and the like. Here, too, a significant relationship, at the 95% confidence level ($r = .31$), was found between scientific success and athletic activity.

What this means is the more your challenge your brain with activities, the smarter and more creative you become.

A separate study by Dean Keith Simonton of the University of California, Davis, was described in the June 28, 1993, issue of *Newsweek*. In a survey of 2,036 scientists throughout history, Simonton found the most respected scientists produced not only more great works, but also more bad ones. They produced. Period.

The bottom line is simple: Use it or lose it. To invent dramatically different ideas for growing your business, your brain has to be in shape.

So what are you doing to exercise your brain?

Practical Tactic: Breaking Mental Constipation

Think back over the past few months. What have you done to stimulate your brain? How many hobbies have you engaged in? How many physical activities? Regardless of your answers, it's time to ratchet up the numbers.

Here are ten ways to stretch your mind. Pick three to do over the next two weeks. Not only will you learn something new, you'll exercise your brain.

1. Read a magazine or book you'd not normally read. Reading is the ultimate mental stimulus. The challenge is to read new stuff. A steady diet of any particular style of book or magazine doesn't grow your brain.

2. Exercise your body. Considerable medical literature shows that exercise has a direct impact on your ability to think smarter and more creatively. Aerobic exercise increases the oxygen flow. And oxygen is critical. Your 3.5-pound brain may represent only about 2% of your body weight, but it consumes some 20% of the oxygen you inhale.

Dr. Cliff Gronseth, M.D., and assistant professor at the University of Colorado, has found that a rhythmic sport, such as running or swimming, is the most helpful for creating ideas. He theorizes the continuous repetitive movements help the subconscious thoughts rise to the top. I agree. I've found that when I'm stumped for an idea, a run or a swim around the lake behind the ranch is highly effective at generating a fresh perspective. And if those aren't reasons enough, exercise also reduces stress, which is known to kill brain cells.

3. Create a craft project you would never otherwise complete. Visit a craft store or local building supply store. Get the plans and build a birdhouse, for example. Better yet, build one without plans. Buy some tools and figure it out.

4. Learn a new skill. Take a class. My grandmother began learning about computers at age eighty-five because, as she said, "I don't want to miss out on anything." Learn to speak French. Take up photography. Your local community college offers a wide variety of classes in subjects you've probably never considered.

5. Cook a meal from scratch. You may not know how to cook, but anyone can follow a recipe. Cooking engages your entire brain—from process and procedures to the creative display of the end result. For truly great recipes, check out http://www.CooksIllustrated.com. They teach you the why and how to create the best of anything.

Scientists tell us that protein is the power food for brainpower. Jean Carper in *The Food Pharmacy* (Bantam Doubleday Dell Publishing, 1991) had this to say: "Shellfish, low in fat and carbohydrates, and almost pure protein, delivers large supplies of an amino acid called tyrosine to the brain, which then converts into the two mentally energizing brain chemicals, dopamine and norepinephrine. . . . Extensive research with both animals and humans proves that when the brain produces [these chemicals] you tend to think and react more quickly, be more attentive, motivated and mentally energetic."

6. Enjoy Music. Listen to music you'd never normally listen to. At the Eureka! Ranch, I make it a point to stock the jukebox with the top ten recordings in all the major music categories. It stretches our minds and tweaks our thinking patterns.

Even better, take up a new musical instrument, even if it's just the harmonica or the kazoo. I recently took up the Great Highland Bagpipe. The dogs howl when I play, and my progress has been slower than I'd like. But I am making progress nonetheless, and in the process, I'm stretching my thinking.

7. Experience new people. Engage in meaningful conversations with new people. These new people could be at your church, your kid's school or next door. Through discussions with others, we gain new perspectives on life and living

8. Write your thoughts on paper. Challenge yourself to write a poem. Don't worry about rhymes. Just articulate your thoughts honestly. Write a piece of science fiction, a mystery, a comedy, a fantasy. The act of crafting a piece in a format foreign to you will expand your mental portfolio.

9. Travel to foreign destinations. It could be overseas, or it might just be to a part of town where you've never been. Engage yourself in the culture of new surroundings. Pick up the local newspaper. Talk to the locals.

10. Visit museums. This is one of the great untapped business resources. Museums are a feast for the brain. Art museums give you the opportunity to stretch your perspective. Science museums challenge your thinking. Historical museums provide three-dimensional visions of other times, other places. While I was writing this book, our family visited COSI (Center for Science and Industry) in Columbus, Ohio. During our day at the museum, I filled two pages with notes on ways to describe and explain the concepts on these pages.

Practical Tactic: Walk the Talk

Talking about something is not doing it. Neither is watching it on TV. Do yourself a favor. Take a break from reading this book, and go out and have a first-person experience.

Walt Disney believed in first-person experience. He used to visit Disneyland on weekends, quietly slipping into shows and standing in lines for rides unnoticed. From these experiences, he created ideas that led Disney theme parks to unprecedented success.

Whatever your business is, I'd like you to take on a new role. Involve yourself in some mundane portion of your business. It doesn't matter what it is—frontline sales, manufacturing, order processing, customer service, even accounting. The key is to immerse yourself in the experience and see, feel and experience what's really going on there.

If you have a landscaping business that has experienced growth, thereby putting you in the office, go back to the front line for a while. Sell a project, then design and complete it yourself. If you own a restaurant, be a waiter for a night. Watch your customers react to the menu, the dècor, the service, the food. Or if you're considering starting a new service business, hire your potential competitor to perform the service for you at your home. If your company has grown to the point that you have a receptionist, take the job yourself for a day. Listen and learn from the questions callers ask. If your company manufactures widgets, work a shift. If you have three shifts, work all three.

As you involve yourself, ask real questions and really listen to the answers. This is not as simple as it sounds. William Isaacs of MIT reports in his book *Dialogue and the Art of Thinking Together* that "An estimated forty percent of all questions that people utter are really statements in disguise. Another forty percent are really judgments in disguise. Only a small percentage of inquires are genuine questions."

After a healthy amount of time, step back and reflect on what you've learned. Use the following prompts to provoke your thinking. Then put your reflections on paper.

- How was your experience different from what you expected?
- Would you want the job you took?
- What can you do to make the process easier?

When I became involved with the College of Piping and Celtic Performing Arts of Canada, my first action was to recommend that all board members take lessons in dancing, piping and drumming. Director Scott MacAuley reported the results: "Putting board members in the classroom gave the issues we discussed a reality that was missing before. Looking back, it was the start of a revolution in our mission. Today, we have an alignment and focus on teaching that's far greater than I ever thought possible."

Stimulus Has a Long Pedigree

The idea of using a stimulus as inspiration is not new. For centuries, artists have borrowed from the natural world to inspire their works. When Robert Frost sees two paths in the woods, it becomes the inspiration for poetry: "I took the one less traveled by / And that has made all the difference."

When making home repairs, it's not uncommon to putter around the workbench looking for miscellaneous bolts, clamps and screws until an inspiration hits. Recently my daughter was working on a science project that stumped us. Together we poked around the garage finding collections of miscellaneous this and that. From this came a solution.

Inventors have been similarly inspired. A waffle iron inspired

Bill Bowerman to create the waffle-bottom running shoe for his University of Oregon running team. That was the beginning of Nike. A buzzard soaring in the western Ohio sky gave Wilbur Wright the inspiration for flight. A stagecoach ride with regular stops for fresh horses gave Samuel Morse the inspiration for the electrical relay. From that insight came the telegraph. Philo T. Farnsworth used the stimulus of the horizontal rows in the hay-field he'd just cut to help create the first electronic TV. The electrons follow the same line-by-line path, creating the perception of a complete picture. A personal hero of mine, Jim Henson, would stroll through art museums when creating new characters. The origins of many of the Muppet characters can be traced back to those walks. I once had the opportunity to present a few new product concepts to Jim and I found him to be a stimulus sponge. Before talking about the "business opportunity," he gave his total attention to understanding the idea, asking real questions and probing to understand completely.

The Four Stages of Creativity When Using Stimuli

The process of creating ideas unfolds in four distinct stages. You are urged to approach each stage deliberately. You may have to force your thinking to stay disciplined as you move from one stage to the next using a sequence that might not feel natural at first. But as you get the hang of it—and you will—your thinking will flow naturally and advance more quickly from one stage to the next.

Stage I: Gather Stimuli. This is the gathering of the raw fuel your brain will process into ideas. Over the next few pages, you'll discover many ways to gather stimuli.

In simple terms, gathering stimuli means to get moving. Instead of sitting and thinking, get out and open your mind. Stuck for ideas for how to promote your business? Take a walk and see what the other guys are doing. Struggling for ideas for new products in your category? Visit the competition in the next city, the next state, another continent. The process of exposing your mind to new thoughts will spark new ideas spontaneously.

Stage II: Multiply stimuli. Having gathered the stimuli your next task is to multiply them through free association. There is a stepwise process for doing this that you will learn soon. However, the greatest method for multiplying stimuli lies in the next chapter on leveraging diversity. When you multiply the stimuli entirely new avenues of exploration open before you. The opportunities for this multiplication are unlimited.

Stage III: Create Customer Concepts. Use multiplied stimuli as fuel for inspiring ideas that offer your target customer an Overt Benefit and a Real Reason to Believe. At this point, don't worry about anything other than what's in it for the customers. Feasibility and practicality are addressed in the next stage.

To encourage this orientation, I challenge groups to suspend disbelief and assume they have unlimited time and money to make their ideas happen. By releasing the pressure to be practical in the here and now, their minds are more alert to creating truly new ideas.

Stage IV: Optimize Practicality. The focus here is on translating the customer-focused ideas into practical concepts that can be designed, developed and delivered profitably. Feasibility is the driving force for this stage, but fulfillment of customer desires through Overt Benefits, Real Reasons to Believe and Dramatic Differences is still the foundation of all work.

The following visual depicts the alternating cycles of divergence and convergence that the four steps utilize.

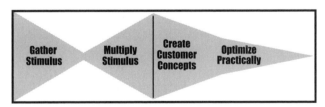

When working on the fourth stage, it is important not to lose the customer focus. A concept that's merely feasible is the most dangerous of ideas. Feasibility gives it a built-in gravitational pull toward being acted on, despite possibly offering nothing for customers.

Customers only care about what's in it for them. They don't care how much hard work it takes you to deliver an idea. Businesses that give priority to internal feasibility over customer benefits are selfish, and selfish people get what they deserve.

When working ideas at this final stage, expect huge and unexpected obstacles to appear out of nowhere. That's OK. In fact, it's good! It's a sign you're working on an idea that has the potential to be dramatically different. Granted, obstacles can discourage you from taking action if you're new to the process. If so, I suggest you look for ways to modify the core customer concept that lets you preserve 80% of the customer benefit while dramatically improving practicality. Doing so can fill your sails with fresh momentum.

An experience I had working with the College of Piping and Celtic Performing Arts of Canada illustrates this. In the summers, the college holds Ceilidhs, high-energy Celtic parties, Monday through Thursday evenings. These parties give the college's pipers, drummers, highland dancers and step dancers, as well as some of the area's finest professional Celtic performers, chances to perform for larger audiences.

The Ceilidhs also raise money for the college. The objective of our inventing session was to create ways to increase revenues of the upcoming summer season. The number of concerts and pricing for the concerts had already been set in published promotional material. Besides that, the season was beginning in five weeks.

We concentrated our search on what we could sell to people who would already be attending concerts. After much discussion, it was agreed that a recording of the music from the summer's show would let visitors "relive the magic" of the college's Ceilidh. It would be a high-value, one-of-a-kind remembrance of their summer vacations. Everyone agreed on the benefit, and the reason to believe was strong because it would be a recording of the performers they'd just seen. Having defined the customer idea clearly (stage three), we then moved on to optimizing practicality (stage four). Here the real world dealt us a blow to the solar plexus. There wasn't time to book a studio. There wasn't money available to pay for recording sessions and mastering of the CD. The last show wouldn't be finalized until a week before the opening.

Problems slammed into us one after another. There were enough problems to warrant giving up. But Scott MacAuley and Sharon Smith of the college are not the kind of folks to give up. They built the college into the world's top year-round bagpiping school by focusing on the end customer benefit then working out details.

Clearly the benefit was great to both the customers and the college. How could we modify the idea to retain the benefit yet enhance feasibility?

Further discussion turned to the professional performers booked for the summer. What could we offer them? How could they help make this CD happen? The question hit a spark in Scott. He realized the performers could help via the recordings they already had. A plan was hatched to get permission to borrow tracks from the musicians' previously released CDs.

Wow! We had found it. If we didn't have to pay for recording, mixing and editing, we could produce the CD in record time. In exchange for the performers' recordings, they received the Overt Benefits of (1) sampling their recordings in high-quality company, (2) phone numbers and Web links in the liner notes for listeners' ease in ordering the artists other CDs and (3) being granted carte blanche permission to sell their other CDs from the stage.

Just a few weeks later, the College of Piping Celtic Festival 2000 CDs arrived.

The CD proved to be a great success. And because the CD was inexpensive to produce, the profits were even more impressive—a

College of Piping CD

net of better than 70%. And it happened because Scott and Sharon didn't give up. Having created a clear customer concept, they worked it and worked it until they found a way to make it practical.

(If you'd like to order a CD or learn to play the bagpipes at one of the college's week long summer camps, visit http://www.collegeofpiping.com.)

As you approach your own ideas, focus first on the customer. Then work practicality. **When you hit a wall, don't give up. Hold onto the foundation of what's in it for the customer, and continue to work modifications until you find a way to defeat the practicality challenges.** Find a way to go over it, under it, through it or around it.

Practical Tactic: Mind Dump

Each brain has twelve trillion brain cells. Each brain cell is capable of ten thousand connections with other brain cells. Given the number of items stored in your brain and the number of possi-  ble connections, your potential to create new combinations is nearly limitless. The challenge is to leverage these connections in a manner that makes them workable in the real world.

Mind Dump is a tactic with an impressive track record. Of all the techniques used at the Eureka! Ranch, it has the highest average effectiveness score.

The goal of Mind Dump is to unload the contents of your brain onto a sheet of paper. Think of it as picking your brain up by its ankles, shaking it and using whatever falls out to create ideas.

Part of the value of Mind Dump is its releasing nature. It turns down the mental noise we bring with us, freeing us to craft new ideas rather than replaying old ones over and over.

There are many ways to do a Mind Dump. You can go solo or use it effectively in small groups of two to six. The process uses a dramatically simplified version of MindMapping, a long-established display thinking technique created by Tony Buzan. For the greatest efficacy with Mind Dump, get some small sticky notes, such as Post-its. You'll also need some downloaded forms (instructions for this later) or plain sheets of 8 ½" x 11" paper.

Stage I: Gather Stimuli

Step 1 Write your objective on a sticky note and place it in front of you. This should be as specific as possible. What do you want to create? What problem do you want to solve? What do you want to improve? Whom do you want to reach?

Step 2 As rapidly as possible, free-associate on the challenge. When you think of the task at hand, what comes to mind? What are your first instincts? What people, places or things do you associate with the challenge? Use the prompts below to help your brain make different connections.

Additional Coaching
- Write one thought, one idea per sticky note.
- Don't force. Let your mind go limp.
- Ignore spelling and handwriting. They don't count.
- Draw pictures if you wish.
- Do it quickly. Just free-associate; don't think
- Set a time limit of three, five or ten minutes.
- Suspend all judgment, open your mind and let the ideas flow onto the notes without prejudice.

Mind Dump Stimuli-Gathering Prompts

•Think Rational First Instinct
- What first comes to mind?

- What are related thoughts?
- What does it mean?

Think Irrational First Instinct
- What are some devious and funny thoughts?
- What are unrelated thoughts?
- What are sarcastic reactions and thoughts?

Think Logically
- What are the facts of the situation?
- What are the absolute truths?
- What are market research facts?

Think Practically
- What can you do that no one else does?
- What are your strengths and assets?
- What are your weaknesses and liabilities?

Think Emotionally
- What are some positives and negatives?
- What would make you proud?
- What feelings are generated?

Think Best and Worst
- What is your best memory in the category?
- What is your worst experience in the category?
- What little pet peeves mean a lot?

Think Perceptions
- What do people believe about you?
- What are you best at?
- What are you weakest at?

Think Overt Benefits
- What do you give customers?
- What is their emotional benefit?
- What is their rational benefit?

Think Rules
- What are the true truths?
- What prevents you from growth?
- What has not changed in years?

Think Dramatic Difference
- What makes you unique?
- Where is the highest profit margin?
- What are you sole provider of?

Think Absurdly
- What if you had unlimited funding?
- What if you had unlimited time?
- What would make competition laugh?

Think Sensory
- What sights, sounds, smells are associated with it?
- What are the textures and tastes?
- How do buyers get feedback?

Think Target Audience
- Whom do you want as customers?
- Who are the biggest buyers?
- Who will soon become buyers?

Think Marketing
- How do customers learn about you?
- What do you say overtly to customers?
- What are possible channels of distribution?

Think Real Reason to Believe
- What qualifies you to offer customers a benefit?
- What do you really do?
- What testimonials do you have?

Think Competition
- How could they destroy you?
- What do you most fear from them?
- Who is best in class?

Think Historically
- What has been key to your success?
- Who has scared you the most?
- What has been your biggest mistake?

Think Aggressively
- How could you most annoy competition?
- How could you double quality?
- How could you cut price in half?

Think Step-by-Step	Don't Think . . . Dream
• How is it made?	• What would be the perfect situation?
• What materials and methods are used?	• What do you wish for?
• What steps can you eliminate?	• What does your dream look like?

Step 3 When time runs out, put your pen down and randomly lay your notes out on a page. If you're working alone, take a break to clear your mind. If you're working in a group, mix everyone's notes together and place them on pages.

  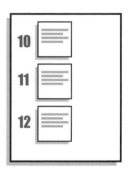

Step 4 Number each note from one to whatever.

Step 5 Having transformed the free-association stimuli from your head to note form, the next step is to select four to work with. I've found it's most valuable if you make true random selection by simply picking a number arbitrarily or rolling a pair of dice. Most people, when allowed to pick and choose, take the path of least resistance by selecting the stimuli that strike them as the easiest to work with. Like it or not, the best ideas often come from stimuli with less obvious connections to the challenge.

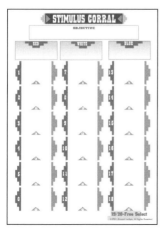

If you were at the Eureka! Ranch, at this point we'd use our Cactus Corral sheet, which provides a special spot for each idea and, on the reverse side, an area for each of the two stages.

Download this sheet from our Web site (http://www.DougHall.com). We

have it in a variety of sizes. If you don't want to download the sheet, you can make your own from a piece of 8 $\frac{1}{2}$" by 11" paper. Simply draw the lines as indicated here and place your selected notes in the sheet's corners.

Having gathered the stimuli from your brain, you now move to the next two stages where you multiply the stimuli (stage two) and then create ideas (stage three).

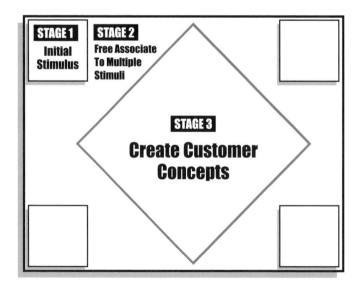

Stage II: Multiply Stimuli

Your next task is to free-associate off the notes you've placed on the sheet. The entire process should take fifteen to thirty seconds. The goal is to provide a number of leaping-off points to work from so you don't become tunnel brained and locked into a single dimension when you start creating ideas.

When stimuli are multiplied in this manner, they take on greater depth, more character. They give off many more sparks that can light new ideas. When working in a group, multiplying of stimuli lets everyone participate in the journey of creating ideas. When we don't multiply stimuli as a conscious step, we end up crafting ideas as if in silos, with only the final output for others to comment on or contribute to. Resist the temptation to leap direct-ly from a stimulus to an idea. The extra fifteen seconds it takes to multiply stimuli is time well spent.

When multiplying the stimuli, your task is simply to free asso-ciate, from memory or spontaneously.

Associate From Memory
- Think of what comes to mind when you read those words.
- Think of all the different dimensions associated with the stimulus.
- Think of things related to the stimulus.
- What experiences have you had that a stimulus calls to mind?

Associate Spontaneously
- Suspend experience and knowledge.
- Relate innocently.
- See, feel, experience as if for the first time.
- Think components and the whole.
- Think emotion.

A quick example: The task is to create ideas for new radio pro-grams. The stimulus is the word music, quite a common element of radio.

If I leap from music to ideas, my thoughts are almost certain to follow familiar patterns of thinking—top ten albums, live con-certs, specialty programming. If, however, I bring a multistage approach to my thinking, the ideas get much richer.

Free-associating on music, I quickly multiplied the stimulus with the following list.

- Mood altering
- Kids' concerts
- Popular music
- Unpopular music
- Local music
- Rhythm and beat

The key with multiplying a stimulus is to do it quickly and without getting tangled up in a lot of conscious thinking. Let your mind skip from one thought to the next without dwelling on anything in particular. When you think of the word, what comes to mind? What else? What else? What else?

Stage III: Create Customer Concepts

Now look at your collection of free associations, considering them individually or in combination. Let your mind leap to ideas for fulfilling your objective. As you create, focus your thinking on Overt Benefits and Real Reasons to Believe. Put the ideas you created in the center of the sheet. I suggest writing them in a free-form format. This lets you make additional connections between ideas.

When crafting ideas by yourself or as a part of a group, there are three operational principles that when followed can increase your productivity.

Quantity Breeds Quality The greater the number of total ideas you create, the greater the number of truly great ones you will have to work with.

Breakthroughs Contradict History Remember what you learned in the Dramatic Difference chapter regarding difficulty of execution. The bigger the idea, the more it will cause absolute chaos for one or more business disciplines. That's OK at this stage. Don't let feasibility constrain your thinking.

Spin All Ideas Into Overt Benefits or Real Reasons to Believe: The two judgment filters you should keep in the front of your brain are Overt Benefit and Real Reason to Believe. Each idea must become either a benefit or a reason to believe. The more you take features and turn them into benefits and the more you take executional elements and turn them into Real Reasons to Believe, the greater the ultimate effectiveness you will reap from your ideas.

Using the music free-association example from before, here some of the ideas for a new radio program.

Free Association	Ideas the Free Associations created
Mood altering	Afternoon "Jump Start Your Day" program
Kids' concerts	"Local Pride": Sunday afternoon showcase of the best of youth
Popular music	"What's Hot Here and Now in Our Town"
Unpopular music	"Planet Original"—world music that's not on the charts
Local music	"Local Pride 2: 100% Locally Created, Performed and Produced"
Rhythm and beat	"Fitness Momentum"—early morning tunes with an aerobic beat, along with motivational DJs who encourage you to keep at it

For purposes of illustration, these are shown as a one-to-one match between free associations and ideas. In the real world, some associations will create multiple ideas while others won't spark any. That's OK. The key is to use the free associations as leaping-off points to spark new connections. Some of these ideas have real benefit, such as "Fitness Momentum." Others are weaker and will require more work, such as "What's Hot Here and Now."

Don't give up when a link doesn't happen in three seconds. Sometimes, it takes a few minutes to find connections. After all relevant sections have been worked individually, select four more notes and start with another sheet of paper.

Continue working these out on more and more sheets until you have a healthy pile of raw ideas. Another way to increase your output is to work each sheet for a period of time, put it aside and then come back to it again. Looking at the sheets after a break can spark new ideas.

Stage IV: Optimize Practicality

Having created dozens of raw ideas, it's time to take a break. In twenty years as a professional inventor, I've found greater productivity when I rest my mind for at least two hours, if not overnight, before I commence refining ideas. As mentioned previously, my personal preference is physical exercise at a relatively high intensity—running, swimming, biking. By removing my body and mind from the challenge, I rest and revitalize my mind, resulting in a fresher, more effective attack.

This last stage is focused on discovering ways to modify the concept to optimize practicality yet maintain the core customer dimensions. Sometimes there is still a need to more clearly optimize the Overt Benefit, Real Reason to Believe and Dramatic Difference. No matter what the approach, the customer elements must remain the core priority.

Process Review

With Mind Dump, we gathered the stimuli from our brains. Later in this chapter, you will learn many other approaches to gathering stimuli that are equally effective. In each of these other cases the means for processing the gathered stimuli is the same: Multiply Stimuli, Create Customer Concepts and Optimize Practicality.

I strongly advise that the paper and sticky note approach be utilized with all of the other stimulus material. I've tried many other approaches to processing stimuli and to date I have not found a more effective approach then the paper system detailed above.

A Brief Discussion of Objectives

Virtually all clients I've ever worked with have had variations of the same objective: "To create ideas to sell more stuff." That said, it's amazing how complicated some objectives are. The following is a client's proposed objective:

> Develop a product line(s) for introduction in 1-3 years in a category (or a niche of a category) where we can achieve dominant share and which has the velocity to maintain distribution with predominately trade (account specific) marketing investments which can be made on an account by account bases (pay-as-you-go basis). From a sales revenue perspective, we've tentatively set a minimum target of $XXX million and would be comfortable with investing all the variable contribution that the new

product generates for 2 years with an ongoing sales/marketing support rate of 20%.

Say what? It's no wonder the company's been having trouble building momentum behind new product ideas. We changed the objective to read as follows:

Create consumer-focused ideas that offer a dramatic difference in their benefit and reason to believe pair.

By focusing on dramatically different ideas, we're guaranteed a higher potential profit margin. By focusing on the consumer, we're also guaranteed to have ideas that are pulled through by consumers—as opposed to being pushed through the system. In either case, a clear objective automatically gives you an advantage.

In 1999, I traveled to the North Pole on dog sled and skis the way Admiral Robert Peary and Mathew Henson did. We started at 88 degrees, about 150 miles from the pole. Our objective was the clearest I have ever experienced in a group endeavor. Quite simply it was 90 degrees North—a singular point on the surface of the earth. There was no confusion about where the eleven of us were heading. Every step north was a step toward the objective. When we hit open water and had to travel west or east to get around it, we were moving away from our objective. When a north wind whiteout caused the ground and sky to become a nebulous, horizonless white fog, we simply traveled in the direction that made our faces hurt most because the wind was coming out of the north. Each night, we checked our Global Positioning devices and learned precisely how far we were from 90 degrees North. Unfortunately for us, when we checked again most mornings, the floating ice cap had pushed us one to three miles south overnight.

Keep your objective simple. The closer you can get your objective to be as clear as 90 degrees North, the more effective your efforts to create ideas will be. If your goal is to increase utilization of a specific resource, be it a manufacturing plant or collection of people resources say that. If your goal is to broaden your customer base, overtly target new customers. If your goal is to increase sales in a certain area, set that as the objective.

Significant creative energy is generated when you can see clearly both where you are and where you want to be. When the distance between the two is clearly visible in your mind, a natural tension builds that can be resolved only by discovering and implementing new ideas.

A Stimulating Discussion

There are two basic types of stimuli: related and unrelated. Each has a place in your idea tool kit. Knowing how to use both will significantly increase your potential.

Homeward Trail: The Power of Related Stimuli

Homeward Trail stimuli are directly related to the challenge. The name Homeward Trail was inspired by the writing of poet David Whyte. In his book *The Heart Aroused*, he tells a story  about a hero who receives the following piece of advice: "Don't leave the old road home for a new one. Go back by the way you came."

Having completed Mind Dump to open your eyes, the next step is to explore the old road home or the Homeward Trail. Earlier, I told the story of how Don and Jeannette had lost their focus with Cavendish Figurines. Their business had become a little bit of this, a little bit of that—a mishmash of a gift shop, a photo site and all manner of elements with no connection whatsoever with fine figurines. By getting them to focus on the Homeward Trail, they found a renewed energy, vitality and sense of purpose.

There's a similar story about Daphne Large Scott, owner of Village Pottery in New London Prince Edward Island. As part of her Eureka! coaching experience, we concentrated on Homeward Trail thinking. We talked about why she and her fellow potter and assistant, Christine Campbell, were in the business in the first place, what they liked best about it, what they liked least about it, what they dreaded about the business.

It became clear that they didn't like the idea of running a factory. And that was what the business was becoming. In fact, when creating mugs, they were careful to make them all the same because customers preferred matched sets. We also learned that, on average, anyone who walked into the shop and bought mugs would purchase two mugs.

Exploring this idea, using sticky notes as described previously, we crafted an idea for a new display and marketing approach for her mugs.

Create Your Own Collection

Each mug we make is a genuine original. As artists we celebrate uniqueness and encourage you to create your own personal collection of mugs to be used and enjoyed by family and friends. To get you started on your own collection if you purchase 3 mugs today—the 4th is our gift to you.

Mug sales skyrocketed. Average revenue per customer rose as well. Instead of buying an average of one and one-half mugs, most customers bought three in order to get the fourth one free. Most important of all, Daphne and Christine could become less like a human factories. They could be true to their passion and create mugs that were unique inspirations, each one different from the next.

Readers may note the price offer and consider that inappropriate. In this case, it's not. With Daphne's business, the incremental cost of a mug in time and materials is low. The greater challenge is that visitors to the shop tend to be tourists who normally make only one stop during their vacations. The promotion is a way to get one-stop customers to buy sets, as opposed to a single souvenir mug.

How to Use Homeward Trail Stimuli

The process of using Homeward Trail stimuli is the same as with Mind Dump. The stimuli come from reviewing the situation close at hand, as opposed to emptying it out of your brain. At its most disciplined, you jot observations on sticky notes as you review the world as it is, then you use the notes in the same process as before.

I recommend you honor the process. At the same time, I understand that most small business owners have a short attention span. Instead of being disciplined,

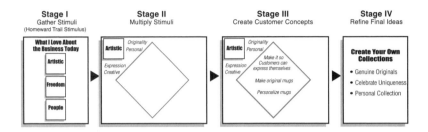

small business owners want to leap from stage one to stage four. They see sparks of ideas and immediately want to focus on feasibility issues. That's OK—as long as you end up with bottom-line ideas that work. But if you're unsuccessful with the Homeward Trail stimuli tactics that follow, it may be that you're skipping necessary stages. By skipping stage two, you reduce the breadth of potential from the stimulus. By skipping stage three, you reduce the focus on customers—both in terms of Overt Benefit and Real Reason to Believe.

Starting with stimuli that are related to your task, you will follow a natural progression of ideas from the known world to the world of imagination. Or said in the same manner as when discussing Dramatic Difference, you are moving from the relevant to the unexpected.

Relevant ➡ UNexpected

This approach is the underpinning of the common challenge to think "outside the box," the box being defined as the current situation.

Ten Tactics for Finding Effective Homeward Trail Stimulus

Homeward Trail stimuli are about taking another look at the basics of your operation. When we lead Eureka! Inventing sessions, we take responsibility for gathering the stimuli. Here are ten effective methods we've found for finding Homeward Trail stimuli that work. In some cases, the stimuli center on ideas or insights. In other cases, they take the form of physical "stuff" that we gather for use in creating ideas.

In all cases, I personally use the sticky note system for gathering the raw stimuli and the sheet system for turning the stimuli insights into practical ideas.

1. Create a Competitive Strength Balance Sheet: The *first* thing to do is gather samples of your product offering and those of your competition. If you're a service company, the marketing brochures or pages from Web sites will serve the same purpose.

Based solely on the information communicated on the packaging, brochures or Web sites, dvelop a balance sheet listing the strengths of your offering and the competition's. If your business segment doesn't have many materials, use what you can find. For example, compare the yellow pages ad from your pizza restaurant with what the competition has.

Use the World Wide Web to compare how you do business with how companies in other towns, states or countries run and manage their company.

2. Observe Candid Comments: For the next month, ask every customer why he chose you. How did he learn about you? Listen closely. Ask the questions, then don't talk. Listen with intensity. Resist the temptation to edit comments to fit your personal view of your business. Write down what the customer says.

After you've gathered some perspectives, compare what your customers say with what you say. Are the reasons customers do business with you the same reasons you proclaim in your marketing materials? If not, why not? It's not uncommon for small business people to neglect simple ideas, thinking they're too obvious. **Remember: Nothing is obvious to a customer who has never done business with you before.**

3. Review Your History: The quintessential Homeward Trail stimulus is to go back to the beginning of your company. Review scrapbooks and old advertisements. If you're not the founder, find her and review the early history. Why was the company formed? Where are its roots? Are you true to those roots now? How has the business changed? Why? Have the changes been for the better?

4. Look at Your Front Door: With many small businesses, a simple change of the signage hanging out front can be a huge help. We talked earlier about Stefan's restaurant, with the confusing sign that marketed "Epicurean Food and Wine." Other examples of this type of opportunity include Don and Jeannette of Cavendish Figurines. When I walked outside their facility, underneath the name Cavendish Figurines were the words "Factory Outlet" plastered on the side. I shook my head. A factory outlet is a place where you purchase overruns and defects. Call it a studio, an artist's studio, an Old World figurine workshop—just don't call it a factory outlet when you're trying to sell relatively expensive fine figurines. The same goes for Village Pottery. Instead of offering crafts, the sign should identify the shop as an artists' studio and gallery. And, most importantly, put the names of the artists on the sign. Compare the differences.

The old sign

The new sign

Look at your "front door," be it the home page of your Web site, your brochure or the front of your retail establishment. What does it say about you? What is implied but not overtly stated? As you take your tour, mark your observations on sticky notes to create ideas with later.

5. Experiment With Kitchen Chemistry: Gather all materials associated with the actual application of your product or service. Work your way through these materials, using them as directed. Also use them not as directed and see what happens. Look at the elements themselves and at the way they relate to one another. If, for instance, you sell paint, consider how it interacts with various kinds of brushes. If you sell steak sandwiches, consider how their taste interacts with various types of soft drinks, beer, wine and salty snacks. If you sell investment advice, consider the actual costs required to send a child to college.

Small business people tend to have a close-in understanding of their businesses. They see trees but no forest. With our clients at the Eureka! Ranch, I sometimes find myself working with executives who are far removed from the real world. To bring reality to the surface, we go to elaborate lengths to bring the issues alive. Over the years, we have

- Planted a garden of weeds so clients could experience their weed killer
- Bought junkyard sale furniture so clients could scrape and spray paint it
- Gathered dump trucks, fire engines and other big trucks to check their suspensions
- Sent clients with ten dollars each to buy breakfast at a convenience store
- Gathered more than two hundred beverages so clients could mix new concoctions
- Got cars purposely dirty so clients could clean them top to bottom
- Had clients sign up for online banking during a session
- Loaded SUVs with gear for camping, vacations and everyday life
- Had clients call their own customer service departments with challenging problems
- Had clients call customer service with simple problems (with terrible results, unfortunately)
- Created, mixed and cooked hundreds of different foods
- Had clients carry and lie in a burial casket (yes, you read that right)

Go through the usage experience of your product or service from start to finish. Examine each step of the process. Look at the preparation required before using your product and the requirements afterward. Look for problems. Look for big problems, and look for the little things, the pet peeves and little annoyances that cause customer frustration.

If possible, use your product and your competitor's product side by side. Compare and contrast. Smell, taste, feel and listen to the differences. Look at the factual differences and at your perceptions. How are you the same as or different from the competition? When we were working on a new way to cook french fries for convenience stores, we used McDonald's as our comparison, which required us to run across the street every fifteen minutes to buy McDonald's fries so we could compare them with what our new machine was creating.

6. Visit the Scene of the Crime: Put a pack of sticky notes in your pocket and go for an idea walk. Stroll the factory floor or the customer showroom looking for ideas. Reality has a way of sparking ideas that no amount of thinking can create. Over the years, I've had many memorable experiences

- I've traveled on bread delivery trucks at 5:00 in the morning.
- I've toured hog farms in South Dakota from the bloody beginning to the store-wrapped end.
- I've tested experimental boats in northern Wisconsin in November. (One prototype did a little flip. Thank goodness, I was wearing a wet suit.)
- I've sold Avon.
- I've spent emotional time at funeral parlors learning about caskets.
- I've put in time at banks, bakeries and breweries.
- I even spent a few days following members of Congress around Capitol Hill.

As you visit, take note of anything that captures your interest. Record your first perceptions as well as your observations after four to eight hours of watching. Watch with your eyes, ears and nose. Record both the facts and the perceptions of what you observe. If possible, do the same with your competition.

Will Rogers said it well: "People learn more from observation than they do from conversation."

7. Catalog What You Have Going for You: Make a detailed listing of your assets and resources. "What are you proudest of?" is a question I often ask CEOs. What are you known for? Your current skills and areas of strength can provide great opportunities for leveraging potential customers.

There are thousands of ways to organize and execute virtually any business. How you have chosen to organize gives you a combination of natural strengths and opportunities for improvement. The way you approach your business provides the foundation for customer benefits. What do you do differently than the competition?

When considering a food product, for example, my first place of attack is usually the ingredient statement. I'll compare and contrast a client's ingredients with those of the competition. I establish why such and such an ingredient is in the client's product and not the competition's. Or why a certain ingredient is listed more predominantly on the client's label than that of the competition. When I spent some time coaching the Montgomery Inn, a restaurant group in Cincinnati, I noticed that the first ingredient on the BBQ sauce label was tomato. All of their competitors had water as the number one ingredient because they used a cheaper process to make their sauce. From this was born a very successful marketing campaign declaring "tomato is our first ingredient."

8. Review the Next Best Option: Open your mind beyond your current category. If a customer couldn't get his hands on your service or your competitor's service, what could he do? This approach is especially valuable when it comes to growth. If you can find ways to bridge effectively from your category to others, you have an opportunity for significant net extra growth.

If you're a landscaper, what are the do-it-yourself options available to your customers? If you're operating a sporting goods store that sells canoes, what rental options are available in your area? If you're in a rock band, what are the DJ and karaoke options available for entertainment?

Your mission is to look closely at the next category over. By understanding options customers have outside your category but in the same general vicinity, you can open your eyes to new opportunities.

9. Step Back and Look at the Big Picture: Consider your business and category from the broader perspective. To paraphrase the old adage, look at the forest instead of the texture of the bark on the third tree to the left. If you were a customer new to the category, what would you soon learn?
- Who is genuinely best in class? Why?
- Whom do customers perceive as best in class?
- What competitor has growing momentum?

- What competitor has declining momentum?
- How has the industry changed over the past ten years?
- Where will the category be in the next ten years?
- What are the cost of entry benefits?
- What differences make the biggest differences?
- Who/what has created the biggest news in the past five or ten years?
- What gross generalization does each company stand for?
- What trade-offs do customers make?
- What trade-offs have customers come to accept?

10. Explore Cheap Rent Districts: In every category, there are pioneers and mavericks creating new ideas. Some of them will be tomorrow's giants. Finding these folks is surprisingly easy. Their offerings are so dramatically different, they tend to be more memorable. A true pioneer doesn't understand that he is breaking established laws. He simply pursues what he believes is the right path. Pioneers can be found in the cheap rent districts-the little ads in the back of the trade magazines and the two-sentence blurbs in the "What's New" columns. Their Dramatic Differences earn them mentions.

At trade shows, they inhabit the smallest booths farthest from the entrance to the main hall. Years ago, I remember visiting a 10' x 10' booth, off the main floor in the back of the Dallas convention center where a couple guys were hustling a beverage called Snapple. Eventually they sold the business to the Quaker Oats Company for $1.7 billion. The Quaker Oats Company was not as successful. Three years after they bought the Snapple business, they sold it for $300 million.

Visiting with these mavericks is a stimulus feast. Because of the passion they have for their ideas, they're bursting to tell you their stories. And because of their remote locations at conventions, they generally aren't real busy. The only challenge with them is that it's sometimes difficult to know whether you're dealing with true geniuses or certifiable loonies. But either way, your encounter will help you see your business with fresh eyes.

The Fresh Eyes Challenge

The difficulty with a Homeward Trail stimulus is that it can be hard to look at it with fresh eyes. You almost have to step outside yourself. To quote Copthorne MacDonald from his book *Toward Wisdom*: "We find ourselves still looking at the same old data, but we now see those data in a dramatically different way. We experience another valid—and sometimes more significant—way of understanding what is."

As you explore stimuli related to your challenge, work to maintain a "fresh eyes" perspective. Here are some suggestions for doing that.

1. Explore the business like a takeover specialist would: When a business is acquired, the only way the purchaser can make financial sense of a purchase is by making dramatic changes. Every assumption made in the past is checked and challenged. Resources are quickly reallocated from areas offering little return to areas of greater opportunity.

2. Ask yourself, if you just bought your business, what would be some of your first acts?
- Whom would you fire? (I'm talking employees, suppliers and customers!)
- Whom would you hire?
- What areas of marketing or development effort would you discontinue?
- Where would you deploy more resources?

Sounds like a simple list for improving the business. How about taking action on at least one of those answers tomorrow?

3. Explain to the innocent: The act of explaining the situation to someone with no awareness whatsoever of your situation can bring insights. When you're closely involved in a situation, you tend to develop a shorthand way of thinking about it. When you distill the situation into simple language that neophytes can understand, you're likely to discover fresh insights in information that, to you, is old.

This approach is a favorite of top executives. In a survey I fielded regarding actions they take when feeling brain dead, their number one response was to "talk to someone who doesn't know anything about the challenge."

4. View repeatedly: Sometimes, if you review a stimulus again and again, a shift can occur that opens your eyes to fresh insights. I've found this valuable when making on-site visits. For example, if you have a phone service center, spend three shifts observing. During the first shift, you'll learn the whos and the whats that go on. During the second and third shifts, you'll begin to learn the whys. Or to paraphrase Copthorne MacDonald: "We now see in a dramatically different way. We experience another more significant way of understanding what is."

Borrowing Brilliance: The Power of Unrelated Stimuli

With Borrowing Brilliance, you start with stimuli unrelated to your challenge, twisting and turning them until you give them relevance to the task. The advantage of Borrowing Brilliance is that, by it's nature, it tends to lead you to the dramatically new and different.

Recall that Homeward Trail uses stimuli related to your challenge. Your job is to take the relevant stimuli to the more unexpected.

Borrowing Brilliance works in the opposite direction. It uses stimuli unrelated to the challenge in a process that flows from the realm of the unexpected to areas of greater relevance.

Relevant ➡ UNexpected

Success in both cases requires striking a healthy balance between relevance and unexpectedness. **In other words, you're looking for a difference that makes a real difference for your customers.**

Relevant ⬅ UNexpected

Experience has taught us that unrelated stimuli are not nearly as easy to work with as related stimuli. When we start with stimuli that are relevant, it's easier to believe you'll succeed. Starting with unrelated stimuli requires faith. It sometimes helps if you remind yourself that you're in control. Instead of being lost in the wilderness with a lot of disjointed nonsense, you're making your way back home. Don't stop until you get to a point where you feel comfortable.

Thomas Edison was a great believer in the power of directly Borrowing Brilliance. He said once, "Make it a practice to keep on the lookout for novel and interesting ideas that others have used successfully. Your idea has to be an original only in its adaptation to the problem you are working on."

A great story of using unrelated stimuli is told by the award-winning Canadian singer and songwriter Lennie Gallant. When I heard Lennie tell this story at the annual Rendezvous Rustico, I recognized it instantly as a case of a great idea being created as a result of unrelated Stimuli.

Lennie put it this way:

> I had just got back from a concert tour and was flipping through the channels on the television to relax. One station had a story about the state of the ozone layer and how the hole in the sky was getting bigger. The next channel had a science story about how changes in the environment were causing tilting of the Earth's axis. None of this seemed relaxing so I turned to another channel.
>
> The third channel featured survivors of the *Titanic*. Recognize this was long before the movie came out. They talked about how even after the *Titanic* hit the iceberg, no one wanted to believe that such a thing could happen. In fact, the first few lifeboats went out nearly empty as no one could believe the ship could sink. The story also told of how the band kept playing in order to keep the people relaxed and calm.
>
> The images I'd seen on the television merged in my mind and suddenly I realized that in a way we are all sailing on the good ship planet Earth. And we've got a hole in our side (in the sky) as well. And just like those on the *Titanic*, we don't believe anything's wrong.
>
> From this image came a song I call "The Band's Still Playing." It uses the story of the *Titanic*, but in reality it's not at all about the *Titanic*.

The song is a high-energy, fun song to sing with a very important message. The lyrics are listed below with the kind permission of Lennie. To hear the song, visit http://www.lenniegallant.com and click on CDs/Lyrics.

To order the album, call my good friend Bruce MacNaughton at the PEI Preserve Company at (800) 565-5267.

Warning: If you go to the Web site, you'll get hooked, and you'll probably end up ordering a CD or two. Lennie Gallant is a talented musician and a throwback to the great songwriters of the 1960's who wrote lyrics with real messages.

The Band's Still Playing
All hands on deck, please don't panic
It's probably a drill, there's really nothing wrong

Steady as she goes on the *Titanic*
It can't be too bad, the band plays on

There's lifeboats launched upon the water
Captain's crying, won't you please get in
I don't believe in this disaster
I just don't believe the mess we're in

And the band's still playing
Can you hear those horns
Crying out for our souls
And the band's still playing
The band played hymns
And the band played rock and roll

I'm gonna rearrange all of the deck chairs
I'm going to cover my head, every inch of skin
Trading in my sunglasses for a darker pair
So I won't have to see the mess we're in

This music's got me dancing so fast
You know I really ain't got time to think
Someone said something about a great big hole in the sky
Someone said "last call," time for one more drink

(c) Copyright 1996 Revenant Records. All Rights Reserved.

A Surefire Remedy for Cranium Constipation

It's all too easy to narrow our thinking and end up squandering our time rearranging the obvious. When the desire for ideas is intense, we quickly move to tough-it-out machismo mode, as we attempt to grunt and groan our way to original thoughts.

Borrowing Brilliance is like a giant mental can opener. When we open our minds to unrelated stimuli, a vast array of fresh new options becomes available. Remember the story of Dr. Rosenzweig's rats. Stimuli made their brains smarter. So it is for you, too.

Seven Tactics for Finding Effective Borrowing Brilliance Stimuli

Borrowing Brilliance is about stretching your mind. Forcing you to take unrealted stimuli and find ways to make them connect is the equivalent of two-a-day practices at football camp or running suicides (don't even ask!) on a basketball court. When we lead Eureka! Inventing sessions for clients, we take responsibility for gathering the stimuli. Here are a collection of effective sources we have found for finding Borrowing Brilliance stimuli that work.

Open Yourself to Serendipity: The first thing you need to do is become comfortable with serendipity. This term was coined by British Prime Minister Horace Wallpole in 1754. It means "combining a fortunate accident with wisdom." Serendipity is about relentlessly transforming every stimulus you come in contact with into potential idea sparks. Serendipity is not about random chance. Rarely does it occur without an engaged mind. It requires one part awareness, one part preparation and one part optimism.

For serendipity to occur, you must be relentless in applying everything you see, hear, experience and feel against your challenge. You can consciously spark serendipity by exposing yourself to new stimuli and being open to finding answers in unexpected locations.

- As you drive, use highway billboards and store signs to spark your brain.
- Channel surf like Lennie Gallant did, looking to make connections.
- Walk through the zoo or the woods, and think how Mother Nature solves challenges.
- Visit Main Street or the mall "shopping for answers."

Paul Schurke, leader of the North Pole expedition I was a member of, has a great belief in the power of serendipity. When challenges faced us, from punctured stove fuel cans, to fractured frames on our dog sleds, to injured teammates and even damage to our satellite phone Paul continued to believe in the power of serendipity. In each case, intensive training, alertness for opportunities and 100% faith in success led to solutions to all challenges the high Arctic tossed at us. For example, when we faced a 50-foot-wide stretch of east-west open water that blocked our northward travels, we floated ice blocks out onto a slight bend in this river of water and waited. Within twelve hours, a cold front moved in dropping the wind chill temperature from -10 to -40 degrees. The blocks of ice froze creating a fragile yet sufficient stepping-stone bridge and we were off to the north again.

Leverage the Best of . . . : Borrowing Brilliance stimuli that have pedigrees of greatness as evidenced by winning awards can be especially effective. News services, industry trade associations, research organizations and magazines are a rich source of lists of the "best of" virtually anything. Often, behind many of these award winners lie hours of thinking, research and development.

Shop your favorite bookstore and you'll find books detailing the best advertising, best packaging, best direct-mail programs of the year.

The trade association you belong to often gives awards to the "best of" at annual conventions. When they do, release your ego and call, visit and talk to the winners personally. Probe deeper than what's published. What are the true keys to their success? If the winners are fellow small business owners, the odds are they'll share their learning with pride.

Take Advantage of Academic Wisdom: University professors are required to publish their research findings. As a result, thousands of academic journals have been created that serve as repositories of academic wisdom. Admittedly, the reading is slow, tedious and often mind numbing, but it's worth the journey, as the resultant ideas are often priceless.

Reading academic journals has been the primary stimulus for the ideas that have made me wealthy. One spring I gathered a stack of about 14 inches of academic papers detailing "the world's wisdom" regarding market research methods. Over the next six months, I would read an article here and there when I had a moment. When I went on a business trip, I would take a dozen articles with me to read on the plane. It wasn't easy. Sometimes I would have to read them two or three times to understand what they were talking about. By the time fall came, I had the vision for an entirely new type of market research methodology. That concept became the AcuPOLL Precision Research Company. AcuPOLL was so successful I was able to sell it for a healthy profit within three years of founding it.

Many of the biggest breakthroughs in the development of the Merwyn Simulated Test Marketing System were inspired by reading academic journals. And I still read the journals looking for my next big business idea.

Academic research as a stimulus source has become a regular tool of mine. Whenever my team gets stuck during the development of a new business, I read a dozen articles from the local library. Just reading about related challenges spurs new thinking.

No matter what your challenge, reading academic articles can serve as inspiration. If you have marketing challenges, read articles on trial generation or client retention studies. If you have customer service or employee problems, there are literally thousands of articles that can help you. The library at your local college can show you how to search indexes and order copies of articles. The great thing about academic articles is they contain long lists of references that allow you to easily make connections to additional articles that can help you on your quest.

Before you reject this method as too much work, think again about what these articles contain. Academic articles contain groundbreaking research by the top minds in the world for *free*. Plus, as opposed to popular press books, each article must be reviewed for accuracy and approved by two to three experts in the field before being published.

Academics have a much tougher standard of validation than popular press publishers. It's for this reason that I regularly review our research results, including all the data on these pages, with a set of academic professors.

Shop for Ideas: Move your feet and walk though the marketplace.

You'll find ideas. Wal-Mart founder and entrepreneurial legend Sam Walton used to "learn by walking around." Walton was usually in his office half of the time, from Thursday until noon on Saturday. But the other half, Monday through Wednesday, was spent in the field interacting directly with customers and employees and seeing what the competition was up to. The competitor's latest innovation might just be something Wal-Mart could adapt and do better.

The director of packaging at a Fortune 50 food company told me recently that walking through unrelated categories was his most powerful source of ideas: "When I'm stuck for an idea, I walk through the beauty aids category, the alcoholic beverages category, anyplace but the food category. To find a unique food packaging idea, I need to look at categories other than food. "

Look closely at what the major corporations are doing. Whenever you see the introduction of a big new product or service, the odds are that millions of dollars worth of market research are behind it.

Watch ad campaigns. If a leading pizza firm advertises three varieties of pizza, the odds are those are the best-sellers.

Observe retail space allocations. If a certain style of microbrew beer has more facings of space on the store shelves, the odds are that style sells the best.

Learn what's selling in a given category. Most juice drinks are initially offered in citrus, tropical punch and berry varieties. That's because surveys of customer interest indicate that these three flavors have the broadest reach. Knowing this, you can appeal to the broad market with unique offerings by simply making modifications to each base flavor—Lemon Citrus, Banana Tropical Punch and Coconut Berry Blend.

Look closely and observe what the big guys are doing. It's a *free* resource you can use to help you leap to new ideas.

Pump Up Your Brain: When I'm really challenged for an idea, I will often take a walk in a totally unexpected place and force myself to create twenty-four ideas—big, small or otherwise—before I go home. Flea markets, garage sales and street markets are filled with eclectic stimuli that can inspire new thinking. Walk, think, invent ideas while visiting them.

It's a habit I got into when I had my magic show. Early on, I had no money to buy fancy magic tricks, so my primary sources of props were flea markets and garage sales. I would leave early on a Saturday morning and paw through other people's "junk." Once I purchased a toilet seat for twenty-five cents. The price was right, and it just felt like something we could use as a prop. When I got home, my brother and I thought and thought about what to do with it. Then Eureka! we created a funny gag where my brother would "pull a rabbit" out of the toilet seat. The result was a totally original and funny skit that we did for years.

Many communities feature home and garden exhibitions, boat shows, car shows, even children's shows. Watching and observing what's new and what attracts people's attention can be a powerful source of education.

Carnivals, county fairs, arts and crafts festivals offer opportunities to study various styles of marketing. I make it a point to look for the booths that attract the most people. I'll stand, watch and study, all the time trying to discover what it is about the booth that attracts attention.

It was in the world of New England county fairs that I first learned marketing. Working a fair booth for a summer, week after week, was for me an accelerated M.B.A. in marketing. You quickly learn about merchandising, pricing and, most importantly, how to distill your message into but a few provocative words.

At a fair, you have to be overt in your pitch because the competition for the money of the folks walking past your booth is fierce and the level of "stimulus noise" from competing booths is extremely high. When you get your pitch right, it's like printing money. When your pitch is wrong, you make nothing. I learned quickly how to pitch my magic and juggling kits

My magic bunnies magic trick pitch went something like this: "Free magic tricks. Give your honey a bunny. Learn to perform magic in minutes. Tested on my little sister to make sure it's easy enough to understand." Interestingly, without knowing it, at the age of sixteen, I was offering a Real Reason to Believe as part of my pitch.

And here was my pitch for selling juggling kits: "Hi folks [making eye contact with a young couple walking down the midway; couples were the best target as the guys would always buy anything for their gals]. Have you ever tried to juggle three tennis balls or baseballs?" Then, following the nod, "Give me three minutes and I'll give you both your first juggling lesson free. I know you can both do it. I've taught over five thousand people to juggle." Then following a quick lesson, I'd pitch them my juggling kit that contained a set of balls and everything they needed to learn to juggle. When I was on a roll, I would sell the kits as fast as my girlfriend (who in time became my wife) could assemble them.

Important to note is that it took me some time to learn how to refine my pitch. Hours of testing and learning went on before I found out how to make my pitch efficient and effective.

In the "real" business world, the equivalent of the carnival is the business trade show. I am a big believer in utilizing trade shows as a low-cost method for experiments on how to refine your marketing message. What is the equivalent of the trade show in your industry that you can use as a learning experience?

Gather and Review a Portfolio Collection: Reviewing collections of stimuli centered around a specific dimension of your challenge can be very effective at stretching your mind. If your business requires regular promotions, a file of every promotion that catches your eye, in any category, can be very powerful.

At the Eureka! Ranch, we have a number of collections we have found particularly helpful.

- Cookbooks are useful in creating new ideas for foods and beverages.
- Restaurant menus are useful for creating experiential concepts. Menus, when done right, bring together benefit and reason to believe with highly synergistic imagery.
- Color chips from paint stores are a great way to stretch our minds for new products. We'll take a color and force ourselves to create ideas for new drinks, foods and beauty aids that would use the color. What "signals" does the color communicate?
- Greeting cards are great for exploring ways to articulate emotional benefits. For instance, if you own a pub or catering business, congratulations or celebration cards could help inspire language for a new marketing message. And any business could benefit from using cards that express love and thanks as inspiration for customer retention programs.
- Direct-mail offers are rich stimuli sources for new mailings.

The brochure from Canyon Ranch, America's number one rated exercise spa, served as inspiration for our brochure when we first opened the Eureka! Ranch. Our newly built office was for creating great ideas, not healthy, beautiful bodies; however, there were many analogies I could leverage in designing our new brochure.

Practical Tactic

Borrowing Brilliance stimulus is about keeping your eye open for concepts that inspire you. Over the next week save every piece of junk mail you get. At the end of the week, sort through the pile quickly, deal the pieces that catch your eye in one pile and those that don't in another. Next, lay out the ones that caught your eye. What do they have in common? What "brilliance" could you borrow for your marketing pieces?

Take Advantage of the Secret Trend-Spotting System

The stories detailed on the covers of magazines provide a down and dirty way to identify trends. Magazines' covers feature stories that their research and trend experts say are hot with potential customers. Magazines feature these stories on their covers in order to increase newsstand sales.

I keep a collection of magazines such as *Good Housekeeping*, *People*, *Time*, *Fortune Small Business* and *Inc.*, in order to keep track of what's hot in the marketplace. They are a rich source of stimuli for ideas.

Business guru Tom Peters uses a similar system for inspiring his business insights. In an interview with John Grossmann for the October 2000 issue of *Sky* magazine, Peters said, "I'll wander into O'Hare for a two-hour flight and I'll grab eight to ten magazines. Maybe none of them will be business magazines. I'm just looking at what's happening in the world. One of my secrets to success is religiously reading Section D [Life] of *USA Today*, which tells me what's happening culturally."

Another hot trend area is direct-mail catalogs. The mantra for success in mail order is identifying hot items prior to broad-scale distribution. Once an item is widely available, customers will not be willing to pay the shipping costs and take the time to have it delivered.

Try this tactic now. Go to your local bookstore and visit the magazine section. Your first assignment is to look just at the magazine covers. Don't bother to open the magazines. Look at magazines from many different, unrelated categories. On a stack of sticky notes, detail six to ten stories or trends from the covers of the magazines that jump out at you. Next, take a seat and use the notes as stimuli for creating new ideas. Free-associate on the trends, then keep working the concepts until you create at least a dozen ideas for growing your business.

Your second assignment is to select a couple small business magazines and read the articles detailing how other small businesses have become successes. It's especially important that these businesses be unrelated to your own. As you read, write on sticky notes specific principles, learning and lessons that the small business owners found especially important. When you are finished reading, you should have a healthy stack of "small business wisdom." Next, use those notes as sources of inspiration for creating new ideas as you've learned previously.

Quick Process Summary on Exploring Stimuli

1. **Stimuli fuel the brain.**
   - Stimuli set off a chain reaction similar to how the brain works.
2. **Fuel your brain.**
   - Use it or lose it.
   - Read.
   - Exercise.
   - Create.
   - Learn.
   - Cook.
   - Appreciate music.
   - Experience new people.
   - Write.
   - Travel.
   - Visit museums.
   - Work a new job at your company.
3. **There are four stages of creativity when using stimuli.**
   - Stage I: Gather Stimuli.
   - Stage II: Multiply Stimuli.

- Stage III: Create Customer Concepts.
- Stage IV: Optimize Practicality.

4. **Homeward Trail stimuli are related stimuli.**
   - Take from relevant to unexpected.
   - Create a competitive strength balance sheet.
   - Observe candid comments.
   - Review your history.
   - Look at your front door.
   - Experiment with kitchen chemistry.
   - Visit the scene of the crime.
   - Catalog what you have going for you.
   - Review the next best option.
   - Step back and look at the big picture.
   - Explore cheap rent districts.

5. **Borrowing Brilliance stimuli are unrelated stimuli.**
   - Take from unexpected to the relevant.
   - Open yourself to serendipity.
   - Leverage the best of . . .
   - Take advantage of academic wisdom.
   - Shop for ideas.
   - Pump up your brain.
   - Gather and review a portfolio collection.
   - Take advantage of the secret trend-spotting system.

Some Final Thoughts on Exploring Stimuli

As the folks at Nike say, just do it.

Take the time to gather the stimuli and work with them. I promise you tons of ideas will come to you.

And for those of you who say it's too much work, get over it. The work it takes to gather stimuli is a fraction of what it will take to turn your idea into reality.

The last thought I have is to reinforce the importance of putting all ideas on paper and using the disciplined system as outlined in the section on Mind Dump. The more you write, the more you will make true progress with your thinking. And the more you will begin to assemble a portfolio of thoughts that even if not applicable today could be the idea you need tomorrow. The Chinese have a saying that relates: "The weakest ink lasts longer than the strongest memory."

Talking and thinking instead of writing and doing is a common ailment of my clients. I'll never forget a meeting I had with Donna, a world-famous industrial designer at a leading computer company. The meeting took place at her cutting-edge design center, a modern building built to look like an old factory, complete with wood beams and floors and industrial grids and girders. The conversation was going nowhere. In my classic informal manner, I was asking Donna, "What about this. . . ," "What if . . . ," "Might it be possible if . . .," The answer to all questions was "We did that. We've done that. We've tried that." I smelt a rat. Either this lady was a genius or I wasn't being told the entire truth. Acting as naive as possible, I asked if it was possible for her to go get me some of the drawings from their archives. "I'm kind of a visual person," I explained in my best naive entrepreneurial way. "It would help my simple mind understand why those ideas didn't work if I could see them."

Then I grabbed my cup of coffee and let silence fill the air. Silence has a way of making people say things to fill air. And Donna did. I don't think I've ever seen anyone put their conversation into reverse as fast as Donna did. "We don't keep good archives. . . . It would take me a long time to find them. . . . Well we haven't drawn all of them. . . . The designers and I have thought of those things. . . . We know this industry well enough to know when it's not necessary to waste time. . . . We don't believe in following customer trends; we feel it's our job to set the trends."

Don't let yourself get caught in the same trap. Don't reject previous thoughts. Instead, consider them as initial stimuli points to build new ideas around.

Writing and rewriting is the least costly and most effective business prototyping system available. I often recommend to my corporate clients that they have each idea team member describe in writing what he thinks the "big idea" is for his company to pursue. The process is initially painful as the managers and team members soon learn that (1) they all see a different idea and (2) what they thought made sense doesn't when they read it on a computer screen.

The good news is that if they have the persistence, dedication and commitment to keep at it they will soon articulate an idea that can energize and excite all company departments and all trade and end user customers.

The advice is simple. Write it. If you can't write it, you don't have an idea that can ever become a sales success.

CHAPTER 11

Multiply Your Brain by Borrowing Others

This chapter details how to leverage the diversity of viewpoints from others to help multiply the potential from your stimuli. This chapter also provides some detailed insights into how your brain works and your core thinking style. With this learning, you can dramatically enhance your personal effectiveness.

Second Law of Capitalist Creativity: Leverage Diversity

You exponentially multiply the power of stimuli when you seek the ideas, opinions and judgments of diverse perspectives.

A stimulus is the catalyst that sparks the reaction that creates ideas. Diversity is the fuel that turns the spark into a chain reaction of continuous idea creation. The greater the diversity of opinions and perspectives you gather, the more effective you will be in creating ideas that can truly grow your business.

Former United States President Woodrow Wilson understood the value of leveraging diversity. He once said, "I not only use all the brains that I have, but all that I can borrow."

In our research, we measure the breadth of diversity in a group by assessing participants' levels of agreement or disagreement with the following statement: "I felt the participants in my group provided and offered diverse viewpoints in the generation of new ideas." Controlling for all other variables, we find that the greater the diversity, the greater the number of practical ideas that are invented.

Upon hearing the term diversity, some may connect the concept with government-imposed legal requirements for diversity of hiring and equal opportunity. That is not the scope of this book or my point of expertise. When I speak of diversity, I'm talking as a

	Number of Practical Ideas Invented
High Stimulus	46.0
Medium Stimulus	29.9
Low Stimulus	18.5

capitalist. Diversity is a tangible tool for helping you think smarter and more creatively.

The North American colonies of the United States and Canada are proof positive of the power of diversity. Immigrants came to the new lands from around the world. They brought with them their perspectives, views and unique thinking styles. The collaboration and, yes, the disagreements between diverse people are what made the USA and Canada so great!

Historian Joseph Ellis in *Founding Brothers: The Revolutionary Generation* (Knopf, 2000) articulated the value of diversity in the formation of the United States:

> The achievement of the revolutionary generation was a collective enterprise that succeeded because of the diversity of personalities and ideologies present in the mix. Their interactions and juxtapositions generated a dynamic form of balance and equilibrium, not because any of them was perfect or infallible, but because their mutual imperfections and fallibilities, as well as eccentricities and excesses, checked each other in much the way the Madison in Federalist claimed that multiple factions would do in a large republic.

The acceptance and leverage of diversity was then and is now the core strength of the United States and Canada. Readers will note the overt mention of Canada. My mother was a Canadian and while I am a citizen of the United States I am deeply proud of my Canadian roots.

Ideally, within your own company, you have highly diverse individuals working for you. If you don't, then you need to "rent them." The following exercise encourages you to seek out diverse perspectives.

Try It Now: Type up two or three of your ideas for how to articulate your Overt Benefit from chapter three. Your task is to get the reactions of one dozen people. The process is simple.

1. Explain Objective: Explain how you are attempting to define clearly what the Overt Benefit of your product or service is.
2. Let Them Read Idea: Show them a single piece of paper with your statements of benefit typed on them. Don't hype or promote. Ask their opinions of the written words.
3. Actively Listen: Open your ears and mind to their perceptions and reactions. Don't defend, redefine or explain. Take detailed notes of all reactions for later review. If the readers display confusion, you have your answer. The most important thing is to listen and observe their reactions. When a response is not what you expected, seek to understand the source of the comment. When you can open yourself to the broader perspective of the comment, you will gain true wisdom.

When I'm intensely working on a new idea, I ask everyone I see for an opinion. I'll ask total strangers what they think. I've had seatmates on planes read book proposals, fellow soccer parents read brochure copy at halftime of our kids' game.

If you want to dramatically improve your advertising, show it one-on-one to fifty people. Ask them directly what the benefit is and what makes them believe the benefit will be delivered. Ask them what they perceive makes your business offering dramatically different. Listen closely. It is what they perceive, not what you intend, that counts.

Find people who are direct opposites of you and bounce ideas off them. Like people make for like ideas. Unique people make for unique ideas. Walk the halls and lunchrooms and just ask them. You'll be surprised how far people will go to help you if you just ask!

The Surface Source of Diversity

Our initial perspectives are often based on our experiences and expertise. Those in manufacturing look at ideas and immediately assemble production factories in their minds. Those in legal immediately look for potential lawsuits. Those in sales search their minds for customers who would be easy first sales for the new idea. Research and development experts review past experiments for a perspective on potential feasibility.

Each of these focused viewpoints is valuable in helping you develop a three-dimensional perspective regarding your new product, service or business. By listening to each discipline and building on that thinking, your idea develops richness and perspective that can dramatically enhance probability of executional success.

Diversity Can Cause Chaos

Based on the above, diversity sounds like a utopia, doesn't it? So why do so many businesspeople avoid it?

The answer is because the more different perspectives you gather, the greater the discussion, debate and outright fighting that can occur.

Sadly, many businesspeople don't have the guts or the courage to face conflicting opinions. They would rather be like ostriches and stick their heads in the sand to avoid conflict at all cost.

When everyone is engaged and involved, conflict happens. That's life. The only caution is to make sure that the conflict stays content focused and doesn't degrade into personal attacks.

In the city of Philadelphia, intense and high-spirited debate created the United States. In the city of Charlottetown, intense and vigorous debate created Canada.

When I start a project, I let teams know that I fully expect vigorous debate. To make my point clear, I poke them a little by stating, "If we don't have vigorous debate, then someone here is a major cost savings opportunity." I'm not trying to pick a fight; I'm trying to encourage all team members to help the cause by telling what they believe.

Marketing Physics Is the Key to Leveraging the Power of Diversity

In the early days of the Eureka! Ranch it was not uncommon for multifunctional teams to debate the strengths and weaknesses of ideas well past midnight each night. Since we've instilled 100% training of all client teams before creating ideas, the productivity of the debating has improved dramatically. Now, each person has a common focus for her discussion. Specifically, the three laws of Marketing Physics give us a common language and collective goal. Debates today are laserlike focused on how the concepts will serve and motivate customers or consumers.

Practical Tactic: Musical Chairs

Musical Chairs is a stimu-
lus-gathering tactic used at
the Eureka! Ranch. This
method is designed to force
you to look at the world
from someone else's seat.

When we face challenges, we tend to develop reflexive reactions based on our personal points of view. The goal of Musical Chairs is to force us to stop, turn off the autopilot and open our minds to new perspectives.

The overall process is the same as what you learned in the Homeward Trail section of the previous chapter. Instead of starting from related or unrelated stimuli, you utilize different people's viewpoints as your starting stimuli.

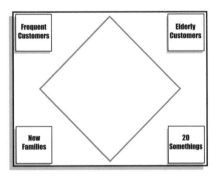

This illustration shows a page that lists different people to use as initial stimuli. In the area closest to one of the labels, write free associations that come to mind when you think of that person or group. Translate the free associations into relevant Overt Benefits and Real Reasons to Believe, and write them in the center of the page.

Variations of Musical Chairs

Over the years, we have successfully used many variations of Musical Chairs.

Functional Departments Think like your company is a big company with many departments. What would be the needs and desires of each of the following departments?

- Marketing and PR
- Manufacturing
- Legal
- Sales
- Purchasing
- Advertising
- Engineering
- Customer Service
- Research and Development
- Human Resources

Specialty Customer Segments Think of extremes of your customer base. What are unique offerings that could especially delight them?

- Competition's customers
- Frequent switchers
- Customers with special needs
- Love technology
- Concerned about health
- Concerned about the environment
- Your most loyal customers
- Customers with no category experience
- Price-conscious customers
- Scared to death of technology
- Live life to the fullest
- Believe in the power of people

Demographic Groups The population of the world is continuously shifting—baby boomers age and new immigrants move to town. What are each group's specific opportunities for growth?

- Active senior citizens
- New to town
- Youth of all ages
- Men or women
- Inactive senior citizens
- Longtime locals
- Families of all life stages
- Various ethnic groups

We have found it effective when focusing on people to cut out pictures from a magazine to represent various user groups. By visualizing the people, it is sometimes easier to articulate what they are thinking.

What Would (Who) Do This approach focuses on what specific people would do. The values, perspectives and wisdom of those you know or know of is used as a mechanism for broadening perspective.

For example, what would your grandfather, your mother, your favorite teacher in school recommend that you do? When I'm stuck for an idea, I often reflect on what my personal hero, Ben Franklin, would do when faced with a similar challenge. You can use celebrities or historical figures as points of inspiration for original thinking about your challenge.

Takeover Time A variation of what was discussed earlier under The Fresh Eyes Challenge is Takeover Time. This is a popular variation of Musical Chairs. Here we make the assumption your organization has been taken over by a well-known company. What values, cultures and belief systems would the new managers bring to the challenge? How would they look at the issues? What would be their approach to your business? How would they run it? What would they change?

You can select any company you wish to use as a source of inspiration. The following are common ones we use at the Eureka! Ranch. I've added some statements to provoke and excite thinking.

- Nike: Authentic performance . . . how winners win
- American Express: Service, service, service
- Disney: Storytellers
- Godiva Chocolatier: Indulgent decadence
- World Wrestling Federation: Entertainment rules
- Taco Bell: The fastest and the cheapest
- The Ritz-Carlton: Your private home away from home
- America Online: The McDonald's of the Internet
- Harley-Davidson: The politically correct way for executives to be rebels
- Ben & Jerry's: The sixties attitude in an ice cream tub
- Barbie: Idealism at its worst or best (depending on your perspective)

Practical Tactic: Don't Sell Me

This tactic is particularly good at helping you define the Overt Benefit your business will offer to customers. It forces you to look at the world through the eyes of others.

Customers don't want to be "sold" anything. Rather, they want to have their wants and needs satisfied. The exercise Don't Sell Me is a stimulus-creation exercise that focuses your thinking on a customer's perspective.

Step 1 Define what your business is in a generic sense, and detail it on a piece of paper in the following format.

If you own a restaurant, your statement would read as follows:

Don't sell me a restaurant dinner. Sell me _____.

If you own a dance studio, your statement would read as follows:
Don't sell me dance lessons. Sell me _____.

Step 2 Now complete the statement looking at the world from the eyes of your customers. You can use a generic customer as your frame of reference or one of the specialty segments detailed in the Musical Chairs prompts above.

Write each response on its own sticky note, and collect the notes on a sheet of paper.

For example, your answers to the business challenges listed above might be

Don't sell me a restaurant dinner. Sell me _____.
• Escape from the evening dishes
• A new taste adventure
• A moment of romantic intimacy
• A great taste experience without any health guilt

Don't sell me dance lessons. Sell me _____.
• Increased self-confidence for my child
• A feeling of belonging for my child as part of a dance group
• Early experiences of onstage performing
• An opportunity to learn discipline

Step 3 Take the sticky notes from the sheet, and then follow the process detailed for Musical Chairs. Free-associate, then create ideas.

My wife and I love the College of Piping and Celtic Performing

Arts of Canada. The college is located in Summerside, Prince Edward Island, Canada, just a short drive from our island farmhouse in Springbrook. We also have a great love for the island and its people. When looking for a way to give back something to our island home, we came upon the idea of offering scholarships to island youth to take bagpiping or Celtic drumming at the college.

Discussions with Scott MacAuley, the college's director, and Ken Gillis, the president of the college, led to the creation of the Doug & Debbie Hall Pipe Band scholarship, offering free lessons once a week to any island child age eight to eighteen.

When we announced the offer at a press conference, I also related the challenge we would face in gaining the interest of the island youth, who are more prone to playing ice hockey than playing the bagpipes and wearing kilts.

To create the advertisement for the program, we turned to Don't Sell Me as our tool. The statements went like this.

Don't sell me bagpiping. Sell me a job.
Don't sell me bagpiping. Sell me pride and accomplishments.
Don't sell me bagpiping. Sell me friendships.
Don't sell me bagpiping. Sell me travel with the band.

From these raw ideas was developed the following newspaper advertisement.

The ad worked. On an island where ice hockey rules, we went from two classes of beginners to twenty-seven classes. And we had over 150 kids on the waiting list!

The Secret to Finding Great Diversity—Passion

Some people live life at half speed. Others attack life with every ounce of energy and enthusiasm in their bodies. If you want the most powerful help with your challenge, find people who live a full-tilt life. Those who are passionate about just about anything-sales, music, painting, engineering, coaching a kids' baseball team-have a natural vitality that will energize their perspectives on your challenge.

A Dutch study reported in the January 1, 1999, edition of *USA Weekend* ("What Happens in the Brain of an Einstein in the Throes of Creativity?") demonstrated the power of passion. The study

WANTED:
Island Youth to Band Together

PEI youth, ages 8 to 18, you have a unique opportunity this fall to receive **FULL TUITION Scholarships** for the College of Piping for lessons in bagpiping or snare drumming. Scholarships are provided by The Doug & Debbie Hall Pipe Band Scholarship Program fund. All you need is a spirit of adventure and a willingness to learn.

Benefits of Playing the Pipes and Drums

- **PRIDE**: Being a key participant at PEI's world famous College of Piping.
- **EXCITEMENT**: Of learning to play from some of the world's greatest teachers.
- **FUN**: It's a great group of people who know how to have a GREAT time.
- **TRAVEL**: Opportunities to travel with the pipe band.
- **JOBS**: One enterprising piper earned over $2,500 playing his pipes this summer.

PHOTO CREDIT: DOUG AND TORI HALL

Criteria for applicants:
i. Scholarship recipients will be youth between the ages of 8 and 18 years.
ii. A resident of Prince Edward Island.
iii. Each student must give serious consideration to joining The College of Piping Pipe Band once they are musically capable.

A Scholarship includes:
i. A one-hour weekly group lesson.
ii. A one-hour monthly band practice from January to June.
iii. Use of a practice chanter or drum pad and sticks.

What is expected of a scholarship winner:
i. A thank you letter for the Patrons, Doug and Debbie Hall.
ii. Recipients will be expected to attend classes and practice regularly.
iii. Recipients must demonstrate a commitment to learning.

Value of a Scholarship:
The total value of the scholarship is approximately $500.

How to apply:
Applicants will be required to complete an Application and Enrollment Form by Wednesday, September 6, 2000 for the fall semester commencing Monday, September 11, 2000. The scholarship packages are available at: The College of Piping, 619 Water Street East, Summerside. Answers to FAQ's (frequently asked questions) are included in the packages and are also available on our website at: **collegeofpiping.com**

The newspaper advertisment

examined what separated chess masters from the higher-level chess grand masters. Each group was tested on a wide range of dimensions, including IQ, memory, reasoning and attitudes towards chess. No differences were found in the classic thinking areas of IQ, memory and reasoning: "The only difference: Grand masters simply loved chess more. They had more passion and commitment to it."

Seek and find people who are passionate about anything, and you will find a vital energy source for new thinking about your business challenge.

Three Specialty Sources for Diverse Perspective

There are three other sources that are particularly helpful when looking for new perspectives: rookies, workers and retired workers. Rookies or those who have been with a business for only a short time have the power of first impressions. When we start new jobs or companies, we are filled with new thoughts and ideas. In time, the pressures of the day-to-day world cause our brains to become aligned with the established views our companies' cultures.

When you hire someone new for inside your company, or even outside-an attorney or accountant-spend time listening to him as well as briefing him. Every few days or weeks overtly ask questions.

- What surprises you about how I run my business?
- How is the business different than you thought it would be?
- What could we change to make it more effective?
- What three things would you suggest for change?

The next powerful group of people to tap into is frontline workers, the everyday people who make the business function. My father worked as an engineer in the pulp and paper industry. As a youth, he worked on paper machines and learned firsthand the amount of wisdom and knowledge the frontline workers had. He taught me the power of asking the machine operators what they thought.

When I was at P&G, I made it a point to tour the factories where the product I was responsible for marketing was made. To truly learn, these were set up as long tours so I would have time to talk one-on-one with as many of the workers as I could.

Today, I still tour client factories whenever possible. In private, one worker's comment shocked me so much I wrote it down. It's from a fifty-something-year-old employee who tried to create change yet was met with little support: "When I started at the plant, I suggested lots of new ideas for our production area. The bosses weren't interested. They wanted to do it the way they'd been doing it for twenty years. After being told no a dozen times, I stopped making suggestions. I still try out ideas, but only when the bosses won't notice what I'm up to."

Ask your frontline workers what they think. Ask the folks who make your product, deliver your product and answer the phones when customers call with complaints. They know what's going on better than any so-called specialist can ever know. However, you have to take the initiative to ask if you want to learn.

Think about your business. Whom can you learn from? Whom are the frontline people you can seek out for their wisdom and perspective?

The last powerful group to learn from is retired workers. The youthful generation, with their love of technology and change, is wonderful. Seniors, however, have a sense of balance and wisdom that cannot be learned in a classroom. Plus, they are refreshingly direct and honest with their comments.

Seek out those who have retired from your industry. Ask for their perspectives and advice. Don't be surprised if what seems like an entirely new situation wasn't faced by them some twenty years ago.

Think. What veterans can you call for advice? Whom can you talk to who has the "long view" of history and can help put things in perspective? Who is the smartest person you've ever known in your industry?

Don't ever be afraid to overtly ask the opinions of rookies, workers or veterans. Everyone feels flattered to be asked his opinion. Just be respectful of others' thoughts. If they agree to tell you their thoughts, you have a responsibility to listen respectfully.

A Final Source of Diversity: Thinking Styles

How we approach the world is defined by our thinking styles. There are a number of different surveys you can take to quantify your thinking styles. In my experience, the most effective is called the Herrmann Brain Dominance Instrument (HBDI).

The HBDI is a 120-question diagnostic survey that provides an in-depth profile of how you think and approach problems. We have had hundreds of clients complete the entire HBDI profiler prior to attending Eureka! sessions. By analyzing their thinking styles versus their productivity at creating ideas, we have gained considerable insight.

We've used the HBDI to develop a top-line measure of thinking style called the B.O.S. (Brain Operating System) Profiler. Before going further, I would like you to complete the profiler.

B.O.S. Profiler

Please rate yourself on the following dimensions by circling the number between the two descriptors that best describes you.

1. Idea Realist	1	2	3	4	5	6	Idea Builder
2. Rational	1	2	3	4	5	6	Emotional
3. Process Oriented	1	2	3	4	5	6	People Oriented
4. Neat and Organized	1	2	3	4	5	6	Messy and Chaotic
5. Trust the Facts	1	2	3	4	5	6	Trust Gut Instinct
6. Predictable	1	2	3	4	5	6	Spontaneous
7. Logical	1	2	3	4	5	6	Visionary

There are no right answers; there are no wrong answers. Circle the number that instinctively defines the true you.

This simplified thinking-style test gives a snapshot overview of your primary orientation. It has been validated through two separate analyses as being highly predictive of your true left/right orientation as determined by the HBDI.

For a more in-depth profile I recommend you consider purchasing a full HBDI analysis at http://www.hbdi.com. Hermann International is generously offering readers of this book a 20% discount on the cost of a complete HBDI profile purchased via the Internet. To take advantage of this offer, simply complete your assessment and on the secure online payment form enter BRAIN BREW where it asks for a special offers code. (Note: This offer is a generous gift and may be discontinued at any time.)

Quick Background on Thinking Styles

Thinking style research was born with the work of Roger Sperry, Joseph Bogen and Michael Gazzaniga in the 1970s. They discovered much about how the brain works as a result of disconnecting the two halves of the brains of patients with incurable epilepsy.

From this effort, the concept of right brain and left brain was born. Based on testing, it was learned that the two sides of the brain have separate and distinct functions. The left side of the brain is where logic, analysis and organization occur. The right side of the brain is where emotion, vision and intuition occur. In a simple sense, the left is about the details, and the right is about dreams. To be successful in developing profitable business ideas, you must leverage both details and dreams.

Whole Brain Orientation

Those who have strengths in both areas are called whole brain individuals. They have the ability to access both styles of thinking. Note, having the ability doesn't mean that they take action with it. If they're not careful, whole brain individuals can become mentally lazy and simply lean toward one side or the other in their behavior. Whole brain orientation can be personally difficult because your vision of both sides can result in an inability to make decisions and a frustration of not being able to fulfill each to its maximum.

I am a whole brain type. In researching this book, I had the ultimate brain test conducted. I had my brain wired up with a dozen electrodes. My brain activity was then measured as I completed a number of tasks. What the brain scan found was that both sides of my brain acted nearly simultaneously. For example, when I do math problems, both sides of my brain light up as I both calculate and visualize the numbers.

This whole brain or dual brain orientation fits my personality. I am as passionate about statistics and science as I am about the arts.

Calculating Your B.O.S. Profiler Score

Analyzing your results is simple. Simply add the numbers you have circled.

If your score is 0 to 25, you have a logical left brain orientation.

If your score is 26 to 30, you have a whole brain orientation.

If your score is 31 or above, you have a radical right brain orientation.

Who Is Best at Creating Ideas?

Conventional wisdom holds that, to be creative, you must be right brained. As shown below in a survey of innovation experts, creating ideas is seen as more the world of right brain individuals and defining business strategies the focus of left brain individuals.

Average Ratings

	Left Brain	Right Brain
Asked for advice on new ideas	7.8	9.1
Asked for advice on business strategies	7.7	6.3

All questions use an 11 point scale: Rarely = 0, Often = 10.

Results are significant at the 95% confidence level or greater.

It is said that unless you think from the right side of your brain, you'll never feel the muse, howl at the moon, get in touch with your inner child or quack like a duck.

Shifting to a right brain orientation is particularly difficult when you realize that most businesspeople are left brain in orientation. Analysis of surveys of some 311,207 individuals by Herrmann International finds that most adults lean logical.

Percent Distribution (Sample of 311,207)

Logical left brain	44.2%
Whole brain	27.4%
Radical right brain	28.3%

The Truth About Who Is Most Creative

The reality is that in general a whole brain balance is most effective when it comes to creating Capitalist Creativity ideas, that is, ideas that are relevant yet unexpected.

It just makes sense. To be effective with business ideas, you can't simply dream big thoughts like the artist, poet or musician. To be effective, you must blend those inspirations with the strategic logic of Marketing Physics and the realities of profitable execution.

Measurement of clients as part of our quality control charting program provides confirmation of the power of whole brain balance. A total of 265 participants were measured as part of 38 innovation work groups. Using the Herrmann Brain Dominance Instrument, the work groups were segmented based on their collective thinking styles. When groups had strengths in both left brain and right brain thinking, they were dramatically more effective than groups with strengths in only one of the two thinking styles.

Number of Quality Ideas	
Whole brain skilled	37.1
Left brain skilled and not right brain skilled	31.8
Right brain skilled and not left brain skilled	31.6

The Good News Is You Can Get Whole Brain Results

By reading and applying the laws detailed in this book, you can generate whole brain effectiveness whatever your current thinking style. I know this is the case because of the transformation in client results we have seen since initiating training in the learning presented here. Since adding training, we have seen an improvement in all thinking styles. Today, all groups more closely match the level of our top groups. In the analysis detailed below, some 822 participants were measured during 124 work groups.

Number of Quality Ideas	
Trained whole brain clients	38.1
Trained left brain clients	38.5
Trained right brain clients	38.1

Logical Left Brains Are Easier to Work With
Than Radical Right Brains

Historically, it has been preached that when it comes to innovation the right brain style is more effective than the left brain style. As someone who works on the front lines, I can tell you that it's just plain wrong. It makes no difference what thinking style you have when it comes to bottomline effectiveness.

Everyone has an equal potential to create in a whole brain manner. However, at the Eureka! Ranch, we've found logical left brain types significantly easier to work with when it comes to creating than radically right brain types. Left brain people seem to rationally understand the need for stretching their brains. Conversely, it often takes more work to get right brain teams to focus and make disciplined decisions. The comments of one recent right brain client explains the situation well: "These ideas feel really great but I feel like we're still missing something. I can't really say what it is . . . it just feels that way."

Net, it is usually easier to get a left brain person to open up than it is to get a right brain person to become more disciplined.

An assembly of comments from top scientists, some Nobel Prize winners quoted in a *Creativity Research Journal* (see chapter ten) supports our finding.

It is an interesting point that scientists like music, read poetry, read books and are I think in general intelligent, interested in politics, and so forth. No poet, no painter has ever tried to study a little mathematics to know about the new things in this new world. The scientific world is extremely beautiful. I'm much more interested— I mean, if you ask me what I really care about—I care about the beauty in science; and this novelty of discovery is a really aesthetic pleasure. It's just comparable, I think, to any other of the great artistic emotions. It isn't rational. It's beyond reason.

If there are two cultures, the scientists are the ones who have had both. It's the nonscientists who have a separate culture.

I find that a student of the arts, for example, is completely ignorant of science and proud of it, but a student in the sciences, if he is ignorant of art will be attempting to make up the deficiency.

The Thinking Styles Are True Opposites

Left brain and right brain people are true polar opposites. When they work together, great accomplishments are possible. When they don't respect each other's skills, all-out war can result.
We offered pairs of words to various businesspeople and had them identify which best described themselves. They could vote for either phrase directly or somewhere in between the two. At the 95% confidence level, the differences between the two groups are clear. **The two thinking styles' personalities are like oil and water.**

Left Brain	Right Brain
Serious	Humorous
Down to earth	Sophisticated
Boring	Exciting
Saver	Spender
Trust the facts	Trust gut instinct
Neat and organized	Messy and chaotic
Profit is the purpose of ideas	Ideas are an expression of myself
Prefer scientific method	Prefer to "sense" a solution to a problem

It's important that as you interact with others in the operation of your business, you clearly recognize these kinds of differences. By leveraging the unique perspectives of others, you can dramatically increase everyone's perspective.

Employees of many of my corporate clients are forced through a funnel of conformity and made to walk alike, talk alike, think alike and act alike. It's done in the name of discipline and corporate culture. This is not diversity. Leveraging diversity is about taking advantage of the unique abilities of each individual.

We must learn to appreciate and respect the views of all individuals. The fact that they see the world differently is not wrong. It's just them.

To be happy in life, people do not have to become like you.

In fact, our research finds absolutely no differences in happiness between the brain styles. There were no differences on any of the following assessments.

- How would you rate the quality of your life?
- How would you rate the meaningfulness of your life?
- Disagree/Agree: I am doing exactly what I have always wanted to do.

In general, most folks are happy with who they are and what they are doing in life.

In a broad sense, thinking style is behind much of the differences between the sexes. In fact, the Herrmann people tell me that their research indicates that most first marriages are between people who have directly opposite thinking styles. It is thought that we are initially attracted to partners who are different as they fill in the gaps in our own thinking styles. For many, this makes for rewarding lifelong relationships.

However, the uniqueness can wear on individuals' nerves, and unless the differences are recognized and regarded with respect, those charming differences can soon become huge annoyances. The high emotions of an individual or one's intense logical analysis of every detail can soon drive a marriage to divorce.

Interestingly, the Herrmann folks say that when people marry for the second time, they tend to invert and marry individuals with styles just like theirs.

Maximizing Productivity for Right and Left Brains

Everyone can be equally effective at creating ideas, but the path to success is different for each thinking style. The following tips provide direction on maximizing your personal effectiveness. Read all the tips. Understanding the opposite style will make you more sensitive to differences in individuals and help you coach others who are different from you. If you are whole brain in orientation, it's important that you explore both of the other orientations as you exist in both spaces.

Tip 1: Approach Creative Challenges From the Proper Direction.

The two styles of thinking approach idea creation from opposite directions. As the data below indicates, those who lean more left brain tend to be more effective when focused on a structured, realistic premise. Those who are more right brain in orientation utilize a more unstructured and fantasy-focused approach.

Average Ratings

	Left Brain	Right Brain
I am more creative with structured techniques.	5.9	4.2
I am more creative with unstructured techniques.	6.4	8.3
I am more creative with a realistic premise.	7.2	5.2
I am more creative using fantasy.	5.1	7.9

All questions use an 11 point scale: Disagree = 0, Agree = 10.

All results are significant at the 95% confidence level or greater.

This 180° opposite approach can be best explained if we use the Dramatic Difference definition of "relevant yet unexpected" as the goal we seek. Those who are more logical left brain in orientation are more comfortable starting from a relevant and grounded orientation and expanding out to the unexpected.

Those who are more radical right brain in orientation find it more effective to start from the unexpected and unstructured and move to practical relevance.

If you're more left brain oriented, this means you should start your creative efforts from the facts and data associated with the situation. However, this alone is not enough. You need to recognize that opening yourself up is necessary to create ideas that offer a true point of difference. Practical plans are of no value if they are fundamentally the same old stuff simply served up in a new way. **Don't let yourself become the builder of practical yet boring ideas.**

If you're more right brain oriented, this means that you should start your creative efforts from the big-picture, no-constraints orientation. However, you should also recognize that this is not enough. Your job is not complete when you have a big thought. You must take responsibility for defining the details that are required for profitable business success. Dreams will stay dreams until they are given strategic and executional discipline. Don't let yourself become a builder of ideas that become unfulfilled fantasies.

Tip 2: Leverage the Type of Stimulus That Is Most Comfortable to You.
There are natural preferences for each kind of thinking style. Those who are of the left brain style find comfort in using stimuli that are related to the challenge. Those of the right brain style feel constrained when dealing with the reality of related stimuli. Their clear preference is to start with a stimulus that is unrelated to the challenge and work it until they discover a big, bold idea that is a true original.

Average Ratings

	Left Brain	Right Brain
I am more creative using related stimuli.	7.7	5.4
I am more creative with unrelated stimuli.	5.6	8.4

All questions use an 11 point scale: Disagree = 0, Agree = 10.

All results are significant at the 95% confidence level or greater.

If you are the left brain type, this means focusing on the Homeward Trail sorts of exercises. Build your confidence and skill here before moving on to the unrelated Borrowing Brilliance approach.

If you are the right brain type, it means the opposite. Let your mind run with unrelated Borrowing Brilliance stimuli. Use the laws of Marketing Physics to provide personal discipline. Having gained confidence in your ability to bring relevance to your visions, you can learn how to leverage the power of using related stimuli.

Tip 3: Leverage the Energy of Right Brain Types as a Source of Energy for Change.
Each brain style has very distinctive strengths. As the direct adjective pairs below indicate, right brain thinkers can be leveraged as an energy source for change. These are the nonconformists, dissenters and rebels. Against all odds, they will help develop the momentum to cause great things to happen.

Left Brain	Right Brain
Cautious	Adventurous
Common sense	Big dreams
Silent supporter	Cheerleader
Rule maker	Rule breaker
Conservative	Liberal
Predictable	Spontaneous

If you have left brain traits, recognize that your practicality and cautiousness could cause you to go the way of the dinosaur; that is, you could become extinct! Wake up and smell the coffee. The natural way is growth. You need to take a few risks here and there if you are to make a real name for yourself in the world. The laws of Marketing Physics can be your greatest resource in this challenge. The three laws transform random chance into a disciplined effort where risk is manageable.

If you find it difficult to gain the momentum to change, get a right brain partner or trusted business advisor, a person who is *not like you*. Use that associate as an energy source to fuel change.

If you have right brain traits, recognize your gift of spirit. You are the energy that inspires big things to happen. In many cases, you are the spark that leads an entrepreneur to leave the work-for-a-boss world and start her own business. You must lead the need for change. Without your spirit of adventure, nothing new will ever occur.

Don't despair when the left brains don't stand and cheer with you. It may amaze you to know they're often highly supportive of your emotional energy; they just don't show it. You have an important role in the evolution of your business. You are the spark that sets off the chain reaction of growth. If in doubt, take action! Now! As the saying goes, it is always easier to ask forgiveness than to seek approval.

Tip 4: Understand That Left Brains Are the Discipline That Transform "Ideas" Into Reality.

Those of a left brain orientation turn dreams into reality. They are the doers, the planners, the disciplined idea builders who turn the sparks of an idea into an enduring reality. Here are more adjective pairs that confirm this statement.

Left Brain	Right Brain
Critical	Forgiving
Planner	Dreamer
Rational	Emotional
Logical	Visionary
Process oriented	People-oriented
Disciplined	Free-spirited
Lead with head	Lead with heart
Think before talking	Talk before thinking
Idea realist/builder	Idea dreamer
Perspective	Passion
Think	Talk
Ready, aim, fire	Fire, aim, ready

"How you see yourself" adjective pairs. Differences significant at 95% confidence level.

If you are left brain skilled, recognize that you have a responsibility to provide leadership in the translation of visions into practical reality. Do not wait for the right brain types to make their ideas practical. It may never happen. Take their ideas and work them, enhance them, modify them until you discover a way to turn them into practical reality.

If you are right brain skilled, recognize that dreams are nice but they won't pay the bills. Never whine about how "your idea is being killed." For your dreams to become reality, they will need to be modified. When the left brainers start changing to enhance feasibility, defend with all your might the Overt Benefit, Real Reason to Believe and Dramatic Difference. All else is optional. If you find it difficult turning your ideas into practical realities, get an opposite-oriented partner or trusted business advisor. Find the most logical, rational, results-oriented left brainer you can. Inspire that person and get out of his way. Continuous change and creativity are huge barriers to the production and operation of a profitable factory.

Tip 5: Find Common Ground for All Styles.

As you can see, each thinking style has a reason for existence. Neither is more or less important than the other. Instead of having war with each other, use the laws of Marketing Physics as your common ground. Left brainers, use Marketing Physics as a way to find courage as you move to uncharted areas. Right brainers, use Marketing Physics as a way to lend discipline to your imagination.

The best way to find common ground is to use the power of the written word. Don't allow right brainers to preach with emotion or left brainers to debate with logic. Focus your energy into transforming your unique abilities onto the written page.

Our research indicates that on average, both left and right brain individuals have the same level of confidence in their ability to write. However, the kind of writing and the way they approach it are very different.

Average Ratings

	Left Brain	Right Brain
I enjoy writing that is highly precise.	7.0	3.0
My writing is more playful than serious.	3.7	6.1
I write to help make logical decisions.	5.7	4.1
I write to inspire and make people feel good.	5.8	8.1
I need a clear picture of what I want to say before writing.	6.2	4.0
Writing is more about emotions than process.	4.1	6.1

All questions use an 11 point scale: Disagree = 0, Agree = 10.

All results are significant at the 95% confidence level or greater.

When you work together, there is great potential for articulating disciplined ideas that generate significant customer excitement. Left brainers have the ability to define with precision. Right brainers have the ability to breathe life into the prose. To make the process efficient, I suggest the following process.

Step 1 Talk for a few moments about the ideas you have.

Step 2 Individually translate your thoughts into written words.

Step 3 Swap what you've written and aggressively edit each other's work.

Step 4 With an open mind talk about what you each wrote and rewrote. Use as a guide to your discussion the three laws of Marketing Physics: Overt Benefit, Real Reason to Believe and Dramatic Difference.

When writing with my longtime creative partner David

Wecker, this is the approach we use. When writing by myself, I make it a point to first lay in the left brain logic and discipline then give the writing a rest then come back and rewrite from the more inspirational right brain perspective.

Writing in a whole brain fashion is not dissimilar to building a house. First, you need to build a sturdy, left brain foundation. Then you must add the right brain-inspired finishing craftsmanship. In the end the house is both strong and beautiful.

Practical Tactic:
Mixing Stimuli Using 666

The differences between thinking styles can be a huge challenge. My all-time favorite technique for creating ideas is called 666. I like it because it works. I also like it because it engages both sides of my brain. The 666 technique is an easy way to leverage both related and unrelated stimuli.

The 666 method allows you to force-associate dimensions of your challenge in patterns and pairs you would not normally consider. Because of the technique's gamelike nature, it provides a safe common ground for right brain and left brain individuals to work together using both related and unrelated stimuli.

It's called 666 in irreverent recognition of my ten years working at Procter & Gamble. I realize this number is thought to have some evil connotations. P&G has been the subject of rumors it was evil because the corporate logo supposedly had the number 666 hidden in it. I can say without a doubt that while not all P&G managers are angels, none that I ever met is truly a devil. So with apologies to those who find the name offensive, here's how it works.

Step 1 As with all Capitalist Creativity efforts, define clearly what your objective is.

Step 2 Looking at your objective, identify two key dimensions associated with your task.
Step 3 Quickly list six options for each of the two dimensions.

Step 4 Select one of the following unrelated categories as a third category. Or if you wish, create your own third category.

Sensory	Trends
1. Smell it	1. Everyone's getting older
2. Taste it	2. Customers want personalization
3. Feel it	3. Instant information
4. Touch it	4. Miniaturization
5. Hear it	5. It's a global economy
6. See it	6. Experiences rule

Zoo Time	Moods
1. Kangaroos hop	1. Happy
2. Snakes slither	2. Sad
3. Caterpillars transform	3. Guilty
4. Lions roar	4. Angry
5. Cheetahs fly	5. Excited
6. Ants dig	6. Anxious

Types of Movies	Continents
1. Comedy	1. Antarctica
2. Drama	2. Australia
3. Horror	3. South America
4. Action	4. Europe
5. Historical	5. North America
6. Western	6. Asia

Holiday Cheer	Science Stuff
1. Christmas	1. Evolution
2. Thanksgiving	2. Biology
3. Halloween	3. Nuclear
4. Passover	4. Experiment
5. April Fools' Day	5. Photosynthesis
6. Valentine's Day	6. Cellular level

Words That Rhyme With June	Colors
1. Balloon	1. Black
2. Noon	2. Royal purple
3. Cartoon	3. Pure white
4. Spoon	4. Green
5. Cancun	5. Red, red, red

6. Prune	6. Brilliant yellow

Risks	Words That Begin With G
1. Skydiving	1. Grapefruit
2. Speeding	2. Grandma
3. Scuba diving	3. Gold
4. Skateboarding	4. Gingerbread
5. Bungee jumping	5. Green
6. Space travel	6. Grass

Step 5 Write your three lists on one sheet, and roll a die three times to select one item from each list. Write the three items on separate corners of your idea creation sheet, and cross them out from the lists.

Step 6 As before, free associate in the corners then smash-associate the thinking in the center of the page using one, two or three of the stimulus phrases as fuel for your imagination.

Note, the way this is designed, two of the selections will be related stimuli. The third selection will be to varying degrees unrelated to your challenge. This mixture of thoughts will help shake your brain into finding new patterns of thought.

Step 7 When ideas start to slow, roll the die again and select three more items from the list. Repeat steps five and six. If you roll a duplicate number in a column simply move to the next higher number. Continue until you have used four or more of the items from each column.

Here is an example of how to apply 666 to your objective.

If your mission is to grow sales for your fine furniture repair business, you might list the following dimensions, options for each and unrelated third category.

Customer Segments	Marketing Resources	Words that Begin with G
1. Loyal customers	1. Direct mail	1. Grapefruit
2. Customers out of our area	2. Current customer loyalty	2. Grandma
3. Former customers	3. Sales force	3. Gold
4. New to town	4. Trade shows	4. Gingerbread

| 5. Rich people | 5. Sign out front | 5. Green |
| 6. Middle class families | 6. Community groups | 6. Grass |

A random role of three dice identified 4, 3, 5

| 4. New to town | 3. Sales Force | 5. Green |

Multiply the stimuli:

New to Town
- Movers
- Changed jobs
- Don't know where to go

Sales Force
- Limited time . . . it's just me
- Whom do I know

Green
- Money
- Lawns
- Green hills
- Kermit the Frog

You'll note how the other lists had an influence on how all the stimuli became expanded. You'll also notice how elements of feasibility worked their way into the free associations on sales force.

Working with these stimulus statements, the following ideas were developed.

Rapid Repair: Align with moving companies or insurance companies to make repairs of injured furniture within forty-eight hours of moving into the home.

Fine Woodwork: Expand business to include repair and replacement of wood trim in homes. Before people move into a home they might be interested in repairs. Maybe even focus exclusively on staircases-railings and steps.

Kids' Classes: Align with groups such as Cub Scouts, Boy Scouts, Girl Scouts to offer Saturday classes to teach woodworking.

Santa's Repair Shop: Market services as creating new gifts through the repair of "family treasures."

Hint: The items you select are intended to be fuel for new ideas. They are not meant to simply become one sentence. Done properly, each stimulus sets off a chain reaction of ideas.

At the Eureka! Ranch, we use giant bulletin boards for this exercise. On the boards, we'll sometimes pin up pictures of potential customers or even research reports to use as stimuli.

Quick Process Summary on Leveraging Diversity

1. The greater the diversity, the greater the breadth and depth of thinking.
2. Use these great sources to look for diversity.
   - Rookies: Those new to the company have the freshest perspective.
   - Workers: Frontline people have a unique understanding of customers.
   - Retired Workers: Retirement provides a unique perspective and honesty.
3. Thinking styles are a source of diversity.
   - They impact how we approach challenges.
   - They impact the best way for us to create ideas.
4. Left brainers are logical.
   - They are most effective working with related stimuli.
   - They take ideas that are relevant and add unexpectedness.
5. Right brainers are radical.
   - They are most effective working with unrelated stimuli.
   - They take ideas that are unexpected and add discipline.
6. Whole brainers have dual strengths.
   - They have the ability to access both thinking styles if they push themselves.

Final Thoughts on Leveraging Diversity

To leverage diversity, we must go beyond tolerance of others and drive ourselves to fully understand the viewpoints of others. The greater the diversity of our experiences in the world of business and in life, the greater the wealth of experiences we have to draw upon as we seek new ideas.

We challenge our children to explore new experiences. We need to similarly challenge ourselves as adults. When we are exposed to new experiences, we stretch our brains. As my good friend and fellow innovation author Chic Thompson says, when you blow up a balloon with air, even when the air leaves it never returns to the same size. So, too, when you expand your true understanding of diverse perspectives, your brain will never be the same.

The goal of teaching you about thinking styles is not to encourage you to change. Rather, it's to help you make the best use of who and what you are now.

Some will say I should instead focus on encouraging everyone to become whole brained. I don't believe that's practical. Sure, a creative evangelist may be able to create a temporary change in the thinking style of a forty-year-old engineer with twenty years of experience. That's fine in theory. But what happens when the pressure is on? When management, the marketplace or competition requires bold, original thought, will our engineer listen to the evangelist or will he be more inclined to revert to his natural state of mind? I think the odds are good he will do the latter. Thus, my focus is to help you use the strengths you have to make a difference right now.

A few years ago, I spent an evening with the famous venture capitalist Arthur Lipper III. It was an inspiring and memorable evening. Arthur is a veteran of the real world of new business start-ups. In his book *Thriving Up and Down the Free Market Food Chain*, he explained his view of what's needed for success.

Successful entrepreneurs, in strange and wonderful ways, combine right-brain dominance, producing the necessary creativity, and left-brain needs of discipline and focus. Truly successful entrepreneurs combine the features of Pablo Picasso and General George Patton.

Friends, as Ben Franklin said over two hundred years ago, "We must all hang together, or most assuredly we will all hang separately." The time to open your mind is now. If you open your ears and listen, there is a high probability you will be amazed at what you will discover.

CHAPTER 12

Go For It! Turning Thoughts Into Reality

You have learned how to use the power of stimuli and diversity to fuel your ability to create ideas. In the last of the three laws, you learn how to face your fears and win against them. In addition to inspiration, this chapter features practical, tactical techniques for tangibly reducing the impact fear has on your actions.

Third Law of Capitalist Creativity: Face Fears

Your potential to achieve is limited only by the level of your fears.

The depth of stimuli and the breadth of diversity fuel your ability to imagine new ideas. But they come alive only in proportion to the extent that you are able to face your fears. Fear directly destroys your ability to create and craft new ideas.

For an idea to amount to anything, it has to be made into something and put into action. Ben Franklin spoke of this challenge: "Well done is better than well said."

In Eureka! Inventing sessions, we track the level of fear through responses to the simple statement "For whatever reason I did not say all the ideas that came to mind." We believe that not giving voice to your ideas is the first indicator that fear is taking root. The data shows that as fear increases, creative productivity declines.

What this means is that at even this early stage of simply discussing ideas, fear has an impact. When we have "full-body fear," such as what takes root when a business is going through tough times, we lose the ability to recognize the kinds of opportunities that can inspire genuine growth. **If people can't even talk about ideas, there is little to no chance they can take action on the**

Number of Practical Ideas Invented	
High Fear	30.9
Medium Fear	33.7
Low Fear	42.2

kind of dramatically different ideas necessary to make a tangible difference.

Everyone has seen a highly successful idea in the marketplace that she's thought of before. However, thinking isn't doing. You don't get any money in your cash register for thinking of ideas (unless you're in my business, where that is our key deliverable). You only get money when you give voice to the whispers of your imagination and take action on them!

What is most concerning about the research results above is that they were gathered at the Eureka! Ranch during actual client projects. And the ranch is supposed to be a "safe haven" for original thinking. It's a specially designed environment where clients work with an equal number of specially trained Eureka! Ranch Trained Brains. The staff, process and environment are carefully designed to ignite a pioneering attitude among client participants.

If we can detect this kind of impact from fear during inventing sessions at the Eureka! Ranch, the impact beyond the ranch must be even greater. Qualitative feedback from corporate clients indicates it could be greater by a factor of ten or more. It's conceivable, then, that fear could be reducing the gross idea output of some organizations to a mere 10% of their respective potentials.

In the world of small businesses, the stakes are even higher.

Instead of risking faceless shareholders' money, we're gambling with our own cash. Success with an initiative means we can afford a family vacation. Failure means . . . well, let's not focus on the cost of failure while talking about courage.

Recall the validated equation presented earlier. Fear truly does have a direct neutralizing effect. **To double your number of bottom-line ideas, you can either double your production or cut your fear in half. The impact is the same.**

$$\text{\# of Quality Ideas} = \frac{\text{Stimuli} \; \text{Diversity}}{\text{Fear}}$$

Fear is part of the human condition. *The New York Times Magazine* (February 11, 2001) featured an article, "Exuberance is Rational," on Richard Thaler of the University of Chicago Graduate School of Business. Thaler is considered one of the world's most progressive and enlightened economists. In the interview he said, "Most people are 'loss averse' meaning they experience more pain from losses than pleasure from gains."

Thaler went on to give the following example he'd discovered from basketball. He looked at basketball games in which a team was behind by two points and there was time for just one more shot. In this situation, a three-point shot is successful 33% of the time. A two-point shot succeeds 50% of the time. However, if the two-point shot goes in, the team must play overtime, in which there is again a 50% chance of winning. Thus, to win the game by taking a two-point shot initially, the team must both make the two-point shot and win overtime. If we do the statistics—50% probability of making the first shot times 50% probability of winning in overtime—the team that takes the two-point shot has only a net 25% chance of winning.

Bottom line, going for the two-point shot provides a net 25% chance of winning the game. Going for the three-point shot gives a 33% chance of winning the game. Thaler explains, "Still most coaches go for two. Why? Because it lowers the risk of sudden loss. Coaches, like the rest of us, do more to avoid losing than they do to win."

It's human nature for us to do more to avoid losing than to win. In many cases, "fear dragons" control us to such an extent that we consciously make bad decisions despite knowing better.

This contradiction in the human spirit is the reason that living a life based on principles, be they from the Bible, Stephen Covey, or the pages of this book, is so valuable when making business decisions. When we live principled lives, we have shields of protection against the fear dragons that want to control our destinies.

We All Have Fear Cancers

Fear is a cancer that takes root in your spirit often without notice. In time it grows and multiplies until before you know it you are faced with a life-threatening situation.

When we look closely at our research data from clients, it becomes clear that fear left unchecked becomes an endless loop.

1. The greater the fear, the less ideas are spoken.
2. The less ideas are spoken, the less ideas are realized.
3. The less ideas are realized, the greater the fear.
4. Go back to 1.

We must break this cycle!

We all have fear cancers within us. You have fear. I have fear. If you are alive, stretching and growing, you have fear. As Mark Twain said, "Courage is resistance to fear, mastery of fear—not absence of fear."

It is not possible to eliminate fear. All we can do is expose our fears to the light of day and confront them. Fear is about uncertainty. And life is uncertain. Life is a collection of probabilities. And there is no such thing as a 0% or 100% probability.

Fear is fundamental to anyone with the courage to be a pioneer in any area. At one level, fear is a good thing, as it causes us to pay attention to details that can be the difference between success and failure. When fear grows from being an internal system of checks and balances into taking control of our actions, it becomes life threatening.

Once you let fear take root, it can assail you from a thousand different places. Fear comes in a vast range of varieties and incarnations. Some fears come from within; others are inflicted on us by circumstances or people around us. There's a fear of failure. A fear of being laughed at. A fear of being politically incorrect. A fear of saying something someone will think is stupid. A fear of the unknown. A fear of change.

Fear is greatest when things are going badly. And this is just the time when courage is most needed. In "The Effects of Organizational and Decision-Maker Factors on New Product Risk Taking," a study reported in the *Journal of Product Innovation Management* (J. Mullins, D. Forlani and C. Walker, 1999, Vol. 16)), the authors observed that our most recent success rates predicted future risk taking. Businesspeople who had recently been successful were found to be significantly more likely to take a future risk. Conversely, those who had recently failed were dramatically more risk adverse.

The gravitational force of fear is contradictory to our needs. When times are good, fear is low, yet we don't have as great a need for it. When times are bad, fear is high, just when we need courage to take bold actions to correct the business.

When you're wrapped up in fear, whether consciously or unconsciously, you don't speak your mind. You don't take a stand. You accept standards of quality that you know are substandard. And once you've allowed your standards to slide, you are on a path to self-destruction. Said Ben Franklin, "It's easier to suppress the first desire than all those that follow."

How You Face Fears Is Your Choice

In business and in life, you can take the well-traveled path or you can blaze your own trail. But to be a true trailblazer—one who creates history instead of one who sits back and waits for it to be made into a movie—takes courage.

I wrote an entire book on this subject called *Making the Courage Connection*. In retrospect, the title was a huge mistake. Talking about courage put a "positive spin" on the concept of fear. It softened the edge off what is socially difficult to speak of.

Following Marketing Physics and Capitalist Creativity training at the Ranch, numerous managers have told me that they have no fear. I tell them to remember that thought for the next few days. **You cannot judge your fear when not facing a dangerous decision.** It's common that twenty-four hours later, when clients are faced with bold and brash ideas, they find fear gripping them. As one client said recently: "Doug, I didn't think I had any fears, but now that I am faced with having to commit to taking actions on dramatically different ideas, I realize I'm filled with fear."

It's easy to sit on the sidelines of life and say you're brave. It's another thing to be on the front line in the face of battle and make what you perceive to be a life-threatening decision.

The first step toward confronting fear is to recognize its very real existence. Recognize that when you rationalize why you can't do this or that, you are actually covering your fears. Left brain types are particularly good at finding logical, rational arguments to help hide the real issue: They're scared of taking action.

We find comfort in keeping things the same. When we take action, any action, there is a level of uncertainty. The sad truth is that the only way to generate significant growth in your business is to change. And change requires letting go of where you are and daring to try something new.

So What to Do About It

Courage to confront fear must come from within you. That said, here are some simple tactics for helping you in your battle.

Fear Battle Tactic 1: Do the Right Thing.

It could very well be that this tactic provides the one and only way to truly face your fears. When you are taking action on the right things in the right way, fear has no chance of taking root.

And the singular best way to discover if your proposed action is "right" is to examine it in the context of the three laws of Marketing Physics, as discussed earlier. When your efforts are focused first and foremost on the customer-offering Overt Benefits, Real Reasons to Believe and Dramatic Differences—you truly know that the odds of success are on your side.

Truth has a power that transcends all fears. Truth and a sense of right caused Rosa Parks to refuse to give up her seat to a white man on a bus in Montgomery, Alabama. Truth and a sense of right caused patriots to toss King George's tea into Boston Harbor. Truth and a sense of right gave Nelson Mandela the courage to stand up against apartheid and be imprisoned for twenty-eight years.

The power of truth is a concept that even contemporary leaders preach.

> When we have truth on our side, there is a straight-forwardness, a confidence that comes with it.
>
> *Dalai Lama*

> This much I know is true: The companies that succeed will be the ones that make their ideas real and that stand for what is true.
>
> *Scott McNealy, Chairman and CEO, Sun Microsystems*

> The big losers in the future are going to be the companies that sell mediocre products and services expertly.
>
> In the old world, you could fool customers through great advertising and great marketing and that isn't going to work anymore.
>
> *Jeff Bezos, Founder and Chairman, Amazon.com*

> As long as I have known the world I have observed that wrong is always growing more wrong, till there is no bearing, and that right, however opposed, comes right at last.
>
> *Ben Franklin*

One way of finding the courage to seek out change is to involve yourself in a pursuit in which you truly believe. If you're passionate about your cause, you're more inclined to take risks on its behalf. You're more inclined to push boundaries.

A story about my daughter, Kristyn, further illustrates the

point. When she was ten, her mother enrolled her in a karate class. Kristyn was the only girl in a class full of boys. Since she was the "odd man out," she had to put up with a good deal of teasing.

At the end of the session, there was a sort of karate recital for parents. At one point during the program, the students were called on to break a board with a kick. The first boy broke the board. The second and the third tried but failed. Then it was Kristyn's turn. There was some snickering from the boys as she took her place on the mat, assumed the stance and focused on the board.

Then she got that look on her face. I've seen that same look on her mother's face. Kristyn raised her leg, lashing out with a cobra-like kick that split the board in two. At that moment, the room became quiet. The snickering stopped. It's not easy to snicker when your mouth is hanging open.

Afterward, I asked Kristyn what she'd been thinking. Boys who were much larger than she is hadn't been able to break the board. She said, "You know girls can do anything boys can do, right? Well, I had to prove it to those boys."

It boiled down to Kristyn's belief that she was standing up for the entire female gender. In her mind, all girls and women were on her side. She had the power of being right. And that all added up to a personal commitment and passion. The board didn't stand a chance.

When you believe, you'll find intense passion and courage. It doesn't matter what you're doing. In business, if you honestly offer your customers an Overt Benefit, a Real Reason to Believe and a Dramatic Difference, you're offering value. You're offering something that your customers can put to good use. Courage and passion become your allies, because when you do the right things in the right way, it's easy to drum up the courage to move forward, speak out and make a difference in the world.

The truth is, we almost always know what we should do. In almost any situation, our internal compasses point to the right thing to do. We may even believe we're going to go ahead and do the right thing. But if we've failed to drive away fear, it will shut us down every time. We let our fears short-circuit our own abilities, our potentials and our lives. We prevent ourselves from being what our inner nature would direct us to be.

When you feel it happening to you, listen to the voice inside you, the one urging you to do the right thing. Listen to its protests and act on them.

Think Now . . .

Are you offering your customers an Overt Benefit? If not, why not?

Are you offering your customers a Dramatic Difference? If not, why not?

What is the right thing to do for your customers?

Have you written your concept? **The written word is the best defense against floating fears.**

Fear Battle Tactic 2: Use Pain to Motivate Gain.

If the pursuit of truth does not motivate you to change, the only other option is to face the reality of pain. This is not the most enjoyable means for finding the courage to change, but it is highly effective.

It's a matter of lesser pain. When your business hits the absolute rock bottom, the pain of change all of a sudden feels far less unbearable than continuing the current path.

The greater the business urgency the more effective a team is at articulating and creating big, bold ideas. Surveys conducted with clients prior to attending the Ranch show a direct relationship ($r = .498$, 99% confidence level) between participants' feelings of "urgency towards taking action" and their brainstorming effectiveness. In addition, perception of urgency also correlates with participants' perceptions of their companies' "courage to take action" ($r = .507$, 99% confidence level). When we feel great pressure and urgency to do something—now—it is a lot easier to find the courage to create something bold.

The impact of personal pressure on delivering results can also be seen in a survey we conducted with innovation experts. Fully 68% felt they are more creative when they face a deadline.

It's a simple matter to change when business is bad. Our challenge is to learn to accept change when business is good, before the natural cycle of rise and fall takes its next turn. To accomplish this, we must follow the advice of Picasso: "The first act of creation is often an act of destruction." To create a sense of urgency, it helps if we can create or inspire within ourselves a healthy amount of dissatisfaction with the established way of thinking.

Generating a healthy disrespect for authorities is easy when we are just starting in a business. The challenge is how to create urgency when we are already in a business, feeling a little comfortable and facing no urgent threats. Looking toward the future world of changes with great clarity can inspire change. Reading the writings of any of the popular "business trend" experts can inspire fear-many make a living declaring that the sky is falling.

Alternatively, you can just be honest with yourself and look back on your own life. Look back to what you were doing six months ago. Have you grown? Are you smarter? If not, it's time to take action, because the natural way of any living thing is growth. If a tree is not growing, it is dying.

As mentioned earlier, any truly innovative initiative is going to cause major chaos and turbulence to someone, somewhere. As the American writer Oscar Wilde once said, "An idea that is not dangerous is unworthy to be called an idea at all." Anyone who opposes your concepts is inevitably one who represents the status quo that you are trying to upset.

Recently, after reviewing some particularly radical concepts, the top-ranking client made a statement that was remarkable in his honesty: "I'm feeling nervous . . . feeling that we're talking about things that we shouldn't be talking about." I asked him if that was OK. "It's fine," he replied. "It's just something I've never felt in my fifteen-year corporate career at the company."

Probably the greatest barrier to change is success. When all is good, it is easy to fall into comfortable complacency. I worked recently with a company that within the past two years had become number one in its industry by being bold. Sadly, once the business achieved success, the managers lost their passion and courage. Their primary focus became "not messing up," instead of continuing on the path of bold innovation that carried them to leadership.

Acceptance of who we are and how we're doing also infects us if business is declining. I worked with a client who had a product that, once upon a time, was a huge success. But by the time she came to me, the product had barely survived ten straight years of continuous sales declines.

The client asked me for ideas. She told me she wanted something bold, something even a bit . . . wild and crazy. So with passion and diligence, we created a portfolio of ideas far removed from anything she had done before.

She came back and said, "Doug, I don't think you understand

how we run our business."

The way I see it, my clients pay me to tell them the truth, painful as it may be. So I replied that with ten years of declines, what did she know about running a business?

To which she huffed, "Well, you know, Doug, it could have been worse."

It could have been worse? *It could have been worse?*

Whom was she trying to fool? What has happened to us to make us believe that ten years of sales declines are acceptable? What cosmic forces conspire to lead an individual to admit that, "OK, business isn't all that hot—but on the plus side, I'm no dumber than my predecessors." She made it clear she wasn't willing to learn. Even with her abysmal sales record, she was unwilling to give up what was familiar. She was unwilling to change.

Not that it's an easy lesson to learn. Another client from a Fortune 50 company asked for help in defining the "reason for being" for a multimillion-dollar division. He wanted what in business circles is known as a fundamental strategic mission.

We conducted a Eureka! session. The client and his group returned to their East Coast headquarters. Four weeks later, he called to say the vision we'd crafted had been successfully sold to the president, the CEO and the board of directors.

I was amazed. How had he managed to sell the strategy to the organization in such a short time?

Somewhat sheepishly, he told me I was under the wrong impression. It hadn't really been a month. It was more like thirteen months.

"The first twelve months we spent grappling with the realization that where we were wasn't working," he said. "Once we came to grips with the fact we needed to change, the change came easy."

It's an everyday truth: We have to be willing to leave where we are before we can experience real change. As Franklin said in the 1745 edition of *Poor Richard's Almanack*, "no gains without pains."

Think about your business. After having optimized your Overt Benefit and Real Reason to Believe, have you been honest with yourself? Is your proposition truly something exciting or could you, should you start a program to reinvent yourself?

Think about your situation. Are you happy with where you are? Has your business fulfilled your true dreams? Have you set goals that stretch your capabilities? Or have you set modest, conservative, same-old-stuff objectives that make no waves.

Fear Battle Tactic 3: Try, Try, Try Your Way to Courage.

If you want to find courage to succeed, increase your idea failure rate by a factor of ten.

The more ideas you consider, craft and reject, the greater your courage will be to pursue ideas that offer real potential. Ben Franklin spoke of the value of never giving up: "It is true that there is much to be done, and perhaps, you are weak-handed; but stick to it steadily, and you will see great effects; for constant dripping wears away stones; and by diligence and patience, the mouse ate in two the cable; and little strokes fell great oaks."

A clear measure of a person's or a corporate culture's courage is the number of failures. Show me a person who never fails, and I'll show you a person who isn't living life to the fullest, someone who is not fully engaged to his potential.

You cannot score in hockey or basketball if you don't take shots. So, too, in business you cannot create real change unless you try something truly different. Recently I met with a three-billion-dollar-a-year company that leads its category. A review of the business's history found that over the past ten years, it has conducted serious testing on only thirty new ideas a year. Any wonder they have virtually no new products? To grow a three-billion-dollar-a-year company, management should be looking at three hundred if not three thousand new product ideas a year.

Now think of your situation. How many ideas for new marketing campaigns, new products or services have you written on a piece of paper or actually tried? Remember, thinking doesn't count as really trying. Thinking is not doing. If you're like most businesspeople, the number of real ideas considered over the past year, five years or ten years will be embarrassingly small.

For a small business, not trying new ideas means you have given up your primary competitive advantage versus larger companies. Momentum in the marketplace is created in the same way that it's defined in physics books. Momentum equals mass times velocity.

In other words, you can be big and massive, spending tons of money and having tons of people work for you, or you can be fast and nimble and focus on velocity. There are no other options. It's

MOMENTUM = Mass X Velocity

understandable when a big company, with meetings, committees and layers of management is unable to think and test ideas. However, it is inexcusable for a nimble entrepreneur to not do so.

When you take a shot on new ideas, your successes and, most importantly, your failures offer you a resource of strength that provides fortitude when you face real adversity. One of the greatest gifts of my trip to the North Pole was the day we traveled in a near total whiteout. I hurt my knee that day, and with each step it felt like a knife was being twisted and poked into me. With the wind whipping at us directly from the north and no ability to see up from down, we trudged on. At one point, the whiteout became so strong I literally had to get on my hands and knees to find the trail of the team in front of us.

That day was one of those proverbial character-building moments. Or as Arctic explorer and our guide Paul Schurke calls them "a gift from the high Arctic." I survived. And today when things seem bad, I turn back to that day and realize that I've faced much worse in my life. From that day I gain strength. So, too, from your failures do you gain strength.

Another advantage of crafting lots of ideas is you expand your horizons of understanding. The journey of exploring new ideas opens your mind to new thoughts. Just as climbing a mountain range provides a new view to the world beyond, the act of writing and defining new ideas opens you to new opportunities.

Exploring lots of ideas is not without challenges. As Charles Schwab said in an interview for a *Fortune* article, "The World's Most Acclaimed Companies" (October 2, 2000), "To introduce new ideas, you have to be able to take a lot of ridicule."

Consider the events of your own life over the previous six months, the previous year. How many times have you failed spectacularly? If you run out of fingers keeping count, congratulations! You have the courage to take risks, which means you have the courage to grow.

History is clear on the virtues and value of taking risks. Consider the sport of baseball. From Babe Ruth to Reggie Jackson to Sammy Sosa and Mark McGwire, the players who slug the most home runs have always been the ones with the most whiffs. In 1998, Sosa and McGwire both broke Babe Ruth's record for home runs in a year. They also were number 1 and number 4, respectively, for highest number of strikeouts that year. It's yet another illustration that it takes courage to be great. It takes a willingness to strike out. Babe Ruth himself once said, "Every strike brings me closer to the next home run."

Think about it. A baseball player is considered to be great if he bats around .300. In other words, if he fails only twice for each success, he's a superstar.

So what about you? Does the prospect of failing keep you from trying? Are you willing to let even one failure happen? Or is there something that prevents you from stepping up to the plate? If so, what is it? What steps can you take to remove the obstacle?

What's the alternative? Consider this: In a Cornell University study, senior citizens were asked to describe their greatest regrets. Some 75% of the respondents expressed more regret for actions that weren't taken as opposed to actions that were taken, even those that turned out badly.

So just do it. Take that job offer. Raise your hand in protest. Go out on that blind date. If it turns out badly, time will heal the pain. On the other hand, if you turn down the job or keep your mouth shut or tell that blind date thanks but no thanks, you'll never know. No amount of time will keep you from wondering what might have been. And when you're sitting there in your rocking chair at the nursing home, you'll look back on a lifetime of woulda, coulda, shoulda.

Often you don't know how things would have turned out. However, sometimes the alternative path becomes very clear. You read in the paper of the success of the company you almost went with. You meet the guy you turned down for a date in high school. Or even more commonly, the competition to your company goes to market with an idea that you had but didn't pursue.

Watching the success of what could have been ours causes far greater pain than any short-term failure could.

Mark Twain knew it: "Twenty years from now, you will be more disappointed by things you didn't try than by the ones you did. So throw off the bowlines. Sail away from the safe harbor. Catch the trade winds in your sails. Explore. Dream. Discover."

We must learn how to commit ourselves. If we stand at a crossroads in the woods looking down a path, we can only see as far as where the path bends. No amount of staring from where we stand can tell us what lies beyond the bend. The only way to see the next horizon is by committing ourselves. It is only by walking down the path and looking around the bend that we can with intelligence decide if it's a path we wish to follow.

At my company, my position on trying is clear. I value success. I value failure. It is the nonaction of standing and staring down the path that drives me crazy.

Fear Battle Tactic 4: Reduce the Cost of Failure and Increase Your Courage.
Our fears are in direct proportion to what is at risk. The greater the cost of failing, the greater our level of fear.

It's easier to be aggressive with change when the cost of failure looms small. In the business world, we can use this truth to our advantage by creating methods for experimentation that accelerate the cycles of failure and success so that, when we do fall short, we fail quickly and inexpensively. It's a matter of creating prototyping systems that allow us to make a little, sell a little and learn a lot.

The first of these systems is examination of the idea through the written word. The act of organizing your thoughts on paper will expose many flaws. This is the true value of business plans. Rare is it that the plan as written becomes the action as taken. The value of the plan lies in the organizing of the thinking.

Ideally your paper prototype starts as a simple set of paragraphs that defines the proposition from a customer's perspective. Following this it becomes a full-blown brochure, direct-mail package or press release that provides greater details that support the core premise.

Rarely would a business fail if at the start the founders wrote a one-page, tri-fold brochure that defined their offering with clarity. When you define your idea with clarity, you have some defense against the forces of fear. Softly defined ideas provide a poor defense against highly defined and often exaggerated fears.

Having written, rewritten and rewritten your idea till it is unquestionably clear, the next stage is to make a "works like" prototype. Works like prototyping is about rapidly and cost efficiently simulating the customer experience. It doesn't have to be pretty or even mass producible. The key is to simulate the end experience so to provide guidance to development and reduce fears.

Jim Davis, the creator of the comic strip *Garfield*, described to me his passion for prototyping: "If we have a truly different idea, the best way to sell it is to help the client visualize it. We'll take our idea, dress it up, draw it, paint it, set it to music and prototype it. Many times, we go to dramatic lengths to demonstrate your ideas. If our clients can see it as we see it, chances are they will embrace it."

If you plan a restaurant, cook your specialty.

If you intend to offer tax preparation, create the forms and processes customers will complete to have their taxes done.

If you intend to have a retail store, create a prototype of the front windows or primary displays. I once coached a corporate team in the creation and execution of a radical new retail concept in a biblical forty days and forty nights. Critical to our success was the rough prototyping of the store concept in a warehouse prior to moving into the actual retail space.

If you intend to offer a software system, find a way to manually execute it. For the first two years of development, the Merwyn Simulated Test Marketing model was broken into a collection of modules that ran in spreadsheets and flat file databases. We used these low-cost systems for prototyping the system with clients and validating the model. Having worked out many of the kinks, we then spent the time and money to build a full relational database that was Web enabled.

In the early days of video on demand at hotels, the prototyping system involved someone slipping a videotape by hand into a VCR that was then switched to connect to the guest's room.

Over the years, I have seen companies successfully conduct ultra-low-cost test markets using vending machines, restaurants, convenience stores and college campuses.

By rapidly executing prototypes, you gain the wisdom the scientist gathers when conducting test and learn experiments. Change is the natural way—in fact, it's the only way to inspire genuine growth. It follows then that to be a success in life or business, we must learn to embrace change with the same energy and enthusiasm most people expend avoiding it.

Winston Churchill said it: "To improve is to change; to be perfect is to change often."

Fear Battle Tactic 5: Manage Your Fears Like Your Stocks.
You can dramatically reduce your fears by managing them like you do your financial investments. Invest your innovation time, effort and resources just as you do your money.

Initially invest in a portfolio of innovation options instead of putting everything behind one concept. Split your portfolio among a range of risk levels from short- to long-term concepts. Split your portfolio between easy-to-execute concepts and concepts for which scientific breakthroughs are required.

I advise clients to initially pursue the development of three ideas. When a clear winner reveals itself, reallocate all resources on the winner and either discontinue or put on hold the remaining concepts. This approach increases confidence, as you are able to adjust your level of investment as you learn valuable information about true feasibility and profitability.

The original concept for this system came from a client experience ten years ago. A CEO of a leading corporation asked me to interview the leaders of his company's last three major new product initiatives over the past seven years, each of which had been a significant failure. He wanted to know what had really happened. I spoke with the various team members, asking what their thoughts had been at the sales meeting where their initiative was introduced. Each declared that they pretty much knew their idea would fall short of objectives.

When asked the obvious question of why they continued forward despite having reservations, each in different words said, "I figured it was better than doing nothing, and we had no other alternative available to pursue at the time."

In truth, time has shown that going ahead was not better than nothing. The company's financial losses were significant on all three initiatives. Even worse was the cost to the company's collective self-confidence.

We usually know in our heart of hearts what is right and what is wrong. However, when we feel backed into a corner, we can take actions that in another situation we would usually avoid. Having the same team initially pursue three initiatives prevents them from feeling backed into a corner and thus making a decision that will later be regretted.

Learning to kill an idea may be as valuable a skill as learning to hold the course in the face of great obstacles. People who truly pursue new ideas with passion will have moments when they suddenly realize that they have no chance of success. These are the times when great courage and great leadership is called for. As Ralph Waldo Emerson said once, "A foolish consistency is the hobgoblin of little minds."

Fear Battle Tactic 6: Play Probabilities Not Certainties.

Much of the fear we face is driven by a misguided attempt to find certainty in an uncertain world. There is no such thing as guaranteed success or failure. Life is about probabilities. When you learn to become comfortable with viewing the success or failure of an idea as a probability of success, you increase your comfort with change.

Depending on our thinking styles, we tend to round probabilities differently. A concept with a true probability of 50%, will tend to be rounded to "no chance" by someone with a logical left brain orientation. A more optimistic right brain individual will take that same 50% probability and round it to "a near definite go" concept.

This fundamental difference in rounding-left brainers tend to round down and right brainers round up-can create significant disagreements and very different assessments of risk. We see the same facts as our partners, spouses or employees yet come to very real and different perspectives.

Don't debate the decision as being black or white. Rather, focus discussion on the degree of gray, or the probability. By accepting probability you align thinking closer to the true realities of the world. When we evaluate our decisions in light of chances of success, we more appropriately evaluate the risks associated with each decision.

The other advantage a probability mind-set provides is it makes us look deeper at alternatives. The concept of what to do if an idea fails can be talked about and planned for, without being perceived as a "traitor who lacks faith." For example, we can gain confidence committing to a new product that has only a 45% probability of success if we know the equipment required to produce it has alternative uses for our mainline business.

When we focus our decision making on probabilities, we are more aligned with reality. It also helps us reduce damage to our personal and collective self-esteem if we accept all actions and reactions as part of a probability of life. Instead of blaming ourselves or others, we learn to take failures in stride, knowing that with each attempt, we are coming closer to having lady luck turn up on our side.

When we accept a probability view of the marketplace, we are able to manage risk and fears with appropriate business planning. Our greatest fear becomes not the probabilities known but the challenges unknown.

When we're planning a new initiative at the Eureka! Ranch, we use a system called Compression Planning to identify and quantify risks. It was developed by my good friend Jerry McNellis (http://www.mcnellisco.com). In this planning technology, critical project elements are storyboarded on cards of various colors and pinned to huge easels.

Whenever we are planning a new initiative, I insist on having a blank card pinned on the board as a reminder of our need to be flexible and ready for the unknown. We can never fill in the blank card. Issues will always arise that we never anticipated. As such, that unknown card is the hardest risk to manage. But here, 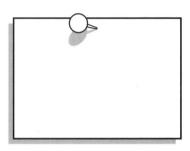 too, by accepting the fact that we can't do anything about the truly unknown, we find comfort and courage to push on.

Fear Battle Tactic 7: Play the Role of Revolutionary Law Breaker.
All businesspeople run their companies using laws and lessons. Some are applied consciously, as when determining what gross profit margin is needed to price goods or services so to insure reasonable net profits. Some are  followed unconsciously, based on feelings developed over many years of experience. Others are based on overt learning acquired over the years-from academic classes, to books and seminars that have been experienced, to the wisdom shared by others inside and outside the business itself.

When working with clients who are well entrenched in their ways, I find it helpful if I give them direct instruction and permission to think like revolutionaries. Having been given overt permission to break the law, clients are opened up to new possibilities.

I call the approach Law Breaker. It involves overtly contradicting "educated" thinking with regards to the business. When executing Law Breaker I utilize the same step-by-step process described earlier under Mind Dump.

Step 1 Define your challenge clearly.

Step 2 On individual sticky notes, list the "laws" or truths that surround your task. What are the "proper" and accepted ways of accomplishing the tasks? What are the facts of the industry? What are the absolutes that are accepted as truths?

The truths you list can be focused on big or small issues. The key consideration is that they guide you, as a sort of shorthand, for the making of decisions regarding your business. The following are provided as prompts to stir your memory bank. Use as many or as few as you feel are appropriate.

• If you were on your deathbed, what would be the three things you would tell your children to always keep an eye on and never forget as they take over your business?

• If you won a twelve-month trip around the world, what would be the three key numbers or pieces of information you would like to have e-mailed to you each day, week or month? Each business has key numbers that are early warning signals. For some it's gross profit margin, for others it's average selling price (after discounts) or customer satisfaction ratings. What fundamental truths do you have that are based on monitoring specific numbers relative to specific standards?

• Faced with $1,000, $10,000 or $100,000 that you were required to spend against the business within seven days, where would you invest the money? Said another way, what is the quick, short-term area that can grow your business?

• Faced with $1 million or $10 million that you could invest in capital equipment or systems over the next year, where would you spend the money? Said another way, what is the capital infrastructure element that constrains your business growth?

• Look back to the early days of your company. What were the lessons you learned early on that are still guiding your actions today?

• When selling customers your category of products or services, the most important considerations are _____.

• Success at your company is most dependent on _____.

• Each industry, marketing area and customer base is unique. What are the distinguishing aspects of your personal situation? For example, you might be faced with a market in which there are lots of older consumers, rich consumers or poor consumers. You may be in a market that is highly competitive, and any action to raise price is destined to fail.

• When sales decline, I know it's time to _____. When profits decline, I know it's time to _____. For my advertising to work, I need to _____. When I hire a new employee or manager, I teach them that for our business we must always _____.

Use as many words as possible to define your personal truths. If you find it difficult to give definition to your truths, focus less on the conscious and explore the unconscious actions you take. Explore how you made recent business decisions. What were the principles and truths that guided your thinking?

Having made your list, select the dozen that are the most critical to your success. This list represents the strategic brains of your operation. The items listed are the wisdom that you believe in. Within these fundamental statements of truth lie both your potential for growth and potential barriers to your growth.

Continuing to follow these truths is virtually guaranteed to provide you with more of the same results. Repeated actions result in repeated reactions.

The mission of Law Breaker is to help you challenge your beliefs and invent relevant yet unexpected ways of approaching your business.

Step 3 One at a time, place each of the laws in the corner of a sheet as was described in Mind Dump. In the area nearest the corner, free-associate the facts, figures and rationale behind the law.

Step 4 In the center of your sheet, break the laws. Shatter them. Defy them in every sense. Force yourself to discover a way to violate each law, to be like a revolutionary confronting an establishment that he had no faith, confidence or respect in.

Step 5 Having destroyed thinking as usual, step back and review the results of your revolution.
   • What parts hold potential as tomorrow's potential truths?
   • What are the ideas you would pursue if you were to start your business all over again—without the burden of your current infrastructure? Ask yourself what stops you from beginning again now.

- What ideas would scare you the most if your competition pursued them?

A number of years ago, I was working with small business owners Wendy and Tim Eidson, the founders and leaders of the first hot and spicy food catalog, Mo Hotta, Mo Betta. During our conversation, I suggested Law Breaker.

When discussing laws of hot food, Tim quickly volunteered, "Hotter is always better. The more heat an item has, the more it sells." It seemed like a reasonable law, so we agreed to work on breaking it.

We multiplied the stimuli from the law "hot is always better."

- Hot coffee is better than cold coffee.
- The song "Hot, Hot, Hot"
- Emergency ward
- Fire

Building customer propositions by contradicting this law took us to a new place. What if we sold the right hot for each person? What if we could tell customers how hot each sauce really was? We recognized this is against the law of hot food, where more is always considered better. However, it might be a way to get customers to purchase more and more sauces.

Tim volunteered that there might be a way to measure the heat using Scoville units, a unit of measurement used in high performance liquid chromatography (HPLC), which basically measures the amount of water it takes to neutralize the heat in a sample of sauce. It's not a precise measure, as each person has a different sensitivity, but it would provide a reasonable estimate of heat level.

It's been a huge success. Here's how they describe the new system on their Web site (http://www.mohotta.com).

HOT! Hot? What exactly does the word 'hot' mean when it's used to describe food? How about 'nuclear', 'fanny-kicking', 'medium' or 'mild'? Just because a label says it's hot, should you believe it? Hot compared to what? With so many different heat scales and terms being used, there is too much confusion and no reference point. We figured it was time to use a standardized scientific heat rating for our catalog that would be universally understood.

The concept worked great. Customers could now make multiple purchases with confidence. It generated so much excitement that Tim and Wendy received purchase offers and sold the business and moved on to new entrepreneurial adventures.

Beware of your internal truths as they are your greatest enemy. The tales of "experts" proclaiming truths that are later proven to be false makes for great reading. Jane O'Boyle in her book *Wrong! The Biggest Mistakes and Miscalculations Ever Made by People Who Should Have Known Better* (Plume, 1999) fills pages with such classics as these:

> The "telephone" has too many shortcomings to be seriously considered as a means of communications. The device is inherently of no value to us.
> *Western Union Memo, after Alexander Graham Bell*
> *offered the rights to the telephone*

> We don't like their sound and guitar music is on the way out.
> *Deca Records, rejecting the Beatles*

> The concept is interesting and well-formed, but in order to earn better than a C, the idea must be feasible.
> *Yale University business professor in 1966, on Fred*
> *Smith's senior thesis that would one day become*
> *Federal Express*

> Stocks have reached what looks like a permanently high plateau.
> *Irving Fisher, Yale University of economics,*
> *October 17, 1929*

> Fantasy doesn't sell.
> It has no patter and is not practical for a child.
> Verse doesn't sell.
> *Excerpts from rejection letters to a cartoonist*
> *who called himself Dr. Seuss*

Then there was this memo that was sent to me by a client friend at a company that was considering partnering with us on distributing Merwyn:

> We should not be connected in any way with Merwyn. It could lower the credibility of [our company] to be associated with it. It seems unrealistic and unbelievable.
>
> *Internal memo at a Fortune 50 company rejecting*
> *Merwyn Simulated Test Marketing*

I look forward to proving this wrong.

Now think about your world. What truths do you proclaim? What changes in your industry are you avoiding? What changes in your business are you ignoring?

A classic story of the power of breaking rules is the tale of Trivial Pursuit. At the time, there were a lot of absolute truths about board games.

- All board games sold for under ten dollars. It was well known that no one would ever pay more.
- Games were marketed to children. Experts on games knew that adults never bought games for themselves.
- Triva games were a well-known niche category of small sellers. When Trivial Pursuit came out, there were about a dozen other trivia games on the market, each generating very poor sales.

A friend of mine, Bill Hill, at the then Selchow and Righter company, was VP of product development. He met with Canadians who had invented Trivial Pursuit and found something special.

- The game materials had a sense of class and sophistication.
- The trivia questions were designed to make it possible to successfully guess at answers when you didn't know for sure.
- The question categories were cleverly selected to make it possible for everyone to feel expert in one or more areas.

Bill told me later, "In playing the game I found it was different. They had taken all the existing rules of games, turned them sideways and somehow the whole thing worked. I felt immediately that it could be a hit in the United States."

It worked. As of the writing of this book, Trivial Pursuit has generated sales of over $1 billion.

If the Trivial Pursuit team had known the "rules," we would not have the bounty of great board games that exist on the shelves today.

Fear Battle Tactic 8: Change Your Frame of Reference.
We can find courage when we change our frame of reference. Instead of focusing on the next week or month, take a longer term or bigger picture view to build your courage to take action.

Let's step back and take a broader view. Compare where you and your business are today versus six months ago, twelve months ago, two years ago, ten years ago. When you realize how much you've grown and evolved, it is easier to look to changes in the future with courage. When you courageously look into the future, you can see dramatic changes that can transform your business.

In our day-to-day world, we usually spend our lives like Lucille Ball in the famous "Candy Factory" episode of her original black-and-white television show. In the show, Lucy and Vivian take jobs at a candy factory. They are responsible for wrapping each candy in paper as it comes down a conveyor belt.

They start out working with diligence, then the line is slowly speeded up. Soon candies are everywhere. Fearing an unwrapped candy will make it through, Lucy sticks them in her bra, in her mouth, in her hat. Chaos breaks lose.

It's one of the all-time favorite *Lucy* episodes. It also shows how most businesspeople live their lives. They are so focused on today's production they have no time to think about the bigger picture.

We must be aware of what is going on around us, but we must not let our vision get locked on it. To survive and thrive long term, we must have a longer-term view of who we are and where we are going.

A solitary focus on the short term can become a controlling instinct. Deer and other animals die on highways every year because of their instinctive reaction to a set of headlights coming toward them. Thayne Maynard, executive director of the Puget Sound Environmental Learning Center, explained why they do it:

> Deer, and most prey animals, have not evolved to respond to the pressures of modern life. When threatened

or under pressure, they, like we, respond more from instinct than forethought. More specifically, deer have a particular "freeze or flight" kind of response. As with lots of prey animals, they know instinctively that if they stand perfectly still it is harder for the predator to know where they are.

In the face of the new danger of cars, deer use the age-old instinct of freezing that is simply ineffective versus a speeding truck.

Time and again I've seen businesspeople act just like the deer. When faced with the stress of a business decision, they try to stand perfectly still (take no action) so to make it harder for the predator to know where they are. Sadly, they often end up like the deer that's facing a tractor trailer at sixty-five miles per hour.

Practical Tactic: Great Escape

Great Escape is a powerful way to set your eyes on a broader view and in the process keep your eyes off the headlights.

Great Escape is about stepping back and refreshing and revising your mind. It can take many forms from sports to recreation to meditation. At the Eureka! Ranch, we execute Great Escape in a number of ways. Sometimes it's a ten-minute burst of video games or an afternoon game of sand volleyball or street hockey. Other times it's a guided meditation designed to cleanse and reset the minds of participants.

I will admit that when the Ranch staff first suggested the idea of a guided meditation, I was a bit skeptical. Meditation seemed to me to be a bunch of New Age mumbo jumbo. However, in keeping with my personal mantra of continuing growth, I endorsed a series of experiments. A collection of special tapes was created featuring the voice-over talents of Trained Brain Hannah Buchanan. When the tests were executed, the quantitative results were clear: This thing worked!

When asked why it worked, clients responded that it gave them an opportunity to step back and look once again at the challenge from a fresh perspective.

The study cited earlier from the *Creativity Research Journal,* which tracked the effectiveness of top scientists over many years, documented the value of diverting your attention from the task at hand. Specifically, only 55% of the scientists reported that solutions came from working directly on the problem. The variety of occasions when scientific ideas came to them was incredibly varied.

When Do Scientific Ideas Arise?	
While working directly on the problem	55%
While working on different, related problem	34%
While working on unrelated problem	21%
While relaxing	24%
While falling asleep or dreaming	31%
Upon awakening from sleep	24%
In the bath or shower	11%
Miscellaneous (exercising, shaving, vacationing)	19%

Here's a step-by-step method for executing Great Escape using the Eureka! Ranch guided meditation.

Step 1 Have in mind a clear understanding of what you are looking for.

Step 2 Go to http://www.DougHall/greatescape.com. On the Web page are instructions for downloading the audio file of our most recent meditation recording. Get yourself comfortable, in a chair or lying on the floor. Hit play on the recording and let the instructions do the rest.

Step 3 At the conclusion of the meditation, you should take a moment to list the perceptions and ideas that are flowing through your head, either the ideas you have generated during your escape or those that come to you upon returning to the challenge with your mind refreshed. Write both what you understand and what you at first don't understand. These prompts are then used to build ideas as detailed previously.

This example of Great Escape involved guided meditation. However, Great Escape can be executed in a number of other manners. At its simplest, Great Escape is about getting up from your office and refreshing your mind through an intense game of basketball, a healthy jog or run or playing some intense pinball for a half hour. Great Escape is about taking your mind off of the challenge at hand and allowing your mental workings to rest and reset themselves.

By stepping back, refreshing our minds and looking at the broader view, we enable our minds to see ideas that were at first invisible to our fear-struck craniums.

Quick Process Summary on Facing Fear

1. Do the Right Thing
   - There is no more powerful way to face your fears.
2. Use Pain to Motivate Gain
   - Use your discontent with today as courage to take charge of your future.
3. Try, Try, Try Your Way to Courage
   - Through constant dripping, water wears away the stone.
4. Reduce the Cost of Failure and Increase Your Courage
   - Prototype and learn at the lowest possible cost
   - Fail fast. Fail cheap.
5. Manage Your Fears Like Your Stocks
   - Always invest in a portfolio of short- and long-term ideas
6. Play Probabilities, Not Certainties
   - Manage the variable nature of risk with an understanding of the odds.
7. Play the Revolutionary Law Breaker
   - Overtly break the rules.
8. Change Your Frame of Reference
   - Step back and look again with a fresh perspective.
9. Remember you have three options
   - Never, ever, ever give up.
   - Sit down, shut up and stop whining.
   - Walk.

Final Thoughts on Facing Fear

Courage cannot be given to you. To find true courage, you must look deep within yourself.

I learned this lesson with intense clarity on my trip to the North Pole. When it's -20 degrees and you're standing on the frozen Arctic Ocean some sixteen hundred miles north of Alaska, your heat must come from within. With day after day of relentless cold, it is not possible to wear enough clothes, no matter how high-tech they may be, and stay warm. You must fire up your own furnace through intense aerobic activity. Your body has a near unlimited ability to generate heat if your mind will engage it in activity. Standing still is guaranteed frostbite. In extreme cases, you may even end up like one of my teammates and lose a toe from the killer cold.

When you go to sleep at night, you are destined to freeze if you simply slip into a cold sleeping bag—your body heat sucked into the sleeping system leaving you perpetually chilled. If, however, you first go for a half-mile, high-intensity run to elevate your body temperature, even the worst of cold can be fought off.

You determine whether you will live a life of fear or of courage. It's your choice. Those with the greatest levels of courage have acquired personal self-confidence through hundreds if not thousands of challenges. From the wins and the losses, they have grown strong.

Poet David Whyte said it well: "Creativity is about coming out of hiding and exposing yourself. Practicing creativity is about humiliating yourself in public."

If you are to make history, you are going to have to break the rules. And breaking the rules means sometimes you win and sometimes you lose. If you are not willing to humiliate yourself pursuing bold new ideas, then give up the capitalist business world.

We find personal strength when the ideas we pursue are those we have a strong personal passion for. When we truly believe in our cause, we have the strength to write the history of the world.

Some cynics might suggest that this sounds fine on the surface but what about the "yes, but's"? As in, "Yes, but what if the boss or bank won't listen?" or, "Yes, but what if the company or my customers won't change?" or, "Yes, but what if my coworkers aren't interested in growing?"

If that's what you're thinking, let me assure you that your options are simple. In fact, you have three of them.

1. Remember Churchill: "Never, ever, ever, ever give up." If in your heart, you believe you're absolutely right, keep fighting. Fight 'til the death if that's what it takes.

2. Take a seat. Sit down, shut up, sell out and stop whining. If you're not willing to fight for what you believe in, you have

no grounds for whining.

3. Clean out your office, pack up your brain and take your talents elsewhere. Ride off into the sunset without looking back. Abe Lincoln freed the slaves.

Let's go over that again. Never give up. Sit down and stop whining. Or walk. It's a free country, and it's your choice.

In the end, having courage to face fear is about more than simply growing a business. It's about getting as much as you can from the time you have on this planet. It's about making a difference. No one will do it for you.

It's your life. Live it how you wish to be remembered.

CHAPTER 13

Frequently Asked Questions About Capitalist Creativity

In the last three chapters you learned the three laws that have the greatest impact on your ability to inspire ideas that have high probability of success. This last chapter answers common questions asked by participants at Capitalist Creativity training programs.

Whenever I create ideas with others, it seems the same ideas come up over and over again. How should I respond?

When you hear ideas that are familiar, that should be a hint that you are onto a rich area. Instead of stopping, it should be your signal to push on with greater diligence. Commit yourself *this time* to making the initial idea a reality.

Relentlessly pursue the concept that seems to always come up. Approach it from all 360 degrees of perspective. Plunge yourself deep into the drama of the idea, allowing yourself to become fully immersed until the true answer reveals itself.

At the ranch you talk about working with groups of people. Do I need a group?

You will be more productive if you work with other people, as stated in law two, Leverage Diversity. Academic research studies have found the diversity of groups to be more effective at creating quality ideas than are individuals. In "Clustering Effect," an article by Gene E. Burton of California State University (*Small Group Behavior*, May 1987), Burton reports that groups created 44%, 50%, 65% and 93% more ideas in various academic research efforts.

Our survey of innovation experts has similarly shown the value of leveraging diversity through utilizing additional people.

Mean Values of Effectiveness of Various Group Sizes (0 to 10 Scale)	
More creative by myself	3.8
With one person	6.1
With groups of three or more	7.7

You can, however, be very effective working by yourself. Simply create a collection of ideas using stimuli then use e-mail and one-on-one discussions with others to leverage the power of diverse perspectives.

What is the best way to manage a group idea-creation effort?

At the Eureka! Ranch, we work with groups that are sometimes as large as twenty-four. To maximize productivity, we break into four groups of six participants each. The small groups are used to create the raw ideas, the larger group to help build on the raw ideas.

Prior to the session, we handle the gathering of stimuli so to maximize group productivity.

Step-by-step the process looks like this.

Step 1. Session Preparation Your ultimate success is based on the breadth and depth of your preparation prior to the session. The first step is to vigorously review your objective. By clearly defining what you are looking for you, increase the effectiveness of every other step.

The clearly defined session objective is used as a guide to gather stimuli to be used to create ideas. Stimuli can be both Homeward Trail related or Borrowing Brilliance unrelated. In addition, we have historically always executed the Mind Dump tactic as the first exercise and 666 as the second. After that, any of the various stimuli sources are possibilities.

We invite the most diverse group of people we can find to help create ideas. We look for diversity of (1) functional skills (marketing, technology, legal); (2) thinking styles (logical left brain and radical right brain); and (3) experience in the business (veterans and rookies).

Step 2. Session Start The most important session component is clear communication of the objective of the session. If the participants are not familiar with the three laws of Marketing Physics, we conduct a quick training effort to teach them the definitions.

We explain the first creative exercise, the stimuli and how to process the stimuli. We also define any special objectives we might have for this specific exercise. Usually we're looking for complete ideas that encapsulate all three laws of Marketing Physics; however, sometimes we focus on one key dimension, such as Overt Benefit, names or Real Reasons to Believe.

Step 3. Small Group Creation We randomly count off all participants into small groups. Each group is then given fifteen to thirty minutes to use the stimuli provided as well as the diversity of their group to invent ideas. The small group effort ends with the completion of the quality control charting form (see http://www.DougHall.com). The results from this survey are used to optimize the process.

From a process perspective, we have found it more effective if the small groups remain in the same room. Having groups work close to each other creates energy. It also leverages a healthy competitive spirit in search of the best idea.

We usually leverage music as well during the small group creation step as another source of energy.

Step 4. Large Group Reporting After all groups have created ideas, they report their top ideas to the larger group with a moderator recording their thoughts on a chart pad or white board in the front of the room.

During the reporting of top ideas, the moderator seeks out additional "builds" on ideas from other participants. In effect, the ideas presented are stimuli for the creation of new ideas by those listening.

At the conclusion of each group's reporting, the moderator leads a round of applause for the group members who offered their ideas. Clapping for each group is a way of providing positive reinforcement to group members and thus reducing future fear. Recall the research reported earlier that indicated that when a businessperson has recently been successful, she is more likely to accept even bigger risks.

Step 5. Repeat Efforts After all groups have reported their ideas the process is repeated. The next stimulus, objective and method is explained and the participants counted off again into new groups for continued idea creation.

We run creation efforts for either a half or full day. At the conclusion of the efforts, participants are thanked and it is left to a smaller team to embark on refining the concepts.

Do I have to spend a half day or full day to create ideas?

The length of time needed is dependent on the breadth and depth of the challenge you are facing. If in doubt, I would suggest spending more time rather than less. Given the amount of time and money it takes to develop and introduce any new business, concept time at the front end is usually a wise investment.

When a problem is highly targeted and specific, I recommend a fifteen-minute Eureka! Blitz approach.

Step 1 Gather two to six people. I suggest having participants stand during the effort as it sets a tone of speed and urgency.

Step 2 Set a fifteen-minute time limit. Give them the challenge and some stimuli to work from. Then just crank ideas. You should handle all recording of concepts. Let the participants just explode with ideas.

Step 3 Inform them at various points how much time is left. When time runs out, stop the effort.

These types of blitz efforts can be highly productive in searching for ideas. They also help rejuvenate and revive the brains of participants as they return to their regular work.

But I have no money. What am I to do?

It is regrettable that you have no money; however, it does not have any long-term impact on your probability of success. The Internet craze of the year 2000 clearly proved that money cannot buy success. Unlimited cash causes lazy thinking.

Clever thinking and a credit card or two can create virtually anything. I started my business in my basement with three credit cards. From those poorly funded beginnings, today exist a debt-free, multimillion-dollar facility and the state-of-the-art computer brain called Merwyn Technology.

Small business owners often tell me they have lots of ideas yet no money to execute them. My answer is a stern tongue lashing: If you're imaginative enough to invent great ideas, you should be smart enough to find ways to cost-efficiently turn those ideas into reality.

With virtually every idea, a little thinking can find a way to develop what I call a "pay as you go" program of introduction. This system involves selling your new product or service in a small market then reinvesting the returns as you slowly but surely expand broadly.

Whoa, some will say, I can't introduce my idea slowly, I'll get copied. I need big money to go fast. Wrong. **If you can be copied that easily, then you don't have a big idea.**

Big ideas are so dramatically different that through a combination of patents, trade secrets and executional barriers, they offer significant proprietary protection. Big ideas change the rules of the game such that the establishment views them as the work of kooks and crazies. Don't worry about theft. Usually established companies are so defensive about who and what they are they refuse to acknowledge your existence—until it's too late.

Focus on what you have. There is nothing you can do about what you don't have.

But my category is old. There are no new ideas that work. What are my options?

This is a ridiculous statement that is believed by the majority of businesspeople. Quite simply, the opportunities to innovate are unlimited. There is a limitless opportunity to discover new ideas. Each innovation introduced into the marketplace acts as stimulus for even more ideas.

The Ned Herrmann group provides perspective on the number of true possibilities. They started with the following assumptions: 12 trillion brain cells in the average human brain and each has the possibility of some 100,000 connections with adjoining brain cells. When you do the math, you find that the number of possible combinations in the brain, if written out, would be followed by 10.5 million miles of zeros!

In the highly competitive categories of foods, beverages, financial services and telecommunications, I estimate that the Eureka! Ranch has created about 24,000 raw ideas over the past fifteen years. While some of the ideas surely are repetitive, the vast majority are original. By assembling different stimuli and diverse groups of thinkers, there appears to be no end to the number of potential ideas for growth for even these heavily worked categories.

The bottom line: Keep thinking. There are millions and millions of ideas yet to be discovered.

I'm too old to learn a new way of thinking. What help is there for me?

Sorry, the data doesn't support your conclusion. For those of you who didn't accept the data presented earlier based on the senior citizens research project (chapter ten), here is some more.

We asked top innovators how creative they are at their current ages and in previous decades. The results show that if we keep our brains pumping with thinking, we get smarter and smarter as we age.

Ratings of Creativity at Various Ages (0 to 10 scale)	
Creativity during early teen years	6.6
Creativity during high school years	7.0
Creativity during twenties	7.4
Creativity during thirties	7.8
Creativity during forties	8.2
Creativity during fifties	8.5

Use it or lose it. American founding father John Quincy Adams said it well: "Old minds are like old horses. You must exercise them if you wish to keep them in working order." **Until they close the lid on your casket and put you in the ground, you have the potential to create magnificent new ideas.** As you age, your memory banks have a richness of stimuli upon which to make new connections.

Why do we have to create so many ideas? Can't we just create one great one?

I would love to be able to just create one silver bullet of an idea that is guaranteed to work. In rare occasions working with Eureka! Ranch clients, we have been able to end up with one idea. However, that one idea was the distillation of the best of the best from hundreds if not thousands of raw ideas. Just as it takes thirty-six gallons of sap to create one gallon of pure maple syrup, it take lots of raw ideas to make one great one.

At the Eureka! Ranch, on average we write up fifteen concepts for every one great idea we discover. And we've been doing this for twenty years! Assuming the Ranch team is three times more efficient than someone inexperienced in idea development, it would be reasonable to predict that some forty-five ideas need to be written up as complete concepts to create one great one.

Quantity breeds quality. The more ideas you write up, the greater the number of really great ideas you have to work with. Fortunately, following the six laws outlined on these pages will make you dramatically more efficient so that you shouldn't need to write forty-five in order to find one great idea.

I have tried to use stimuli but nothing comes. What else can I do?

Some people have a hard time opening their minds to make free associations. Instead of letting the ideas flow, they tend to self-judge their thoughts before they get out of their mouths or onto paper. This is particularly true when left brain and whole brain folks are working with unrelated stimuli for the first few times.

My recommendation is to get stubborn and outwait your logical brain. Take a stimuli and simply think about them, think about them and think about them. In a half hour or three hours, your mind will eventually open up and you'll start to hear free associations, patterns and connections that at first were just a whisper. If you have the endurance to continue to simply think, eventually you will make a discovery that changes your entire view of how to think about your problem.

In your first book you advocated fun. I don't see a reference to it here. What's up?

I'm sorry to say but fun does not matter. In my first book, I claimed that "fun is fundamental" to creating ideas. I also promoted the value of toys, Nerf guns, practical jokes and cool T-shirts. I felt that unless a team was laughing, it could not create big ideas.

In the six years since that book was written, I have measured the impact of fun. Sadly, quantitative measurement has found absolutely no relationship between the amount of fun and enjoyment participants are having and their bottom-line productivity.

I didn't like these findings so I had my R and D team repeat the research only to come to the same conclusion. This doesn't mean that it's important to have pain. It means simply that fun is not critical to Capitalist Creativity success. The critical issue appears to be fear. Fun can be a positive and a negative. In most corporate settings, I've observed fun as a fear builder as the laughs are often at the expense of others' misfortunes.

Today at the Ranch, we've retired our Nerf guns and our water pistols. As good hosts, we still have great food, great music and an inspiring facility filled with art and arcade games. However, we don't rely on the hardware of the building for creativity. Rather, it's the software of diversity of participants and specialized stimuli that gives birth to big ideas.

Any personal tips that you're not telling us?

There are things I do myself that I find personally helpful. As the data on them is weak, I omitted them from the base book. Use your own judgment regarding these ideas' potential to help you.

Doug's Personal Systems for Inspiring Ideas

Trust the power of Dramatic Difference When stuck for an idea I go bold. I trust the data that indicates that the more unique an idea is, the greater the probability of it being potentially brilliant.

Turn up the music I find that classic rock and roll music is a powerful way to stimulate my brain. My preference is for playing it at socially inappropriate levels. High-quality headphones have kept me from being thrown out of my home or office. Scientists have found that high sound levels increase the secretion of adrenaline in humans. In their article, "Noise Busters," in the March 2001 issue of *Smithsonian* magazine, Richard and Joyce Wolleomir reported "The greater the sound, the greater the adrenaline rush. That's why exercise classes crank up the decibels, and rock bands and movies [are so loud]."

Our survey of innovation experts found they agreed with the power of music. Some 72% felt they were most creative with music on. Interestingly, the two most popular music styles for listening to when creating were direct opposites: classic rock (55%) and classical (48%).

When the crowd goes one way, go in the opposite direction. I have found great success following Newton's law that for every force there is an equal and opposite force. Whenever a crowd starts moving in one direction, I look in the other. For example, when healthy foods became hot, I advised clients to look into hedonism. When hedonism became hot, I advised exploring holistic natural foods. It doesn't work every time, however, so you have to be a little cautious, but it's a simple principle that works more times than it doesn't.

When your brain is becoming brain dead, move. I don't sit and stew for long. When my brain slows to a crawl, I move and find another location to do my thinking. At the ranch, I often head for the canvas hammock on the front porch my great-grandfather built or head out to the deck overlooking the lake out back. At home I'll often take my PowerBook computer to a different room.

After a long week of writing this book, my mind was running dry. I then moved to one of my favorite places to write-beside the stone fireplace at the wonderful Joseph-Beth bookstore near my home. Joseph-Beth is a leader in the new generation of bookstores. They were even selected top bookseller in America by *Publisher's Weekly* a few years ago. It's a near perfect environment for doing some serious creating—great coffee, comfortable seats and huge selections of stimulus-rich books.

Coffee, coffee, coffee. Lastly, I am a firm believer in the power of caffeine. Whenever I am creating, I consume vast quantities of the stuff. Various studies have shown that with coffee the mind thinks smarter. In fact, I once did a small base study to measure the impact of coffee. On a Saturday morning, twenty-four people who had had no caffeine of any type that day were given forty-five minutes to invent ideas for new television shows. A second group of twenty-four were given three cups of my Brain Brew coffee before spending forty-five minutes creating ideas. When the resultant ideas were counted, it was found that the coffee gang created 40% more ideas than the decaffeinated group.

I believe in following in the footsteps of such noted coffee lovers as Franklin, Twain, Voltaire, Bach, Beethoven and Brahms. I believe that the power of one's mind is directly proportional to the quantity and quality of coffee one drinks. It's for this reason that I have crafted my own personal brew called Brain Brew. It's available at http://www.DougHall.com with all profits, after expenses, donated to charities focused on children or the arts.

I understand that the impact of coffee on health is richly debated. I'm on the side of Voltaire who reportedly drank some fifty cups of coffee a day. When told that drinking coffee was a "slow poison," the philosopher replied that it must be very slow indeed as he had been drinking that much coffee every day for over eighty years.

My favorite idea. A common question is what is my favorite idea I've ever worked on. "The next one" is my answer. And when it's not, it's time to retire.

Final Thoughts

Thank you, friends, for spending time with my scribblings. This book contains nearly every piece of significant data, wisdom and knowledge that I have gathered over my thirty years of growing small businesses and advising the world's largest corporations.

Much of the learning was gathered the ugly way, through great personal and professional pain. However, in my case it was well worth the journey.

My personal mission at midlife is to help true small business owners avoid many of my mistakes by thinking smarter and more creatively about growing their businesses. As I said in the opening, U.S. census data indicates that 75% of all small businesses fail within five years. What is most depressing about this is that most don't actually fail, but the owners give up because they come to the conclusion that it's just not worth the effort. In effect, they run out of energy.

I can't imagine a worse feeling than to have poured your heart and soul into a small business dream only to conclude that it's not worth the effort—and for the rest of your life wonder what if.

Realizing Return on Your Investment

The only way to realize a real return on your investment in reading this book is to take action. And action must come from you. You must eliminate whining about your challenges and take charge of your business destiny.

While we were traveling to the North Pole, whenever we were facing a particularly discouraging situation of towering pressure ridges or open water, teammate Alan Humphries from Ireland would yell out, "How do you eat an elephant?" "One bite at time," we would reply. The only way for us to get to the pole or for you to grow your business is one step at a time. You must first define your Overt Benefit then your Real Reason to Believe. Having done that you must assess the Dramatic Difference of your business concept. If it's not dramatically different, you must Explore Stimuli, Leverage Diversity and Face Fears to reinvent it and reinvent it and reinvent it until it is.

I cannot guarantee that you will succeed. However, if you commit yourself to genuinely serving customers, the odds of success are significantly stacked in your favor.

Ben Franklin said many things that touch me in many different ways. There is, however, one Franklin quote that precisely captures the essence of my philosophy on living. I recite it at the conclusion of every speech I give. Live it and you will live your life to the potential for which it was intended: **"Up sluggard, and waste not life; in the grave will be sleeping enough."**

EUREKA! RANCH SERVICES

Eureka! Inventing This is the Eureka! Ranch's flagship service. It's available in a range of formats, yet the output is always the same: the discovery of big ideas that are guaranteed to exceed your expectations.

Trailblazer Training This is the highly interactive training program that this book is based on. It has two parts: (1) Marketing Physics and (2) Capitalist Creativity.

Trailblazer Trainer Certification For corporations wanting their own facilitators to conduct Trailblazer Training, the Eureka! Ranch offers a certification program.

Eureka! Ranch Small Business Coaching Centers On a selective basis, Eureka! Ranch technologies are available for organizations dedicated to helping small and medium-sized businesses.

Doug Hall Live Lectures Doug is a kinetic bundle of energy and enthusiasm as he delivers a blast of interactive thinking, laughing and learning.

Brain Brew Coffee This is the "magic elixir" of the Eureka! Ranch. It's available for purchase at our Web site. All profits after expenses are donated to charities.

To learn more visit our Web site or call us.

Doug Hall
Eureka! Ranch
3849 Edwards Road
Cincinnati, Ohio 45255 USA
(513) 271-9911
Doug@DougHall.com

BIBLIOGRAPHY

Books are among the world's most powerful stimuli sources. The following books had a direct impact on the thinking that led to this book.

Applied Imagination: Principles and Procedures of Creative Problem-Solving by Alex Osborn (Charles Scribner's Sons, 1953; out of print). The first book to provide a level of scientific discipline to the world of creativity.

Brain Builders: A Lifelong Guide to Sharper Thinking, Better Memory, and an Ageproof Mind by Richard Leviton (Parker, 1995). A fun book jam-packed with ideas for boosting your brainpower.

Dialogue and the Art of Thinking Together by William Isaacs (Doubleday 1999). An insightful look into how to maximize the value of true diversity.

The E-Myth: Why Most Small Businesses Don't Work and What to Do About It by Michael Gerber (HarperCollins 1995). Must reading for anyone who is running her own business.

Ernest Hemingway on Writing edited by Larry Phillips (Simon & Schuster, 1984). The finest book on writing I've read. The clarity and tightness of Hemingway is my life's writing goal. The words on these pages show how far I have to go.

The First American: The Life and Times of Benjamin Franklin by H.W. Brands (Doubleday, 2000). A fascinating book in which America's first business inventor comes alive.

Fuzzy Thinking: The New Science of Fuzzy Logic by Bart Kosko (Hyperion, 1993). Not an easy read but worth the journey for those with a true passion for understanding the future of thinking machines.

The Heart Aroused: Poetry and the Preservation of the Soul in Corporate America by David Whyte (Doubleday, 1996). A corporate poet with an uncanny insight into the world of work.

In Search of Excellence by Tom Peters and Robert Waterman, Jr. (Warner Books, 1982). The great classic. This book transformed my thinking about business. As a young executive at Procter & Gamble I was inspired to take the path less traveled. And that has made all the difference.

The Innovator's Dilemma: When New Technologies Cause Great Firms to Fail by Clayton Christensen (Harvard Business School Press, 1997). A book that makes you stop and think, think and think again. It presents a compelling case for searching for true Dramatic Differences.

Ogilvy on Advertising by David Ogilvy (Crown Publishers, 1983). The greatest book on advertising ever written. New trends come and new trends go, but Ogilvy's words stand the test of time.

Out of the Crisis by W. Edwards Deming (Massachusetts Institute of Technology, 1982). One of the most important management books ever written. Warning: It's not light reading.

The Path of Least Resistance: Learning to Become the Creative Force in Your Own Life by Robert Fritz (Fawcett Columbine, 1984). Wow! It's a bigger picture view of what can be realized when you fully unleash your creative potential.

The Power of Positive Thinking by Norman Vincent Peale (Prentice Hall, 1952). The greatest self-help book ever written.

Thriving Up and Down the Free Market Food Chain by Arthur Lipper III (Harper Business, 1991). A refreshing, real-world look at what it takes to thrive as an entrepreneur.

Toward Wisdom: Finding Our Way to Inner Peace, Love and Happiness by Copthorne MacDonald (Hampton Roads Publishing, Canada, 1996). A masterful piece of writing that never ceases to inspire me.

Winning at New Products: Accelerating the Process From Idea to Launch by Robert Cooper (Addison-Wesley, 1993). A data-based look at what makes products win and lose. It's our research bible at the Eureka! Ranch.

The Whole Brain Business Book by Ned Herrmann (McGraw-Hill, 1996). The definitive work on right brain, left brain and whole brain thinking.

THANK YOU

Thanks first and foremost to my father Buzz Hall. The inspirations of my father in science, engineering and the work of Dr. Deming are the foundation of this work.

Thanks to the thousands of Eureka! Ranch clients who willingly provided the quantitative feedback and business data that is the foundation of this book.

Special thanks to Tom Peters. In the early 1980s, as a chemical engineer turned advertising executive at Procter & Gamble, I viewed a bootleg copy of a videotape (sounds like Grateful Dead tapes) of Tom preaching the virtues of passion, innovation and skunk works.

The tape and Tom's subsequent books spoke to a discontent I was feeling in the look-alike, work-alike world of corporate America. His words brought back memories of my teen and college years as a magician/juggler and marketer of juggling kits at Vermont, New Hampshire and Maine fairgrounds.

I responded to Tom's challenge. I traded in my passport to the executive suite (becoming Tide Brand Manager) and instead took over the chaotic new product skunk works effort in the food division.

The rebel team was a huge success—in my last year at P&G, the team shipped nine new product/marketing initiatives in twelve months with 10% of the staffing and 18% of the cost of similar types of projects according to a finance department audit.

I am a true believer in the preachings of Tom Peters. I heard the calling in the 80s and took action. His thinking changed the course of my life—he lit the spark that today burns brightly as the Eureka! Ranch and the book you hold in your hands.

I do not presume to come to the literary world with a fraction of his skill. I do, however, come with a hope and dream that one day I, too, will inspire other engineers or managers somewhere in the corporate world to listen to the voices inside and take action on their dreams.

Special thanks to my good friend Tom Wilson for sharing the wonderfully inspired Ziggy cartoons he crafts. For many years Tom has been a part of the Eureka! Ranch Posse, the "best of the best" of Eureka! Ranch Trained Brains. Tom brings creative insight and pure passion for original thinking to our inventing sessions.

It's appropriate that a book designed to inspire business owners and those with a business owner attitude should feature Ziggy. Ziggy never gives up. He always finds the bright side when life throws him a curve ball. Having Ziggy at your side when starting or growing your business will provide a much-needed boost when the going gets tough. I especially like the fact that he's short, balding and tends to prefer bare feet.

Thanks to the Eureka! Ranch Research and Development team: Mike Kosinski, Jeffery Stamp Ph.D., Chris Stormann Ph.D.. The discoveries and thinking articulated on these pages would not be possible without the academic rigor, skill and, most importantly, brains of this world-class team. Thanks to Michelle Martin who pioneered the initial research and who is now one of the world's greatest teachers.

Thanks to the Eureka! Ranch Staff and the Trained Brain Posse: Anne Badanes, Justin Beck, Billay Brooks, Hannah Buchanan, Tim Burke, Tracy Duckworth, Matthew Fenton, Benjamin Franklin, Juliann Gardner, Tod Gentile, Steve Glaser, Bruce Hall, Colleen Harris, Roseanne Hassey, Paul Hobart, Leah Hunter, Mike Katz, Matt Kirk, Steve Klein, Craig Kurz, Sondra Kurz, Heidi McCarthy, Sean McCosh, Chris McMahon, Kari McNamara, Kevin McNamara, Maggie Nichols, Lorrie Paulus, Julie Phillipi, Jane Portman, Anne Raichle, Dave Raichle, Laura Rolfes, Mike Salvi, Jason Saunders, Rob Seddon, Zach Sorrells, Pam Twist, David Wecker, Scott Wells, Tom Wilson.

Thanks to the friends of the ranch whose never-ending support helped make this book possible: Tom Ackerman, John Altman, David Cassady, Nancy DeVore, Mike and Margaret England, Paul Farris, D.A. Fleischer, Bruce Forsee, Steve and Mary Friedberg, Jack Gordon, John Grossman, Margaret Henson, Ann Herrmann, Patty Hogan, Chris Hylen, Lynn Kahle, Kip Knight, Arthur Lipper III, Scott MacAulay, Copthorne MacDonald, Thane Maynard, Austin McNamara, Jerry McNellis, Les Moermand, Mary Ann Naples, Dave Owens, Tim Riker, Eric Schulz, Herbie and Angela Schell, Renee Steele, Dick Steuerwald, Kitty Strauss, Chic Thompson, Tracie Tighe, Andy Timmerman, Andy Van Gundy, Negia York.

Thanks to friends and colleagues who suffered through early versions of this work and whose advice and counsel were critical to whatever success it achieves: Mike England, Richard Hassnoot, Kip Knight, Craig Kurz, Copthorne MacDonald, Thayne Maynard,

Jeff Stamp, David Wecker, Joyce Wycoff.

Thanks to Rob Seddon for his expert management at the hundreds of details associated with making the art and copy work together.

Thanks to the good friends and trusted colleagues of my Young Entrepreneur/World Entrepreneur Forum: Anne Bain, Fred Diamond, John Greiwe, Dan Meekin, Scott Miller, Jay Stoehr, David Uible.

Thanks to my fellow teammates on the 1999 Aspirations Expedition to the North Pole. That experience changed my outlook on life and on these pages: David Golibersuch, Alan Humphries, Craig Kurz, Bill Martin, Celia Martin, Corky Peterson, Paul Pfau, Paul Schurke, Randy Swanson, Michael Warren.

A huge thank you to Lori Pendelton of Prince Edward Island Business Development and the small business owners of Prince Edward Island, Canada, who participated in Eureka! Ranch Small Business Coaching sessions. This experimental program provided critical insights on how to maximize communications effectiveness with small business owners. They include Jeannette Arsenault, Katie Baker, Peter Baker, Tim Banks, the Honourable Pat Binns (Premier of Prince Edward Island), Lee Brammer, Christine Campbell, Tim Casey, Scott Chandler, Mary Crane, Bob Cumming, the Honourable Michael Currie (Minister of Development and Technology of Prince Edward Island), Stefan Czapalay, Brandy Foley, Ken Gillis, Blaine Harbi, Scott Harper, Byron Howard, Jim Johnston, Scott MacAuley, Carol MacLeod, Bruce MacNaughton, Don Maxfield, Ed McKenna, the Honourable Mitch Murphy (Minister of Agriculture and Forestry), John Rossignol, Doreen Sark, Daphne Large Scott, Kent Sheen, Allan Smith, Sharon Smith, Daniel Viau, Shirley Wright.

To those whose names I missed I apologize. I will seek to correct my mistake in future editions.

INDEX

A

academic journals, as stimulus, 215
advertising
    obscure, 15
    optimizing, through Real Reason to
    Believe, 94-96
America Online, free sampling,103
Andrew Jergens Company,
    demonstration of Bioré, 105
arts, communicating experiential
    benefits of, 72–73
Attea, Tom, 74
authenticity, and probability of
    success, 161–162

B

B.O.S. (Brain Operating System)
    Profiler, 236–237
balance sheet, of competitive
    strength, 203
benefits
    communicating
        in headlines, 43–44
        importance of, 44–46
        self-audit of, 46–48
    emotional/experiential, failing to
        support, 121
    rational v. emotional, 70–74
    selling positive vs. negative, 82
    turning into Overt Benefits, 52
    vs. features, 47–50
    See also Overt Benefits
Borrowing Brilliance stimuli, 213-221
    tactics for finding, 213–220
brain
    increasing power of, 178–182
    logical left vs. radical right, 240–241
    maximizing productivity for, 242–248
    "pumping up," stimuli for, 216–217
    workings of, 178–179
    See also thinking styles

brainstorming. See Capitalist
Creativity, Ideas
brand name,
    declining, seeking credibility from,
        120–121
    established, as trademark
        pedigree, 113–114
business
    honesty of claims, and Real Reason
        to Believe, 98–99
    name. See brand name
    reason for starting, 66–67
    See also small business

C

Capitalist Creativity, three laws of, 14,
171–173
    additional research on, 175
    bringing together, 173–174
    See also Explore Stimuli, Face
Fears, Leverage Diversity
Cavendish Figurines, 108–111
celebrity testimonials, 117
client confidentiality, 15–16
coffee, as stimulant, 292
commodity, and pricing 127–128
concepts. See ideas
contests and awards
    borrowing stimuli from winners, 214
    as marketing pedigree, 112–113
cooking, as stimulus, 183
Cooper, Robert, 140, 164
Create Customer Concepts, 187, 196–197
creativity
    four stages of, 186–187
    measuring, 180
    in senior citizens, 180
    See also Capitalist Creativity, three
        laws of
credibility
    damaging own, 121–122
    of Internet, 92–93

and truth, 98–99
See also Real Reason to Believe
customer
    defined, 9, 26
    focusing on, 7, 15. *See also* Overt
Benefits
    having clear news to tell, 140
    observing comments from, 203
    testimonials from, 115–116
    See also target audience

D

data. *See* Statistics
Dave's Place, communicating benefits
    of, 44–46
Deming, W. Edwards, 12–13, 149–150,
    166
demonstration, as Real Reason to
    Believe strategy, 104–105
development pedigree, 111–112
direct mail, varying message in, 25–26
diversity
    chaos caused by, 227
    surface source of, 226–227
    See also leverage diversity
Don't Sell Me, 230–232
Dramatic Difference, 32–33, 125–148
    assessing, 137–148
    and chance of success,130–131
    common mistakes, 153–155
    continuously developing, 136–137
    flowing from Overt Benefit and Real
Reason to Believe, 152–153
    relevance of, 138–140
    three guiding principles, 149–153

E

Ellis, Joseph, 225
endorsements. *See* testimonials
energy, for change, leveraging right
brain energy for source of, 244–245
Eureka! Ranch
    and client confidentiality, 15–16
    research from. *See* Capitalist
Creativity, Marketing Physics, Merwyn
exercise, as stimulus, 182
expert testimonials, 116–117

Explore Stimuli, 171–172, 177–190

F

Face Fears, 173, 254–283
failure
    facing fear of, 265–268
    reducing cost of, 268–269
fear
    choosing how to confront, 258–259
    effects of, 254–258
    managing, like investments,
269–270
    tactics for battling, 259–279
    See also Face Fears
features v. benefits, 47–50
feedback
    sensory, as Real Reason to Believe
strategy, 105–107
    soliciting, 226
focus groups, shortcomings of, 85
frame of reference, changing, 278–279
franchising, as trademark pedigree,
113
free association
    difficulty with, 290
    Mind Dump, 191
free samples, 41, 103

G

Gallant, Lennie, 211–212
Great Escape, 279–281
Griffin, Abbie, 141
groups, working in, 294
    See also Leverage Diversity
growth, sustainable, 145
guarantees as Real Reason to Believe
    strategy, 118–119

H

Herrmann Brain Dominance
Instrument (HBDI), 235–236
Hewitt, Don, 152
Holder, Will, 83
Homeward Trail stimuli, 200–208
    tactics for finding, 202–208

I

ideas
  as business driver, 5–7
  crazy, 142–143
  creating, brain orientation for,
    242–243
  effect of fear on, 254
  evolutionary vs. revolutionary,
    141–142
  executing, without money, 164–165,
    287–288
  generating new, in old category, 288
  inspiring, personal system for, 291–292
  need for creating many,289–290
  putting in writing, 77, 222–223
  quiz to evaluate, 20–24
  into reality, left brains as discipline
    for, 245–246
  shopping for, 216
  system for assessing. *See* Merwyn
imagery, 160–162
industry, following, 121
infomercials, and credibility, 93
Internet, credibility challenge of, 92–93
Island Pewter, 36–38
Island Winds, and Dramatic Difference,
  131–136

J

J.L. Darling Corporation, 104–105

K

kitchen logic, 100–103
knowledge, assumption of, avoiding, 82

L

L.L. Bean, guarantee, 118–119
Law Breaker, facing fear by being,
  272–278
leadership, crafting Dramatic
Difference through, 149–151
Leverage Diversity, 172–173, 224–226
Life Line Health Screening, 81–82
Lipper, Arthur III, 253

M

MacDonald, Copthorne, 209, 210

MacNaughton, Bruce, 106
Magic Moment, 74
market
  size of, 163–164
  See also customer, target audience
marketing pedigree, 112–113
Marketing Physics
  fighting fear by focusing on, 261
  focus on message, 25–26
  as key to leveraging diversity,
    227–228
  and need for advertising budget,
    159–160
  need for employees to understand,
    165–166
  three laws of, 13–14
    identifying, 30–33
    order of, 158–159
      success with, 158–159
  validity of, 38–39
  See also Dramatic Difference, Overt
Benefits, Real Reason to Believe
    vs. venture capital scoring models,
      164
marketing, message vs. medium, 25–26
marketplace behavior, modeling, 34–35
McKenna, Ed, 36–38
media endorsements, 117
meditation, 279–281
Merwyn, 33–38, 302
  analyses
    Cavendish Figurines, 108–111
    Island Pewter, 36–38
    Island Winds, 131–136
    Victoria-by-the-Sea, 59–61
message
  oversimplification of, 83–84
  vs. medium, 25–26
Michelbob's Championship Ribs, 113
mind. *See* brain
Mind Dump, 191-196
  and gathering stimuli,191–195
  and multiplying stimuli, 195–196
money
  executing ideas without, 164–165,
287–288
  See also price

monopoly, creating, 127–128
multiply stimuli, 186–187
music, as stimulus, 291
musical chairs, as stimulus–gathering
tactic, 228–229

N
noise, as stimulant, 291

O
O'Boyle, Jane, 276
objectives, 198–200
applying 666 method to, 248–249
Ogilvy, David, 33
Optimize Practicality, 187, 197–198
Outside Expeditions, 55–57
Overt Benefits, 31, 40–43
as clear mission, 66, 69–70
common mistakes with, 81–85
defining, through Don't Sell Me
tactic, 230–232
Dramatic Difference flowing from,
152-153
focusing on, 61–65
need to communicate, 50–54
in name, 75–77
perseverance in articulating, 80–81
personal passions as, 67–69
putting in writing, 77–80
and Real Reason to Believe, 88–90
synergy between, 123–124
as reason for starting business,
66–67
turning benefits into, 52
unique, focusing on, 85
visualizing, 74–75

P
P.W. Supply Company, 101
pain, as motivation for fighting fear,
256
passion, 232–234
as Overt Benefit, 67–69
patent
as development pedigree, 112
ideas worthy of, 143
pedigree, as Real Reason to Believe

strategy, 107–115
perseverance, in articulating Overt
Benefits, 80–81
personal experience, as Real Reason to
Believe strategy,103–107
perspective
diversity, sources for, 234–235
"fresh eyes," 208–212
Peters, Tom, 91, 219
portfolio of stimuli, 218–219
price
as core benefit, avoiding, 82–83
deep discounts, ineffectiveness of, 41
vs. uniqueness, as basis of purchase
decision, 130–131
Prince Edward Island Preserve
Company, 106
probability, 29–30
of purchase vs. Dramatic
Difference, 130, 139
of success, 3–5
and authenticity, 160–162
focusing on, 271–272
moving beyond, 159
variables to, 160–162
See also Merwyn
productivity, maximizing, for right and
left brains, 242–248
products
experimenting with, as stimulus,
204–206
vs. services, Marketing Physics
and, 164
prototype, 268–269
purchase probability, vs. Dramatic
Difference, 130, 139

Q
quality control, charting creativity, 175

R
reading, as stimulus, 182
Real Reason to Believe, 31–32, 88–91,
123–124
common mistakes with, 119–122
continually refreshing, 122–123
Dramatic Difference flowing from,

155–156
    Overt Benefit to owner, 95
    and Overt Benefits, synergy
between, 120
    proven strategies for communicating,
      100–122
    relative to Overt Benefits, 96–98
    as way to keep business honest,
98–99
related stimuli. *See* Homeward Trail
    stimuli
research process, 28–29
responsibility, crafting, Dramatic
    Difference through, 149–152
Rosenzweig, Mark, 179

S
samples, free, 41, 103
scientific laws, concepts rooted in,
    10–12
Seasons in Thyme, 76–77
sensory feedback, as Real Reason to
Believe strategy, 105–107
serendipity, opening up to, 213–214
services, experimenting with, as
    stimulus, 204–206
signage, 76–77
Simulated Test Marketing system.
    See Merwyn
666 method, 248–249
small business, 7–9
solutions, providing, to nonexistent
    problem, 82
source mark, 114
Spic and Span, demonstration, 104
    statistics
    and analysis, concepts rooted in,
      9–10
    as discovery tool, 27
    research process, 28–29
    See also Merwyn
stimuli
    Borrowing Brilliance, 210–212
    for creativity, 182–184
    gathering, 186, 191–194
    Homeward Trail, 200–208
    See also multiply stimuli

success
    predicted by data–based
      algorithms, 35–36
    probability of, 3–5
    defining, 29
    moving beyond, 159
    variables with, 160–162
    See also failure; growth, sustainable

T
target audience, 54–59
    creating benefit ideas from, 59–61
    defining potential, 58–59
    Overt Benefits to, 54–59
    and Real Reason to Believe, 98–99
testimonials, 115–118
Thaler, Richard, 256
thinking styles, 235–236
    common ground for all, 246–248
    opposite, 241–242
    whole brain orientation, 237
trademark pedigree, 113–114
trends, spotting, 219–220
Trivial Pursuit, as Law Breaker, 277–278
truth, and credibility, 98–99
Turner, Ted, 142–143

U
unrelated stimuli. *See* Borrowing
    Brilliance stimuli

V
value ratio, 146–148
Victoria Playhouse, 59–61
Village Pottery, 200–201

W
whole brain orientation, 237
writing
    putting "big idea" in, 222–223
    putting Dramatic Difference in, 151
    putting Overt Benefits in, 77–80
    putting strengths in, 206–207
    as stimulus, 183–184

ABOUT THE AUTHOR

Doug Hall just might have what we've all been looking for—the happy secret to success.
— *Dateline NBC*

Hall has a habit of thinking big. His credentials are impeccable.
— *Unlimited Magazine, Scotland*

Doug Hall has been named one of America's top experts on business growth by *Inc. Magazine, A&E Top 10, CIO Magazine, The Wall Street Journal* and *DATELINE NBC.*

Doug started his entrepreneurial career at the age of twelve developing and marketing a line of learn to juggle kits and magic tricks. After earning a degree in chemical engineering he joined Procter and Gamble, where he rose to the rank of of Master Marketing Inventor and in one twelve-month period developed and introduced a record nine new business initiatives.

After ten years at P&G he retired to pursue his vision of the American dream. With three credit cards for financing and his basement as his office, he founded what is today known as the Eureka! Ranch.

Doug's focus on data-proven methods has earned the Eureka! Ranch an 88% client repeat rate since it's founding in 1986. A national study found the average U.S. household uses 18 products or services that Doug and his team have helped develop.

Following six years of R&D, Doug founded Merwyn Technology. Merwyn is a patent-pending computer model that helps managers make smarter marketing and business development decisions. *Fortune Small Business* magazine named Merwyn "one of the top emerging technologies in America."

Today, Doug is on a quest to share his data-proven wisdom with owners of businesses of all sizes. The Canadian TV show *Venture* had this to say about Doug: "Hall is a corporate Robin Hood. He takes from his big corporate clients and gives to small businesses. This super consultant helps entrepreneurs rebuild their busiinesses."

Doug and his family split their time between a 170-year-old homestead in Cincinnati, Ohio, USA and a 140-year-old farmhouse in Springbrook, Prince Edward Island, Canada.

Doug can be reached at doug@doughall.com.